Entrepreneurial Behaviour of Family Firms

ENTREPRENEURIAL BEHAVIOUR

This series is dedicated to communicating innovative and multi-disciplinary new research that advances theory and practice in *Entrepreneurial Behaviour*. The series is focussed on expanding the scope of *Entrepreneurial Behaviour* theory and analysis and enriching practice by encouraging multi-theoretical, multi-cultural, and multi-disciplinary approaches.

Key issues explored in *Entrepreneurial Behaviour* include cognition, decision-making, organisational behaviours, and identifying, creating, and exploiting opportunities concerning new products, services, processes, innovations, or ventures from entrepreneurial perspective.

The primary focus will be on the study of entrepreneurs, small and medium enterprises, and family businesses, with a secondary focus on entrepreneurial and innovative behaviours in other forms of organisations, such as non-profits corporations, and public administration.

EDITORIAL ADVISORY BOARD

Entrepreneurial Behaviour of Family Firms: Perspectives on Emerging Economies

EDITED BY

BESNIK A. KRASNIQI
University of Prishtina 'Hasan Prishtina', Kosovo

SASCHA KRAUS
Free University of Bozen-Bolzano, Italy

VELAND RAMADANI
South-East European University, North Macedonia

AND

PAUL JONES
Swansea University, UK

emerald PUBLISHING

United Kingdom – North America – Japan – India – Malaysia – China

Emerald Publishing Limited
Emerald Publishing, Floor 5, Northspring, 21–23 Wellington Street, Leeds LS1 4DL

First edition 2025

British Library Cataloguing in Publication Data
A catalogue record for this book is available from the British Library

ISBN: 978-1-83753-935-2 (Print)
ISBN: 978-1-83753-934-5 (Online)
ISBN: 978-1-83753-936-9 (Epub)

Printed and bound by CPI Group (UK) Ltd, Croydon, CR0 4YY

INVESTOR IN PEOPLE

Contents

About the Editors *ix*

About the Contributors *xi*

Chapter 1 Entrepreneurial Behaviour of Family Firms in Emerging Economies: An Introduction
Besnik A. Krasniqi, Sascha Kraus, Veland Ramadani and Paul Jones *1*

Chapter 2 Perspectives and Challenges of Family Firms in Emerging Economies
Marsela Thanasi-Boçe, Indri Dyrmishi and Selma Kurtishi-Kastrati *11*

Chapter 3 Family Start-up in Oman: Entrepreneurship Ecosystem Perspective
Hafiz Wasim Akram, Léo-Paul Dana, Haidar Abbas and Md. Daoud Ciddikie *43*

Chapter 4 Entrepreneurial Orientation and Firm Growth in Tunisian Family Firms: The Moderating Role of Generational Involvement
Rim Gafsi *59*

Chapter 5 Corporate Social Responsibility and (Organizational) Conservatism in Moroccan Family Firms: Insights from a Qualitative Approach
Hamza Nidaazzi and Hind Hourmat Allah *87*

Chapter 6 Corporate Entrepreneurship of Family Firms in the VUCA World
Tuncay Odabaş and Esra Gökçen Kaygısız *111*

Chapter 7 Gender Bias and Family Firms Leadership in Africa: Evidence from Nigeria
Joy E. Akahome and Ida Skubis 135

Chapter 8 Entrepreneurial Behaviour of Family Firms in the United Arab Emirates (UAE): Navigating Cultural Dynamics and Emerging Market Realities
Anushka Lydia Issac 161

Chapter 9 A Conceptual Model for Exploring Innovation in Family Firms: Integration of Socio-emotional Wealth and Resource-based Theory Perspectives
Shweta Dewangan, Sanjeev Kumar, Pyali Chatterjee and Ankit Dhiraj 183

About the Editors

Besnik A. Krasniqi is a Fulbright Postdoctoral Scholar. He holds an MA and PhD in Economics from Staffordshire University (UK). He teaches Small Business and Entrepreneurship, Innovation Management, and Research Methods at the University of Prishtina in graduate and postgraduate studies. His professional career spans teaching and research in entrepreneurship at Maastricht School of Management (the Netherlands), Indiana University (USA), University of Michigan (USA), Staffordshire University (UK), State University of Tetovo (Macedonia), and Riinvest Institute for Development Research (Kosovo). He has authored several books, numerous research reports, and consultancy assignments. His research work in the area of entrepreneurship, firm growth, institutions, SME finance, informal economy, and transition and emerging economies appeared in international journals such as *Entrepreneurship Theory and Practice*, *Small Business Economics*, *International Entrepreneurship and Management Journal*, and *Economic Systems*. He is a Member of the Academy of Sciences and Arts, Republic of Kosovo.

Sascha Kraus is a Full Professor of Management at the Free University of Bozen-Bolzano, Italy, and a Distinguished Visiting Professor at the University of Johannesburg, South Africa. He holds a Doctorate in Social and Economic Sciences from Klagenfurt University, Austria, a PhD in Industrial Engineering and Management from Helsinki University of Technology, and a Habilitation (Venia Docendi) from Lappeenranta University of Technology, both in Finland. Before, he held Full Professor positions at Utrecht University, The Netherlands, the University of Liechtenstein, École Supérieure du Commerce Extérieur Paris, France, and Durham University, United Kingdom, as well as Visiting Professor positions at Copenhagen Business School, Denmark, and at the University of St. Gallen, Switzerland. In 2022, Clarivate has ranked him among the world's 100 most impactful researchers in Economics and Business by the Web of Science Highly Cited Researchers Reports.

Veland Ramadani is a Professor of Entrepreneurship and Family Business at the Faculty of Business and Economics, South-East European University, North Macedonia. His primary areas of research focus on entrepreneurship, family businesses, innovation, and sustainability. He has extensive work to his name, having authored or co-authored over 140 research articles, 80 book chapters, 12 textbooks, and 28 edited books. He has published in *Journal of Business Research*, *Technological Forecasting and Social Change*, *Review of Managerial Science*, *Technology in Society*, and *International Journal of Entrepreneurial Behavior & Research*, among others. He has received the Award for Excellence 2016 – Outstanding Paper by Emerald Group Publishing. In 2017, he was appointed as a Member of the Supervisory Board of the Development Bank of North Macedonia, where for 10 months, he served as an acting Chief Operating Officer as well. He was ranked, four times in a row, among the World's Top 2% of the most influential researchers prepared by Elsevier BV and Stanford University, USA. He has remained actively engaged in various projects, including those funded by the European Union and universities in Saudi Arabia, Kuwait, and the United Arab Emirates. Additionally, he has offered consultancy services to private companies.

Paul Jones is a Professor of Entrepreneurship and Innovation at the School of Management, Swansea University, UK. He undertakes research into entrepreneurial behaviour and small business management. He is the Editor in Chief of the *International Journal of Entrepreneurial Behaviour and Research*, Senior Editor with *Information Technology and People*, and Associate Editor with the *International Journal of Management Education*.

About the Contributors

Haidar Abbas works as an Assistant Professor at the University of Technology & Applied Sciences, Nizwa (Sultanate of Oman). He holds approximately 10 years of experience in teaching and guiding undergraduate and postgraduate students in India and Oman. During this period, he played several co-academic roles such as Research Coordinator, Training and Placement Committee Coordinator, Business Administration Program Coordinator, etc. He has also participated in several conferences, symposiums, seminars, and faculty development programmes. He has to his credits around 20 research articles and book chapters published in Scopus Indexed Journals and Books. Before joining the academia, he earned his bachelor's, master's, and PhD degrees from Aligarh Muslim University, Aligarh (India). In addition to this, he also qualified University Grants Commission's National Level Eligibility Test for Lecturership with a Junior Research Fellowship (UGC-NET-JRF). He is a Chartered Member of the Chartered Institute of Logistics and Transport, United Kingdom (India Chapter).

Joy E. Akahome is a Senior Lecturer at the Federal University Otuoke, Bayelsa State, Nigeria and a Contract staff of the University of Economics and Human Sciences, Warsaw, Poland. She has an extensive expertise in Entrepreneurship and Marketing. She is a Member of the American Marketing Association, Chicago, USA. Her research focusses on entrepreneurship and marketing. She has previously achieved a Coimbra Group Scholarship at the Jagiellonian University, Krakow, Poland. Her eagerness for future endeavours envisions goals or projects to advance entrepreneurial knowledge.

Hafiz Wasim Akram is an Assistant Professor at the Department of Marketing and Entrepreneurship, College of Commerce and Business Administration, Dhofar University, Salalah, Oman. He holds a Bachelor of Business Management (BBM) from the Magadh University, Bodh Gaya; a master's in International Business (MIB); and PhD from Jamia Millia Islamia in New Delhi, India. He has been a Recipient of a Junior Research Fellowship (JRF) from the University Grants Commission, Government of India. His dedication to teaching excellence is underscored by his certifications as a Fellow of the Higher Education Academy (FHEA) and a Certified Management and Business Educator (CMBE) from the United Kingdom. His research contributions have made a significant impact, with his work being published on esteemed platforms such as Sustainability,

Inderscience, Wiley, and Springer. These publications have solidified his global reputation as a Respected Researcher in the academic community. His particular areas of research interest are logistics and supply chain management, entrepreneurship, and international business.

Hind Hourmat Allah is a Researcher-Professor at Cadi Ayyad University in Marrakech. She holds a prominent role as a Member of the Interdisciplinary Laboratory for Research and Studies in Management of Organizations and Business Law (LIRE-MD) and is responsible for leading the research axis 'Strategy' within the same laboratory. With a dedicated focus on African and Arab economies, her research endeavours encompass diverse areas, including the internationalisation of businesses, the economics of the fishing sector, institutional economics, and family entrepreneurship. Her expertise contributes to the broader discourse on how family firms adapt and thrive in a globalised economy.

Pyali Chatterjee is the Head of the Department at the Faculty of Law, ICFAI University, Raipur, Chattisgarh, India. She completed her Post Doc. fellowship in 'New Technologies and Law' from MICHR – Mediterranean University of Reggio Calabria – Italy, in 2022. Recently, she has been selected for The Central Asian Legal Research (CALR) Fellowship at Tashkent State University of Law (TSUL), Uzbekistan, from April 2023 to January 2024. Her area of expertise includes criminal law, women and law, human rights, and gender studies. ORCID: 0000-0002-3307-0465.

Md. Daoud Ciddikie is an Assistant Professor at Sharda University. He has around seven years of teaching experience and more than four years of industry experience. Since 2013, he has been associated with various academic institutions, such as the University of Delhi, the FORE School of Management, Jamia Millia Islamia, Jamia Hamdard, Al-Falah University, and IGNOU, in different capacities. Before joining Sharda University, he was associated with the India SME Forum as Assistant Vice President (Research) and as Academic Director of the Asian Centre for Economic and Entrepreneurship Development and Education. He has 20 research papers to his credit. He is a Member of academic bodies such as the Indian Commerce Association and the Indian Accounting Association. He has a passion for research and a love for teaching and has guided many students at the graduate and post-graduate levels toward success.

Léo-Paul Dana is a Professor at ICD Business School Paris and a Visiting Professor at LUT School of Business and Management, Lappeenranta University of Technology. He holds the title of Professor at Dalhousie University and is also associated with the Chaire ETI at Sorbonne Business School. A graduate of McGill University and HEC-Montreal, he has served as Marie Curie Fellow at Princeton University and Visiting Professor at INSEAD and at Kingston University. He has published extensively in a variety of journals including *Entrepreneurship: Theory & Practice*, *International Business Review*, *International Small Business Journal*, *Journal of Business Research*, *Journal of Small Business*

Management, Journal of World Business, Small Business Economics, and *Technological Forecasting & Social Change*.

Shweta Dewangan is an Assistant Professor in the Faculty of Commerce at ICFAI University, Raipur, Chhattisgarh, India, with 16 years of experience in commerce and management. She has an impressive track record of publishing over 20 research papers in respected journals like *UGC CARE, Scopus, Web of Science*, and *peer-reviewed publications*. Additionally, she holds a utility patent published in a government journal. She has guided four PhD scholars in the field of commerce and actively engages in diverse research areas. Her book, published by IGI Global, is currently indexed in Scopus, highlighting her significant contributions to the academic community. ORCID: 0000-0002-6539-3357.

Ankit Dhiraj is currently a Senior Research Fellow at the School of Hotel Management and Tourism, Lovely Professional University, Punjab, India. He has completed his regular three-year bachelor's degree in business management from Magadh University Bodhgaya, a master's in Tourism Management from Alagappa University, Tamil Nadu, and pursuing PhD in Tourism Management at the School of Hotel Management and Tourism, Lovely Professional University, Punjab, India. His areas of research interest are Buddhist tourism, wellness tourism, and sustainable practices. He has experience working with different universities in India as a business development associate. He has also participated in various national and international conferences, seminars, and research workshops. He has published more than 10 research papers in Scopus Indexed, UGC-approved, and peer-reviewed journals.

Indri Dyrmishi is an Esteemed Economist with bachelor's and master's degrees, specialising in Project Management. As a Senior Instructor at the American University of the Middle East, he leads the Entrepreneurship Club and represents AUM as Vice-Champion in the Babson Collaborative Association, fostering global educational networks. His background includes instructing in the Finance Department at the American College of the Middle East and managing the Transfer Technology Office at the University of Tirana. In 2014, he was a National Trainer for the EU-co-financed Pacinno project, highlighting his expertise in entrepreneurship, market analysis, and business studies.

Rim Gafsi is a Doctor in Management Sciences. She obtained her PhD in entrepreneurship from the University of Sousse, Tunisia. Her research areas are entrepreneurship, corporate strategy, family firm, business management, and innovation.

Anushka Lydia Issac is a distinguished professional with a rich academic and industry background, uniquely integrating Engineering and Business Management. Holding an Engineering [Hons.] degree and an MBA, she combines technical proficiency with strategic insight. Currently a Lecturer and Program Head for the Pearson Level 3 Foundational Program at Westford, she is also pursuing a Ph.D. in Business with Management, specializing in Flexible Work Arrangements. Anushka holds a 'Fellow' (FHEA) status from the Higher Education

Academy, UK, is a Certified Management and Business Educator, awarded by the Chartered Association of Business Schools and is a Pearson Certified Lead IQA (Internal Quality Assurance), enabling her to provide a holistic and quality-driven learning experience. Her intellectual footprint extends to about 20 publications in Scopus indexed books and conference proceedings, including reputable publishers such as Springer and Emerald. Anushka is not just a passive contributor but an active participant in the academic discourse, having attended numerous conferences and presenting her research at esteemed forums.

Esra Gökçen Kaygisiz is an Associate Professor of the Department of Business at the Faculty of Economics and Administrative Sciences, University of Giresun. She graduated from the Computer Teaching Programme at Fırat University. She completed a master's programme at Bilgi University and finished Business Management Doctorate Programme at Selçuk University. During her master's and doctorate education time, she studied as an instructor at the Computer Programming Programme, Gaziantep University. She has more than 50 international and national research and conference papers. Her research interests are knowledge and wisdom management, human resource management, entrepreneurship, and reputation management with a focus on IT and digital transformation. ORCID: 0000-0002-4950-9508.

Sanjeev Kumar is an Accomplished Expert in Food and Beverage. He currently holds the position of Professor at the Lovely Professional University, Punjab, India. With over a decade of experience in the field of the food service industry, his research focusses on alcoholic beverages, event management and sustainable management practices, metaverse, and artificial intelligence. He has published more than 35 research papers and chapters in Scopus Indexed, UGC Approved, and peer-reviewed journals and books. He participated and acted as a Resource Person in various National and International conferences, seminars, research workshops, and industry talks, and his work has been widely cited.

Selma Kurtishi-Kastrati holds the position of Associate Professor at the American University of the Middle East in Kuwait, where she currently leads the HRM Department within the College of Business Administration. With two decades of academic experience, she has instructed diverse courses in Business and Management. She has authored and co-authored numerous scholarly publications in reputable journals, international conferences, and book chapters. Her research focus encompasses areas such as Foreign Direct Investments (FDI), Corporate Social Responsibility, Sustainability, and Entrepreneurship.

Hamza Nidaazzi is PhD and Member of Interdisciplinary Laboratory for Research and Studies in Management of Organizations and Business Law (LIRE-MD) at Cadi Ayyad University, Marrakech, specialising in family firms and corporation strategy. His doctoral thesis explored the dimensions of organisational conservatism in family firms and was awarded Summa Cum Laude. His research interests include strategic management and organisational culture, particularly within family firms. He has authored several publications in these areas, contributing to the academic understanding of family firm dynamics. In addition to his research, he is actively involved in academic circles, engaging in discussions and initiatives that support the development of management sciences.

Tuncay Odabaş is a PhD Student at the Institute of Social Sciences, Department of Business Administration, Giresun University. He completed his undergraduate education at Atatürk University, Faculty of Economics and Administrative Sciences, Department of International Relations between 2011 and 2015. He completed his master's degree at Giresun University Institute of Social Sciences, Department of Business Administration between 2017 and 2021, and continues his PhD programme at Giresun University Institute of Social Sciences, Department of Business Administration in 2021. Her research interests include human resource management, reputation management, entrepreneurship, and family businesses. ORCID: 0000-0002-5650-3614.

Ida Skubis is an Assistant Professor at the Silesian University of Technology. She has a PhD degree and an MA degree in four languages: English, German, French, and Spanish. She has professional experience in academia and business – she worked in managerial positions for international companies and lived in various countries, such as Spain, Greece, France, and Austria. Currently, she is the CEO of the Housing Community. Her research interests include entrepreneurship; innovations; leadership; decision-making; AI; AI in Management; AI in Linguistics; Ethics of AI; human-centric approach; chatbots; robots: social robots, humanoid robots, sex robots; human–robot interaction; NLP; MT; IE; NER; cognitive technologies. She has participated in numerous international conferences in Poland and abroad and is involved in various AI projects. She is a Reviewer for international journals on the topics of AI. She received numerous scholarships and awards for her scientific research. ORCID: 0000-0002-2447-9832.

Dr. Marsela Thanasi-Boçe is an Associate Professor of Marketing at the American University of the Middle East (AUM), where she teaches various marketing courses at the undergraduate and graduate levels. Holding a PhD in Marketing from the University of Tirana, her research spans digital marketing, customer relationship management, brand management, consumer behavior, retailing, corporate social responsibility, and entrepreneurship. Dr. Thanasi-Boçe is certified as a Digital Marketing Professional by the American Marketing Association and the Digital Marketing Institute. She also completed the Accelerator Mentorship Training Program at the University of California, Berkeley, in June 2023. Her professional affiliations include the European Council for Small Business and Entrepreneurship (ECSB) and the Diana International Research Institute (DIRI). At AUM, she actively contributes to academic and research committees, enhancing academic standards and research quality. Dr. Thanasi-Boçe's commitment to advancing marketing and entrepreneurship education underscores her influence and leadership. ORCID ID: 0000-0001-9117-9453.

Chapter 1

Entrepreneurial Behaviour of Family Firms in Emerging Economies: An Introduction

Besnik A. Krasniqi[a], *Sascha Kraus*[b], *Veland Ramadani*[c] *and Paul Jones*[d]

[a]*University of Prishtina 'Hasan Prishtina', Kosovo*
[b]*Free University of Bozen-Bolzano, Italy*
[c]*South-East European University, North Macedonia*
[d]*Swansea University, UK*

Abstract

Family firms play a crucial role in global entrepreneurship, especially in emerging economies, contributing significantly to job creation, income generation, innovation, and economic growth. As emerging markets expand rapidly, these business families and their enterprises are poised to drive superior entrepreneurial activity in the coming decades (Baltazar et al., 2023; Le Breton-Miller & Miller, 2018). Rooted in familial ties, traditions, and local contexts, these firms exhibit distinctive entrepreneurial behaviors. Understanding these dynamics is pivotal as research increasingly explores the diversity among family-owned businesses. Factors such as familial dynamics, succession planning, and institutional environments profoundly shape their strategies and decision-making processes. This study delves into these complexities, highlighting the unique challenges and opportunities faced by family firms in emerging economies. Insights gained can inform policies and practices aimed at nurturing entrepreneurial ventures in these dynamic contexts.

Keywords: Family firms; emerging economies; entrepreneurship; familial ties; institutional contexts

Entrepreneurial Behaviour of Family Firms: Perspectives on Emerging Economies, 1–10

Published under exclusive licence by Emerald Publishing Limited
doi:10.1108/978-1-83753-934-520241001

Introduction

Family firms are significant in global entrepreneurship, particularly in emerging economies, contributing to job creation, income, innovation, and economic growth. With rapidly growing emerging markets, considerable business families and their companies will be critical sources of superior entrepreneurial activity over the coming decades (Baltazar et al., 2023; Le Breton-Miller & Miller, 2018; Zaefarian et al., 2016). These firms contribute substantially to economic development and embody unique entrepreneurial behaviours shaped by familial ties, traditions, and institutional and cultural contexts. As research on family entrepreneurship broadens its scope and shifts towards exploring the diversity among family-owned firms, it becomes crucial to grasp the distinct features of the institutional environment within which these firms operate in emerging economies. Understanding the varied entrepreneurial behaviours, family dynamics, firm structures, succession, and business group dynamics further underscores the significance of contextual analysis in this field. These contextual dynamics in emerging economies often have unique socioeconomic and institutional contexts, such as less developed legal frameworks, higher market volatility, strong informal institutions, and cultural nuances. Also, the role of families in these societies is quite different from that of the Western world. These factors significantly influence entrepreneurial decision-making and strategies within family firms. Therefore, this chapter delves into the intricate dynamics of entrepreneurial behaviour within family firms, focussing on their role, challenges, and opportunities in emerging economies. By examining the distinct challenges and opportunities they encounter, this chapter provides valuable insights for academics, policymakers, and practitioners seeking to understand and foster entrepreneurial endeavours in these contexts.

Understanding Entrepreneurial Behaviour in Family Firms

The increased levels of entrepreneurial activity within family firms are often reflected through a higher degree of entrepreneurial orientation (EO) (Chakrabarti & Mondal, 2020). The EO has emerged as a concept to analyse firms' mindsets to pursue entrepreneurial opportunities and provides an essential framework to examine entrepreneurial activities (Lumpkin & Dess, 2015). EO is perceived as a strategic mindset characterised by a willingness to innovate, proactively seek opportunities, and embrace risk (Covin & Slevin, 1991). However, contemporary research on EO within family firms offers a divergent viewpoint. Some authors contend that family firms tend to be risk-averse, exhibiting reluctance to engage in entrepreneurial endeavours to ensure future generations' financial and social welfare (Naldi et al., 2007; Short et al., 2009). Conversely, another group of researchers argues that family firms adopt a long-term perspective, prioritising wealth creation and fostering innovation and entrepreneurship within their organisations (Chakrabarti & Mondal, 2020; Salvato, 2004; Zahra et al., 2004).

Entrepreneurial behaviour within family firms is characterised by a blend of familial relationships, firm objectives, personal aspirations, and familiness (see Bağiş et al., 2023, for an extensive review). Unlike non-family firm, these firms often operate within a framework influenced by family values, traditions, and hierarchies. This distinctive environment shapes the entrepreneurial behaviour exhibited by family members involved in the business, impacting decision-making processes, risk-taking tendencies, and innovation strategies. In emerging economies, where family firms are prevalent, entrepreneurial behaviour is further influenced by socioeconomic factors, regulatory and institutional environments (formal and informal), and cultural norms. Such contextual factors range from concentrated decision-making to family members and socioemotional objectives such as preserving intergenerational family control and involvement in the business (Gomez-Mejia et al., 2007).

These firms often serve as engines of economic growth, driving innovation, employment, and wealth creation within their respective regions. However, they also face unique challenges from institutional constraints, market volatility, and succession issues, significantly impacting their entrepreneurial endeavours.

Challenges and Opportunities in Emerging Economies

Family firms in emerging economies encounter a myriad of challenges that influence their entrepreneurial behaviour. Limited access to capital, inadequate infrastructure, and regulatory hurdles pose significant barriers to entrepreneurial behaviour, innovation, and growth. Moreover, navigating complex sociocultural dynamics, including nepotism perceptions and societal expectations, adds another layer of complexity to entrepreneurial endeavours within these firms. As such, there is a need to adapt new governance structures and professional management practices to better respond to the complexities of the institutional environment.

There is an agreement among the authors that the institutional environment can have a significant impact on shaping the entrepreneurial behaviour of firms in general (Hashi & Krasniqi, 2011; Krasniqi & Branch, 2020; Williams et al., 2023) and family firms in particular (Chakrabarti & Mondal, 2020; Dana & Ramadani, 2015; Ramadani et al., 2020; Soleimanof et al., 2018; Zachary et al., 2017). For example, Zachary et al. (2017) argue that entrepreneurial behaviour in family firms is dynamic and changes due to the external environment conditions – it increases during stable environments while decreases during external shocks like a financial crisis as the family tries to protect its socio-emotional wealth (SEW). Particularly in times of crisis, family firms can act and make decisions that are given a higher priority to ensure the firm survival and, thus, also the well-being of the family (Kleve, 2020; Le Breton-Miller & Miller, 2018). Calabrò et al. (2021) support the view by providing evidence that family firms during COVID-19 have adopted strategies not only to overcome the barriers but also to turn challenges into opportunities and manage to emerge from the crisis even stronger than before. Members of the family firms demonstrate a commitment to their companies, even at the expense of forgoing personal gains, to ensure their ventures persevered through the global crisis (Ramadani et al., 2022). The commitment of family members contributes to resilience during crises.

In addition, understanding the formal and informal institutions and their interactions is critical in understanding the behaviours of family firms in emerging economies, often associated with strong informal business practices (Krasniqi et al., 2023; Soleimanof et al., 2018). In some cases, they lack market-supporting institutions or are characterised by strong political control, and family firms tend to cultivate political connections to respond to the failure of legal systems (Dinh & Calabrò, 2019). Such institutional environments increase the political risk and, in turn, may affect the proactive behaviour of firms, often prioritising political connections over proactive behaviour and innovation.

In summary, family firms in emerging economies also leverage unique opportunities to foster entrepreneurial behaviour despite these challenges. Deep-rooted social networks and familial ties often serve as sources of support and resilience, enabling them to weather economic uncertainties and adapt to market dynamics effectively. Moreover, their inherent flexibility and agility allow them to seize emerging opportunities swiftly, driving innovation and market disruption in diverse sectors.

Strategies for Fostering Entrepreneurial Behaviour

To nurture entrepreneurial behaviour within family firms in emerging economies, it is imperative to adopt tailored strategies that address their unique challenges and leverage their inherent strengths. However, family firms' preferences for low-risk strategies could often hinder their adaptability in dynamic and uncertain environments (Stenholm et al., 2016).

Fostering a culture of innovation and risk-taking is essential, encouraging family members to explore new ideas and embrace calculated risks. The literature suggests that proactive behaviour and innovation positively impact the growth of family firms (Casillas et al., 2010; Stebhol et al., 2016). Often, young family members in family firms do not have the same ambitions as the owner-mangers of family firms. The young family members' interests in running the same type of business may be different, and owners/managers can encourage younger and incoming members of business families to launch new companies that are more in line with their priorities and skills (Le Breton-Miller et al., 2004). Many families in business possess flexible resources – financial, human, and relational – that can be leveraged across multiple firms and generations. These resources and strategies may foster entrepreneurial behaviour further and help family firms expand.

Promoting professionalisation and governance mechanisms within family firms is crucial for sustainable growth and succession planning (Clauß et al., 2022; Rovelli et al., 2022). Implementing transparent decision-making processes, establishing clear roles and responsibilities, and investing in leadership development programmes can mitigate conflicts and ensure the continuity of entrepreneurial endeavours across generations. Firms in emerging economies should increase managerial capacities and align new organisational forms to grasp opportunities in the local and international markets.

Furthermore, fostering external partnerships and alliances can enhance the entrepreneurial capabilities of family firms in emerging economies. Such social networks and partnerships help family firms recognise domestic and international opportunities (Kontinen & Ojala, 2012; Kryeziu et al., 2022; Zaefrian et al., 2016). The networking and personal ties of family members provided a range of significant resources, both professional and practical, for access to financial, human informational, and other resources needed to support development and growth (Anderson et al., 2016). Some types of support include but are not limited to borrowing from family and friends, informal finance, and unpaid labour during downturns and financial crises (Krasniqi, 2011). Evidence suggests that the social capital of family firms contributes the most to firms' ability to absorb shocks, reallocate existing resources, and internalise practices that allow firms to cope with future disturbances (Mzid et al., 2019).

In particular, in the weakly installed environment where informal institutions exist (as in many emerging economies), personal entrepreneurial networks can be used to overcome formal institutional barriers or complement them. Business ties among family firms at all stages of the value chain and relationships with banks and regulatory authorities make it easier for established business families to branch out into new lines of firm (Bjornberg et al., 2015). In addition, collaborating with academia, industry associations, and government agencies can provide access to resources, expertise, and market insights, fostering innovation and market expansion opportunities.

Book Structure

This book comprises nine chapters, with the introductory chapter setting the stage. Each subsequent chapter focusses on specific family firm topics within a distinct emerging country.

Chapter 2 – *Perspectives and Challenges of Family Firms in Emerging Economies* is written by Marsela Thanasi-Boçe, Indri Dyrmishi and Selma Kurtishi-Kastrati. This chapter critically assesses the distinctive challenges and opportunities confronted by family firms in emerging economies – a subject that has received scant attention in existing literature. Acknowledging the elevated failure rates prevalent among startups, particularly those within family firms, this research endeavours to unravel the determinants influencing their outcomes. Through a qualitative analysis, the chapter delves into diverse economic, legal, and cultural dimensions shaping these enterprises. It adopts a comparative standpoint, extracting insights from multiple emerging economies to discern trends and variations in the trajectories of family-owned startups. The chapter seeks to bridge the knowledge void by presenting a holistic perspective on the dynamics of success and failure in family-owned startups, emphasising strategic, managerial, and operational facets.

Chapter 3 – *Family Start-up in Oman: Entrepreneurship Ecosystem Perspective* is co-authored by Hafiz Wasim Akram, Léo-Paul Dana, Haidar Abbas and Md Daoud Ciddikie. The focus of this book chapter is on evaluating the potential and challenges encountered by family startups in Oman's evolving entrepreneurial landscape. The chapter delves into the hurdles confronting entrepreneurs, while also shedding light on growth prospects and avenues for innovation within this dynamic market, thereby revealing the unique dynamics of the Omani startup scene. The authors posit that family startups assume a crucial role in bolstering a country's global competitiveness. This is achieved through their ability to attract capital, foster entrepreneurship, and contribute to the diversification of the economy beyond its foundational industries. Moreover, these firms serve as catalysts for social change, addressing societal issues and offering solutions that contribute to community well-being. Consequently, nurturing a robust startup ecosystem becomes imperative for a nation's sustained development and prosperity.

Chapter 4 – *Entrepreneurial Orientation and Firm Growth in Tunisian Family Firms: The Moderating Role of Generational Involvement* is authored by Rim Gafsi. This chapter seeks to explore the impact of generational involvement on the relationship between EO and growth in Tunisian family firms. Conducting a quantitative investigation involving 150 family firms, the research utilises a questionnaire-based approach and employs structural equation modelling through SPSS 22 and AMOS software. The results indicate that not all dimensions of EO contribute equally to growth. Specifically, proactiveness, competitive aggressiveness, and autonomy directly influence growth, particularly in the context of generational involvement acting as moderators. The efficacy of these dimensions in driving growth is contingent upon the active and collaborative participation of various family generations in the entrepreneurial activities of the family firm. This study underscores the significance for family firms to ensure sustained EO when multiple generations are engaged, reinforcing the importance of these concepts for maintaining long-term entrepreneurial focus within family enterprises.

Chapter 5 – *Corporate Social Responsibility and (Organizational) Conservatism in Moroccan Family Firms: Insights from a Qualitative Approach* is written by Hamza Nidaazzi and Hind Hourmat Allah. This chapter delves into the intricate dynamics between organisational conservatism (OC) and corporate social responsibility (CSR) practices within family firms, specifically focussing on the context of Morocco. The study, emphasising the familial aspects of CSR, seeks to unveil how OC influences CSR strategies, outcomes, and broader implications. Employing an exploratory qualitative design encompassing multiple case studies, the research scrutinises three family firms in Morocco. The findings illuminate that OC plays a pivotal role in fostering stable, values-driven, and sustainable CSR initiatives. This is realised through the alignment of shared values, judicious change management, careful financial strategies, a steadfast commitment to legacy, and seamless integration with family values. In essence, this study contributes to a nuanced comprehension of the intricate relationship between conservatism, CSR practices, and familial dimensions. By doing so, it enhances the ongoing discourse on responsible business practices, providing valuable insights into the unique interplay within family-owned businesses, particularly in the Moroccan context.

Chapter 6 – *Corporate Entrepreneurship of Family Firms in the VUCA World* is co-authored by Tuncay Odabaş and Esra Gökçen Kaygisiz. This study sought to establish a connection between the role of family firms in the volatile, uncertain, complex, and ambiguous world and their engagement in corporate entrepreneurship. The examination of corporate entrepreneurship within family firms was conducted in alignment with their corporate logic. To achieve this objective, the study employed a content analysis method, analysing the news available on the corporate websites of seven family companies operating in Türkiye and listed in the 2023 Family Business Index. Thematic coding was applied to the data, leading to the identification of key findings. According to the results, the predominant corporate logic observed in family firms is market logic and efficiency and savings logic. Consequently, the corporate logic of family firms exhibits a hybrid nature, incorporating a blend of market logic, efficiency, and savings logic.

Chapter 7 – *Gender Bias and Family Firms Leadership in Africa: Evidence from Nigeria* is co-authored by Joy E. Akahome & Ida Skubis. This research delves into the motivations and obstacles faced by women in leadership positions within male-dominated family firms in Nigeria. It addresses a critical gap in the literature regarding gender dynamics in these businesses, particularly in the Nigerian context where such enterprises wield economic significance but often exhibit gender biases rooted in cultural and societal norms. The findings reveal three primary motivations driving these women: the pursuit of necessary skills and capabilities, career development aspirations, and a desire to enhance their quality of life. The study also underscores three major challenges encountered by these women: the existence of a glass ceiling effect, adherence to traditional gender roles, and the influence of primogeniture. These challenges contribute to the perpetuation of stereotypes, societal pressures, and the frequent relegation of women to subordinate roles, posing significant hurdles to their leadership aspirations.

Chapter 8 – *Entrepreneurial Behaviour of Family Firms in the United Arab Emirates (UAE): Navigating Cultural Dynamics and Emerging Market Realities* is written by Anushka Lydia Issac. This chapter extensively examines the convergence of family entrepreneurship, cultural dynamics, and emerging markets, with a specific emphasis on the United Arab Emirates (UAE). By scrutinising the entrepreneurial behaviour of family firms, it explores how these entities navigate cultural complexities, exploit opportunities in emerging markets, and impact both local and global entrepreneurship ecosystems. The chapter analyses the dynamic interplay between family dynamics and entrepreneurial pursuits, unravelling their effects on resource allocation, succession planning, risk-taking, and innovation within family firms in the UAE. The inclusion of case studies offers valuable insights into the strategies adopted by family firms in the UAE, contributing to a nuanced understanding of the evolving landscape of family entrepreneurship. This chapter serves as a valuable resource for researchers, policymakers, and practitioners seeking profound insights into the intricate interplay of family entrepreneurship, cultural dynamics, and emerging markets.

Chapter 9 – *A Conceptual Model for Exploring Innovation in Family Firms: Integration of Socio-emotional Wealth and Resource-based Theory Perspectives* is co-authored by Shweta Dewangan, Sanjeev Kumar, Pyali Chatterjee and Ankit Dhiraj. The authors explore the dynamics of innovation within family firms through the lenses of the SEW framework and the resource-based theory (RBT), providing valuable perspectives. When employing the SEW framework, family firms might prioritise the preservation of their traditions and core values, possibly resisting the adoption of new technologies and contemporary business methods. Conversely, according to RBT, family firms can gain a competitive advantage by leveraging and nurturing their distinctive resources and capabilities – such as collective experiences, market reputation, and established networks – to foster innovation and secure a robust market position. By integrating these two viewpoints, family firms can attain sustainable competitive advantages, effectively managing the tensions between tradition and innovation. This holistic approach enables them to innovate while safeguarding their socio-emotional wealth, ensuring enduring success in the continually evolving business landscape.

Conclusion

Entrepreneurial behaviour within family firms in emerging economies is a multifaceted phenomenon shaped by familial dynamics, sociocultural influences, and institutional contexts. While these firms face unique challenges, they also possess inherent strengths that enable them to thrive amidst adversity. Family firms adopt various strategies to navigate the weakly installed institutional environment. Understanding the distinct features of the business environment and family business in emerging economies is critical. Also, by understanding the different features of entrepreneurial behaviour within family firms and implementing tailored strategies, family business owners can unlock their full growth potential as economic development and innovation drivers in emerging economies. To this end, policymakers can design policies to support family firms and provide greater impetus to employment, innovation, and economic growth.

The editors and contributors of this book envision that the compiled chapters will make a meaningful and substantive contribution to the field of entrepreneurial behaviour of family firms. This contribution is especially significant in the context of specific contexts, such as emerging countries. Despite a growing body of research on general business and entrepreneurship in these countries, studies focussed on the entrepreneurial behaviour of family firms remain relatively limited. The existing literature lacks a robust emphasis on these countries concerning family entrepreneurship, and this book strives to bridge this gap.

In light of the scarcity of studies investigating the entrepreneurial behaviour of family firms in emerging countries, this book is positioned to be exceptionally valuable to researchers globally and to those with a keen interest in gaining deeper insights into family entrepreneurship within these regions. It aims to rectify a notable research gap, aspiring to be a comprehensive resource for individuals intrigued by the intricacies of family firms in the unique context of emerging countries.

References

Anderson, A. R., Jack, S. L., & Dodd, S. D. (2016). The role of family members in entrepreneurial networks: Beyond the boundaries of the family firm. In A. Fayolle, S. L. Jack, W. Lamine & D. Chabaud (Eds.), *Entrepreneurial process and social networks* (pp. 236–262). Edward Elgar Publishing.

Bağiş, M., Kryeziu, L., Kurutkan, M. N., Krasniqi, B. A., Yazici, O., & Memili, E. (2023). Topics, trends and theories in family business research: 1996–2020. *International Entrepreneurship and Management Journal*, *19*(4), 1855–1891.

Baltazar, J. R., Fernandes, C. I., Ramadani, V., & Hughes, M. (2023). Family business succession and innovation: A systematic literature review. *Review of Managerial Science*, *17*(8), 2897–2920.

Bjornberg, A., & Nicholson, N. (2015). Emotional ownership: The next generation's relationship with the family firm. *Family Business Review*, *25*(4), 374–390.

Calabrò, A., Frank, H., Minichilli, A., & Suess-Reyes, J. (2021). Business families in times of crises: The backbone of family firm resilience and continuity. *Journal of Family Business Strategy*, *12*(2), 100442.

Casillas, J. C., Moreno, A. M., & Barbero, J. L. (2010). A configurational approach of the relationship between entrepreneurial orientation and growth of family firms. *Family Business Review*, *32*(1), 27–44.

Chakrabarti, A. B., & Mondal, A. (2020). The effect of institutional transition on entrepreneurial orientation of family businesses: Evidence from India. *International Journal of Entrepreneurial Behavior & Research*, *26*(1), 76–97.

Claußß, T., Kraus, S., & Jones, P. (2022). Sustainability in family business: Mechanisms, technologies and business models for achieving economic prosperity, environmental quality and social equity. *Technological Forecasting and Social Change*, *176*(1), Article 121450.

Dana, L. P., & Ramadani, V. (2015). *Family businesses in transition economies*. Springer International Publishing.

Dinh, T. Q., & Calabrò, A. (2019). Asian family firms through corporate governance and institutions: A systematic review of the literature and agenda for future research. *International Journal of Management Reviews*, *21*(1), 50–75.

Gomez-Mejia, L. R., Haynes, K. T., Nunez-Nickel, M., Jacobson, K. J. L., & Moyano-Fuentes, J. (2007). Socioemotional wealth and business risks in family-controlled firms: Evidence from Spanish olive oil mills. *Administrative Science Quarterly*, *52*(1), 106–137.

Hashi, I., & Krasniqi, B. A. (2011). Entrepreneurship and SME growth: Evidence from advanced and laggard transition economies. *International Journal of Entrepreneurial Behavior & Research*, *17*(5), 456–487.

Kleve, H. (2020). Understanding the family business: Different theoretical approaches to the business family nexus. *Journal of Family Business Management*, *10*(2), 145–160.

Kontinen, T., & Ojala, A. (2012). Social capital in the international operations of family SMEs. *Journal of Small Business and Enterprise Development*, *19*(1), 39–55.

Krasniqi, B. A. (2011). Barriers to entrepreneurship and SME growth in transition economies: The case of Kosovo. *Journal of Small Business and Enterprise Development*, *18*(3), 619–635.

Krasniqi, B., & Branch, D. (2020). Institutions and firm growth in a transitional and post-conflict economy of Kosovo. *Journal of Entrepreneurship in Emerging Economies*, *12*(2), 187–204.

Krasniqi, B., Williams, N., Hashi, I., Reçica, F., Lubishtani, E., & Kryeziu, L. (2023). The impact of institutional quality on country-level variations in foreign equity shares in transition economies. *Review of International Business and Strategy*, *33*(4), 581–604.

Kryeziu, L., Coşkun, R., & Krasniqi, B. (2022). Social networks and family firm internationalisation: Cases from a transition economy. *Review of International Business and Strategy*, *32*(2), 284–304.

Le Breton-Miller, I., Miller, D., & Steier, L. P. (2004). Toward an integrative model of effective FOB succession. *Entrepreneurship Theory and Practice*, *28*(4), 305–328.

Le Breton-Miller, I., & Miller, D. (2018). Beyond the firm: Business families as entrepreneurs. *Entrepreneurship Theory and Practice*, *42*(4), 527–536.

Lumpkin, G. T., & Dess, G. G. (2015). Entrepreneurial orientation and firm performance: The role of entrepreneurial orientation and organizational learning capability. *Journal of Business Venturing*, *30*(1), 27–38.

Mzid, I., Khachlouf, N., & Soparnot, R. (2019). How does family capital influence the resilience of family firms?. *Journal of International Entrepreneurship*, *17*(2), 249–277.

Naldi, L., Nordqvist, M., Sjöberg, K., & Wiklund, J. (2007). Entrepreneurial orientation, risk taking, and performance in family firms. *Family Business Review*, *20*(1), 33–47.

Ramadani, V., Memili, E., Palalić, R., & Chang, E. P. (2020). *Entrepreneurial family businesses*. Springer International Publishing.

Ramadani, V., Rahman, M.M., Salamzadeh, A., Rahaman, M.S., & Abazi-Alili, H. (2022). Entrepreneurship Education and Graduates' Entrepreneurial Intentions: Does Gender Matter? A Multi-Group Analysis using AMOS. *Technological Forecasting and Social Change, 180* (7), 121693.

Rovelli, P., Ferasso, M., De Massis, A., & Kraus, S. (2022). Thirty years of research in family business journals: Status quo and future directions. *Journal of Family Business Strategy*, *13*(3), Article 100422.

Salvato, C. (2004). Predictors of entrepreneurship in family firms. *Journal of Private Equity*, *7*(3), 68–76.

Short, J. C., Payne, G. T., Brigham, K. H., Lumpkin, G. T., & Broberg, J. C. (2009). Family firms and entrepreneurial orientation in publicly traded firms: A comparative analysis of the S&P 500. *Family Business Review*, *22*(1), 9–24.

Soleimanof, S., Rutherford, M. W., & Webb, J. W. (2018). The intersection of family firms and institutional contexts: A review and agenda for future research. *Family Business Review*, *31*(1), 32–53.

Stebhol, J., Blundel, R., & Treanor, L. (2016). Reframing family entrepreneurship: Exploring the generational and organizational diversity of family firms. *Entrepreneurship & Regional Development*, *28*(5–6), 384–410.

Stenholm, P., Pukkinen, T., & Heinonen, J. (2016). Firm growth in family businesses – The role of entrepreneurial orientation and the entrepreneurial activity. *Journal of Small Business Management*, *54*(2), 697–713.

Williams, N., Plakoyiannaki, E., & Krasniqi, B. A. (2023). When forced migrants go home: The journey of returnee entrepreneurs in the post-conflict economies of Bosnia & Herzegovina and Kosovo. *Entrepreneurship Theory and Practice*, *47*(2), 430–460.

Zachary, M. A., Payne, G. T., Moore, C. B., & Sexton, J. C. (2017). Time to recalibrate? Exploring entrepreneurial orientation of family businesses before, during, and after an environmental jolt. *International Journal of Management and Enterprise Development*, *16*(1/2), 57–79.

Zaefarian, R., Eng, T. Y., & Tsavorite, M. (2016). An exploratory study of international opportunity identification among family firms. *International Business Review*, *25*(1), 333–345.

Zaefrian, R., Eng, T. Y., & Wiebe, E. (2016). Relational capabilities in entrepreneurial firms: Impact on performance. *Journal of Business Research*, *69*(11), 5040–5045.

Zahra, S. A., Hayton, J. C., & Salvato, C. (2004). Entrepreneurship in family vs non-family firms: A resource-based analysis of the effect of organisational culture. *Entrepreneurship: Theory and Practice*, *28*(4), 363–379.

Chapter 2

Perspectives and Challenges of Family Firms in Emerging Economies

Marsela Thanasi-Boçe, Indri Dyrmishi and Selma Kurtishi-Kastrati

American University of the Middle East, Kuwait

Abstract

This chapter critically examines the unique challenges and opportunities faced by family-owned startups in emerging economies, a topic that has received limited attention in existing literature. Recognizing the high failure rate of startups, particularly in family firms, this study seeks to understand the factors contributing to their success or failure. Employing a qualitative analysis, the chapter explores various economic, legal, and cultural dimensions that influence these businesses. It provides a comparative perspective, drawing insights from various emerging economies to identify patterns and differences in the experiences of family-owned startups. The chapter aims to fill the knowledge gap by offering a comprehensive view of the success and failure dynamics in family-owned startups, with a focus on strategic, managerial, and operational aspects. This approach offers valuable insights for both academics and practitioners, aiming to guide future research and practical interventions to support the sustainability and growth of family firms in these dynamic markets.

Keywords: Start-up venture; family firms; family entrepreneurship; human capital; emerging economies

1. Introduction

Family firms have long been a cornerstone of the global economy (Alkahtani, 2021; Kraus et al., 2023). Characterized by family ownership and management of day-to-day operations (Pieper et al., 2013), they play a pivotal role in global

Entrepreneurial Behaviour of Family Firms:
Perspectives on Emerging Economies, 11–41

doi:10.1108/978-1-83753-934-520241002

economies, often constituting a significant portion of firms, reaching as high as 90% in certain instances (Ramadani et al., 2022). Research indicates that a significant portion of publicly traded companies globally is family-owned (Klein & Blondel, 2002). Remarkably, many of the world's largest enterprises, such as Wal-Mart, Porsche, BMW, Hyundai, and others, started as family-owned ventures (Birdthistle & Hales, 2023).

Despite their historical significance, family firms face growing challenges that jeopardize their continuity. The potential risk of a business's demise, coupled with the founder's exit, underscores a fundamental issue that can be disconcerting for a community, especially in emerging economies with elevated poverty levels (Buckman et al., 2020). The stability of these family firms is crucial for global economic growth, exerting substantial influence on a nation's economy (Kraus et al., 2011; Rexhepi et al., 2018). Therefore, there is a compelling need to develop and adopt a well-established business succession plan to guide family firms.

In this book chapter, we delve into the significant role of family firms in emerging economies and thoroughly examine the unique challenges they encounter. We explore the distinct characteristics of family firms, considering the obstacles they face as well as the opportunities they can leverage to foster growth, ensure longevity, adapt to changing environments, and foster innovation in emerging economies. Additionally, we shed light on the diverse challenges that entrepreneurs encounter in various countries and contexts, providing insights into the hurdles they must overcome during their entrepreneurial journeys. Drawing from both the valuable lessons derived from these challenges and the best practices observed in family firms in emerging economies, we offer actionable recommendations for practitioners across different sectors.

2. Family Firm Concept

Family firms are crucial drivers of economic growth, creating wealth, and jobs, and enhancing the well-being of the nation and its inhabitants. Such firms are characterized by single-family ownership and family members actively directing the company (Ernest and Young (EY) & University of St. Gallen, 2023). They can be seen as a complex interplay between two interconnected subsystems: the family and the business. Both operate with distinct, sometimes, unclear boundaries and rules (Palaiologos, 2017). These subsystems mutually influence each other, significantly impacting the organization's outcomes and operations (Nordqvist & Melin, 2010; Rovelli et al., 2022).

The definitions of family firms vary across different countries, emerging and developed ones, reflecting cultural and operational distinctions. Each country's unique definition reflects its own cultural and operational context. For example, family firms in Portugal are characterized by the active involvement of family members in both ownership and decision-making processes, emphasizing their direct participation in key business aspects (Ramadani et al., 2019; Rodrigues et al., 2023). The UK defines family firms based on their commitment to a culture that seamlessly integrates family-owned values and attributes into the overall operations of the business, emphasizing a cultural aspect, while in the USA, family firms are identified by the presence of at least two family members employed within the company, highlighting the importance of family members as part of the workforce (Gallo et al., 2004). The definition of family firms is related also to meeting the legal requirements in a country regarding ownership and management. For example, in Italy, the family must own a minimum of 50% of the shares, and at least one family member is actively engaged in managerial roles (Cascino et al., 2010).

As the focus of this chapter is exploring family firms in emerging economies, various definitions that describe them in these contexts are provided for reference in Table 2.1.

Table 2.1. Family Firms' Definitions.

Country	Definition	Reference
China	In China, the presence of a family member on the management team is essential, highlighting the importance of family engagement at the managerial level	Gallo et al. (2004)
India	Family firms in India are characterized by a system where a particular family holds the voting control, irrespective of the company's legal framework	Merchant et al. (2018)
Malaysia	Malaysian family firms are defined by both ownership and active involvement in running the company. Specifically, to be considered a family firm, more than half of the company's ownership (at least 51%) needs to be in the hands of family members, and these family members should also play a hands-on role in the company's management	Gallo et al. (2004)
Pakistan	A family firm is typically seen as a small- to medium-sized enterprise with under 250 staff. The majority ownership, over 50%, should be in the hands of family members, often spanning to the second generation or beyond. Moreover, family members should have a significant role in high-level management	Alkahtani et al. (2020) and Khan et al. (2022)
Saudi Arabia	Family firms are characterized by the involvement of multiple family members, through establishment, inheritance, or the transfer of ownership, in the operation of a company's activities across different generations. It involves the participation of more than one family member in the exercise of a company's capital	Alkahtani (2021)

(*Continued*)

Table 2.1. (*Continued*)

Country	Definition	Reference
The United Arab Emirates	The Family Companies Law defined the family firm in the United Arab Emirates (UAE) as a business in which the majority of its shares are owned by individuals belonging to a single family. A family constitutes a "Single Family" where it comprises one individual or a group of individuals all of whom are the bloodline descendants of a common ancestor or their spouses (including widows and widowers, whether or not remarried)	Sergieh and Abdelhamid (2022)

Family firms in emerging nations are characterized by a shared emphasis on familial control and involvement. In each of these countries, a family firm is defined by the way that ownership, management, and generational succession combine family and business. These firms are primarily characterized by the strong involvement of family members in management and ownership spanning several generations. General definitions of family firms, which are defined as small- to medium-sized organizations with majority ownership by family members who frequently play significant roles in high-level management, reflect this tendency.

2.1. Ownership, Governance, and Management

Young family firms tend to exhibit specific characteristics, including their status as sole proprietorships, domestic orientation, focus on niche activities, and relatively small scale. Fernandez's study revealed a positive impact of family dynamics on early-stage business performance. Particularly when family members are actively involved in ownership, management, and labor, family firms initiated with family involvement tend to perform better than those that start without family involvement and later evolve into family firms (Fernandez, 2023).

Due to cultural and historical circumstances, family-owned startups are common in emerging nations such as several in Asia, Africa, and Latin America (La Porta et al., 1999). The list of identified emerging economies is provided in the Appendix. These family firms frequently have long roots in their communities, and their founders rely on familial networks for financial assistance and counseling (Chua et al., 1999).

They are distinguished by governing frameworks that are strongly linked to cherished family values. These ideals frequently lead to a governance framework that places high importance on trust, familial relationships, and informal decision-making processes.

Family firms' management practices reflect the local business environment and the cultural values that surround it. Management in emerging economies, where these startups are common, is relational and trust-based (Chua et al., 2003).

Decisions are made in small groups, where interpersonal interactions and adherence to family traditions dictate operational techniques.

Particularly smaller family firms are often recognized for their swift adaptability to change. This agility was notably evident among large family firms in the Middle East during the pandemic. Many families in the region demonstrated a commendable commitment to their businesses, even if it meant forgoing personal gains, to ensure their ventures persevered through the global crisis (Ramadani et al., 2022). Family firms exhibit distinct characteristics based on the development stage (developing, emerging, or developed) of the country in which they conduct their business, as outlined in a set of criteria (Table 2.2).

Compared to emerging economies, developed economies have sophisticated entrepreneurial ecosystems with diverse ownership arrangements. Startups in these economies frequently attract individual investors, venture capitalists, and institutional investors, who contribute not just finance but also knowledge and connections (Gimmon & Levie, 2010).

Governance in developed economies is more formalized, with an emphasis on openness, accountability, and compliance with established norms. Startups use a more professional, data-driven management strategy. They may adopt lean startup approaches, focusing on market research and scalability, where market feedback, analytics, and agile practices are commonly used in the decision-making process (Blank, 2013).

The 2023 Family Business Index, a collaborative report by Ernest & Young and the University of St. Gallen, reveals intriguing contrasts between family firms in developed and emerging economies across various key indicators (Table 2.3). In developed nations, these enterprises boast an average longevity of 87 years, whereas their emerging counterparts have an average of 66 years. The presence of female CEOs in developed economies stands at 7%, whereas in emerging nations, it's notably lower at 2%. When it comes to the appointment of a family member as CEO, developed economies have a 42% representation, with emerging nations having a slightly higher percentage at 51%.

Although developed and emerging economies exhibit striking similarities in data related to revenues, employee numbers, and shareholding percentages, a substantial disparity arises in the composition of family members on the board. In developed nations, 41% of board members are family members, while in emerging economies, this figure decreases to 23%. This variance can be attributed to differences in corporate governance practices, regulatory frameworks, and the level of competency and trust within the family. In developed nations, family firms may place greater trust in the competence and expertise of family members to sit on the board, while emerging economies may have a more cautious approach, preferring to appoint non-family professionals to ensure effective corporate governance.

Data on the Top 500 family firms in emerging economies are included in Table 2.4. Firms operate in a variety of industries, including manufacturing, consumer goods, energy, and technology. Reliance Industries from India, managed by the Ambani family, has $94 billion in revenues, and SK Corp from South Korea, run by the Chey family, has $85.9 billion in revenues. Companies have been created in the timespan of 1828 (CK Hutchison Holdings) to 2007 (Meritz Financial

Table 2.2. Family Firm Characteristics at Different Development Stages of Countries.

Factor	Developing Economies	Emerging Economies	Developed Economies	Reference
Economic environment	Lower GDP, focus on basic needs and local challenges	Transitioning to middle income, targeting both basic and aspirational needs	High GDP, focus on high-tech solutions, luxury goods, or advanced consumer needs	World Bank (2021) and IMF (2020)
Infrastructure	Limited tech and physical infrastructure	Improving but might face some challenges	Advanced with widespread internet, transportation, and utilities	UNCTAD (2019)
Access to funding	Limited venture capital, reliance on personal savings	Growing venture capital scene, some international interest	Mature investment ecosystem with varied funding avenues	Crunchbase (2020) and Zephyr (2021)
Talent and skills	The talent gap in advanced tech, eagerness to adapt	Increasing numbers of trained professionals	Highly skilled workforce with advanced education systems	World Economic Forum (2020) and UNESCO (2021)
Governmental policies	Underdeveloped regulations, potential corruption	Improving regulatory environment with start-up incentives	Established frameworks with clear guidelines, possibly bureaucratic	Doing Business (2020) and Transparency International (2020)
Cultural attitude	Necessity-driven entrepreneurship, potential fear of failure	A mix of necessity and opportunity-driven entrepreneurship	High acceptance of entrepreneurship, a celebration of innovation, acceptance of failure	Hofstede (2011) and Global Entrepreneurship Monitor (2020)
Market dynamics	Fragmented markets, vast unmet needs, grassroots focus	Rapid urbanization, growing middle class, new opportunities	Saturated markets focus on niche areas or industry disruption	McKinsey and Company (2019) and OECD (2021)

Table 2.3. Top 500 Family Firms' Metrics: Developed Versus Emerging Economies.

	Developed Economies	**Emerging Economies**
Total number of companies in Top 500	356	144
Longevity (avg years)	87	66
Female CEO	7%	2%
Family member CEO	42%	51%
Family members in the board	41%	23%
Revenues per company (avg)	$16 billion	$12.8 billion
Employees per company (avg)	49,032	41,752
Shareholding of the family (avg)	75.6%	75.7%

Source: Family Business Index (2023).

Group). Aditya Birla Group and Hinduja Group are two examples of companies that are 100% controlled by family members. Each entry includes information about the founding family, the company, the industry, and the shareholding.

3. Drivers of Family Firms in Emerging Economies

Family firms are not only integral to the global economy but are also instrumental in driving economic development, employment opportunities, and entrepreneurship, particularly in emerging economies (Ferraro & Cristiano, 2021). The management of such businesses presents a unique blend of opportunities and challenges. One notable advantage lies in their ability to seamlessly embed family values within the company's culture (Chandra & Mathur, 2017). In this section, we will delve into the economic and legal–political factors that shape their success, explore the motivations driving individuals to engage in family firms, assess the role of entrepreneurial spirit, and underscore the significance of entrepreneurship education in fostering sustainable family startups and cultivating human capital.

3.1. Economic Factors

Emerging economies are often characterized by unexploited and dynamic market opportunities, thus creating an encouraging environment for startups. The growing population in emerging economies creates a great customer base for startups. Moreover, increased purchasing power, combined with the growing availability of digital tools and the internet, creates a favorable environment for startups to thrive (Arruda et al., 2015). The favorable environment for innovation encourages startups to experiment with new ideas and business models, which can lead to breakthroughs in their respective industries. For example, Fintech startups are using digital technology to disrupt the financial services industry by offering mobile payment solutions and online lending platforms (Baltazar et al., 2023;

Table 2.4. Descriptive Data on Leading Family Firms Within the Top 500 in Emerging Economies.

Rank in the TOP500	Company Name	Founding Year	Revenues ($bln)	Employees	Jurisdiction Country	Industry	Family Name	Shareholding (%)
10	Reliance Industries Ltd	1973	94	342,982	India	Energy	Ambani	44.30
12	SK Corp.	1953	85.9	114,842	South Korea	Advanced manufacturing and mobility	Chey	32.70
13	Country Garden Holdings Co Ltd	1992	81.1	100,705	Mainland China	Government and infrastructure	Yang Guoqiang	59.30
17	JBS S.A.	1953	65	250,000	Brazil	Consumer	Batista	35.80
18	LG Corporation	1947	63	75,000	South Korea	Technology, media, and communications	Koo (In-Hwoi)	33.70
20	Aditya Birla Group	1857	60	140,000	India	Advanced manufacturing and mobility	Birla	100.00
22	CK Hutchison Holdings	1828	57.3	285,000	Hong Kong	Technology, media, and communications	Li	56.20
25	Idemitsu Kosan Co. Ltd	1911	54.6	14,044	Japan	Energy	Idemitsu	37.60
27	Midea Group Co. Ltd	1968	53.2	165,799	Mainland China	Consumer	He	32.00

28	Hinduja Group Ltd	1919	50	200,000	India	Advanced manufacturing and mobility	Hinduja	100.00
32	Hanwha Corporation	1952	46.2	4,751	South Korea	Advanced manufacturing and mobility	Kim	38.10
35	America Movil SA de CV	2000	41.6	181,205	Mexico	Technology, media, and communications	Slim	52.90
37	Meritz Financial Group	2007	40.3	20	South Korea	Financial services	Cho	69.10
39	Koç Holding A.Ş.	1926	39.1	105,908	Turkiye	Advanced manufacturing and mobility	Koc	64.30
42	Tata Motors Ltd	1945	37.1	73,608	India	Advanced manufacturing and mobility	Tata	46.40
46	Jardine Matheson Holdings Ltd	1832	35.9	400,000	Hong Kong	Advanced manufacturing and mobility	Keswick	50.10
50	Rajesh Exports Ltd	1988	32.6	135	India	Consumer	Mehta	55.60

Source: Family Business Index (2023).

Jalal et al., 2023). Edtech startups are using digital technology to revolutionize the education industry by offering online courses and interactive learning platforms (Renz & Hilbig, 2020).

Family firms tend to reinvest profits, fostering sustained growth. They exhibit resilience during economic downturns, given their long-term vision and community commitment (Amann & Jaussaud, 2012). The performance of family firms correlates with the economic growth of their operating emerging economies. High-growth economies tend to propel family firms to success. Yet, emerging market family firms confront challenges like inflation, currency fluctuations, and infrastructure deficits.

Start-up funds typically come from personal savings, family contributions, and unique loans from local banks deeply embedded in the community (Banki & Ismail, 2015).

3.2. Legal Political Factors (Government Support)

The legal and political climate in which family firms operate has a significant impact on their ability to succeed in emerging economies. Many emerging market governments provide incentives and initiatives to entrepreneurs in order to foster their growth and success. Coşkun et al. (2022) assert that nations with robust property rights, stable political systems, and open government rules have a higher chance of seeing success from their family firms. But family firms in developing economies might also have to deal with issues including bureaucratic red tape, poor contract execution, and corruption (Lin et al., 2010).

Government assistance in emerging economies frequently goes beyond simple financial incentives. Tax breaks, subsidies, and subsidized training programs are examples of such initiatives. Given that family firms do not have the resources of larger organizations, these services are more important. Furthermore, government-led infrastructure development can have a big impact on fostering a favorable business climate that can lead to more efficient operations and possibly cheaper prices.

On the other hand, substantial risks can arise from political instability or policy changes. For example, abrupt modifications to foreign investment regulations or tax legislation may cause corporate plans to be disrupted. Certain areas require family firms to manage intricate legal frameworks and bureaucratic processes, thus impeding their adaptability and capacity for expansion.

Additionally, as Paun (2019) points out, public funding is essential in fields where innovation is vital. Family firms can enhance their market presence and invest in new technology by gaining access to government-backed loans or grants. However, some family firms may find it difficult to navigate these financial streams due to the complex regulatory processes involved.

3.3. Family Firm as a Career Option

Working for a family firm can be chosen for a variety of reasons, including goals and motivations. Some people are motivated by the desire to continue a treasured family custom, while others see value in the exceptional chance to collaborate directly with close family members. Furthermore, a lot of people view working in a family firm as a means of achieving independence and financial security (Pittino et al., 2020).

The desire to carry on the family tradition is a strong incentive. Family firms are not only commercial enterprises but also symbols of a legacy that has been passed down through the centuries in many cultures. One of the major motivators may be the duty to maintain and improve the family's success and reputation. This feeling of legacy frequently creates a strong sense of dedication and purpose, strengthening a person's bond with the company.

Collaborating with family members provides a special fusion of interpersonal and professional ties. Mutual trust and similar values are crucial in this helpful and understanding work environment that can be fostered by this dynamic. It can, however, also make it difficult to strike a balance between personal and professional limits (Agarwal et al., 2016). Due to the complexity of these interactions, it is necessary to use efficient communication and conflict resolution techniques in order to maintain family peace and corporate success.

Furthermore, family firms might be attractive since they provide a certain level of financial independence and security. Being a part of a family firm sometimes entails having a stake in its success, which may serve as a strong incentive for many. This kind of involvement frequently entails a feeling of independence and the chance to have a direct impact on the course and expansion of the company. Additionally, it might give a feeling of financial security, particularly for companies with well-established brands (Jahmurataj et al., 2023).

In addition to these aspects, one important consideration in family firms is the potential for both professional and personal development. People might have the opportunity to take on a variety of roles, acquiring a wide range of knowledge and expertise. This adaptability can be especially alluring early in a career when exposure to many business facets can offer priceless learning experiences.

3.4. Entrepreneurial Mindset and Education

An entrepreneurial ecosystem pillars have a positive impact on the family firm performance (Alkaabi et al., 2023). According to Brazeau (2013), the entrepreneurial spirit is a complex idea that includes ambition, inventiveness, taking calculated risks, and having a forward-thinking perspective. This mentality is essential to the success of any company endeavor, but family firms require it even more. Leaders in these organizations need to be able to welcome and manage the risks that accompany new opportunities in addition to seeing them and taking advantage of them. In a business environment that is changing quickly, family firms must be proactive in order to thrive and adapt.

Leaders of family firms are frequently faced with the difficult problem of balancing the demands of their families with the objectives of their companies. This necessitates striking a careful balance between promoting innovation and change and upholding family values and customs. In this situation, exhibiting an entrepreneurial spirit entails appreciating the family firm's past and history but still being forward-thinking and receptive to new ideas.

The significance of entrepreneurship education that is especially suited to family firms is emphasized by Soares et al. (2021). Family firm members can stay competitive by having current knowledge of market trends and new breakthroughs thanks to this kind of education. Additionally, entrepreneurship education can impart useful skills in areas like company administration, capital raising, business plan preparation, and business opportunity identification. These abilities are necessary to navigate the dynamic and complex corporate environment of today.

Katz (2003) highlights the transformational impact of entrepreneurship education even more. It's important to foster an entrepreneurial mindset in addition to teaching knowledge and abilities. Creativity, resiliency, and a willingness to question the existing quo are traits of this attitude. Fostering an entrepreneurial spirit inside family firms can result in more creative practices, improved market adaption, and a more solid foundation for long-term success.

Moreover, succession planning can benefit greatly from entrepreneurship education. It equips the upcoming generation of family business owners with the knowledge and perspective needed to take over the firm. This preparedness entails embracing technology changes, comprehending the nuances of contemporary business processes, and formulating growth strategies that are sustainable.

In conclusion, the longevity and profitability of family firms depend on the entrepreneurial spirit in conjunction with focused entrepreneurship education. Family firm owners may make sure their companies are relevant, competitive, and able to survive generation after generation by adopting these components.

3.5. Human Capital

Human capital is a key ingredient in the success of family firms. This human capital includes the family's tacit firm-specific knowledge, hard work, and extraordinary commitment (Baù et al., 2020). According to Howells (1996), tacit firm-specific knowledge is knowledge that is unique to a particular firm and is difficult to codify and transfer to others. This type of knowledge is often embedded in the minds of experienced employees, including family members. For example, a family firm that has been in operation for generations may have a deep understanding of the local market, its customers, and its suppliers. This tacit knowledge can give the family firm a competitive advantage over its rivals.

Family firm members are also known for their hard work and extraordinary commitment to continuing their family firm from generation to generation. This approach can be seen as a major factor in the success of family firms. They are often willing to put in extra hours and go the extra mile for their business to thrive.

Based on a comparative analysis of two entrepreneurs who started businesses in different countries, Troilo (2010) emphasized the importance of considering motivation and environment in entrepreneurship. Motivational factors, such as financial gain and the desire for challenging work, vary in importance depending on the context. For example, in Nigeria, family firms' motivation is economic survival (Banki & Ismail, 2015).

4. Navigating Challenges of Family Firms in Emerging Economies

4.1. Challenges

Launching a new firm is a multifaceted and intricate endeavor, and it's important to recognize that the nature of this journey can differ significantly based on the location, culture, and economic conditions in which entrepreneurs find themselves (Ramadani et al., 2017). Family firms, in particular, face a wide array of challenges that necessitate thoughtful and effective solutions to secure their lasting success. These challenges encompass the ongoing balancing act between family and business priorities, the recruitment and retention of skilled personnel, and the process of transforming the company into a more professional and sustainable entity (Alkahtani, 2021). It's essential to examine these challenges systematically:

- *Entrepreneurial environment*: The entrepreneurial landscape, while influential, can be contradictory. In Tanzania, despite efforts to promote entrepreneurship through education, self-employment rates among graduates have declined. Factors such as a changing political climate, strong family bonds, international connections, and improved financial systems create a favorable environment. However, obstacles like limited start-up capital, cumbersome banking and taxation systems, trust issues, inadequate technology infrastructure, corruption, and competition from cheap imports deter graduate entrepreneurs (Mwasalwiba, 2012).
- *Contextual unique challenges in emerging economies*: Entrepreneurs in emerging economies like Vietnam face distinct challenges related to motivation, resource access, and the overall entrepreneurial ecosystem (Troilo, 2010). In Nigeria's Obudu Mountain resort destination, family-owned tourism micro businesses encounter challenges related to traditional family structures, demographics, start-up funding, motivation, training, and succession planning. These businesses predominantly involve male management with extended family support. Start-up funds typically come from personal savings, family contributions, and community-based loans (Banki & Ismail, 2015).
- *Sustainability and succession*: Sustainability is a pressing issue for family firms, especially those entirely managed and owned by the family. Research in the UAE underscores the need for effective succession planning, strategic foresight, and robust corporate governance to ensure their enduring success (Oudah et al., 2018).
- *Management dynamics*: Management within family firms is distinctive, often featuring family members with early exposure to the business. This overlap between ownership and management can pose legal and sustainability challenges. Some businesses have addressed this by separating ownership from management and appointing independent professional boards. Additionally, generational differences in management approaches may arise, and personal family issues can influence decision-making (Alsharif, 2019; Oukil & Al-Khalifah, 2012).
- *Ownership and control*: In Saudi Arabia, corporate governance principles have gained prominence. However, many family firms, despite adopting joint-stock structures, remain family-dominated, considering the company as private property (Aguilera et al., 2011; Alkahtani, 2016).

- *Minority shareholders' rights*: The governance of family firms in Saudi Arabia involves minority shareholders' rights. Shareholders can establish clauses and terms in shareholder agreements, aligning them with relevant statutes. These agreements are crucial for safeguarding interests, managing disputes, and establishing exit processes (Al-Habshan, 2017; Williams, 2019).

4.2. Common Reasons for Failure

A study by Start-up Genome delved into the primary reasons for start-up failures. Marketing mistakes emerged as the most prevalent issue, with 56% of startups facing challenges due to a lack of product-market fit. Before committing significant resources, startups are advised to validate market demands. Team-related issues, including gaps in domain expertise and internal conflicts, accounted for 18% of failures. Financial challenges were cited by 16% of startups, emphasizing that while over half didn't have a set budget and were predominantly self-funded, money is crucial mainly for growth, not initial validation. Technology issues, representing 6%, primarily stemmed from premature heavy investments before market validation. Operational issues, significant for businesses with physical products, comprised 2%, while legal problems, more pertinent to sectors like food and finance, also constituted 2%.

In addition to the above-mentioned, the authors highlight some other indicators of failure of startups when they are family firms (Basco, 2013; Chrisman et al., 2005; Poza, 2013) as provided below:

- Conflict among family members may lead to disagreements over business strategies, succession, or resource allocation. Extensive family involvement, particularly in ownership and labor, may decrease the likelihood of successfully transitioning from a nascent business to a young and thriving one (Fernandez, 2023).
- Due to a lack of adaptability, family firms in many cases in emerging economies show resistance to change or acceptance of new technologies. Furthermore, they show an inability to pivot in the face of market challenges. In certain situations, there is over-reliance on traditional methods where family firms fail to adopt modern business practices or technologies.
- The high failure rate among family firms can be attributed to family members in top management lacking the resources and capabilities to adapt to market fluctuations. To thrive in the digital age, family firms must embrace digital entrepreneurship, utilizing technologies like artificial intelligence, internet of thing, and virtual reality (VR). This involves converting existing resources and capabilities into a digital environment and modifying business models to align with market demands. Strategic thinking in family firms differs from non-family ones, as they focus on long-term survival and ownership. Policymakers should facilitate resource adaptation for digital entrepreneurship (Khan et al., 2022).
- Poor financial management and over-reliance on internal family funding make family startups in innovative sectors face specific challenges in attracting capital, especially in the early stages (Paun, 2019).

- Lack of succession planning and sustainability – Succession planning involves the complex process of transferring management control from one family member to another, entailing the selection and training of successors, communicating these decisions to family members, and defining the post-succession strategy and roles (Umans et al., 2020). The lack of succession planning poses challenges to long-term sustainability (Banki & Ismail, 2015). In Saudi Arabia, where Islamic Law dictates wealth distribution among family members after death, the third-generation takeover sparks conflicts among family members, impacting roughly 90% of family firms (Al-Sheikh, 2013). Successful transitions become further complicated by the challenge of passing the business to potentially unprepared heirs to take over (Ignatius et al., 2017).
- Reputation damage can be caused by scandals or ethical issues that tarnish the business's image (Ramadani & Hoy, 2015). The image is ruined also when they don't deliver on their promises of providing high product quality and customer service.

The list of reasons for family firms' failure is by no means exhaustive as different industries and specific regions may have additional factors that influence success or failure.

5. The Family Firms' Road to Success in Emerging Economies

5.1. Critical Success Factors

The performance of family-owned businesses in emerging economies depends on some critical success factors, which are essential elements that significantly influence their ability to succeed and achieve long-lasting success. These factors vary based on the specific context related to emerging economy and industry. Some predominant critical success factors we identified from the literature are provided below:

- *Effective succession planning*: A well-thought-out succession plan is crucial for family-owned startups. It involves identifying and preparing successors within the family to take over leadership roles when needed ensures a smooth transition of leadership and minimizes disruptions when the founding generation steps down. It helps maintain stability and continuity in the business (Banki & Ismail, 2015).
- *Strong governance and management*: Implementing robust governance structures, including the separation of ownership and management, and appointing professional managers when necessary. Clear governance helps in making strategic decisions objectively and mitigates conflicts of interest between family members. Professional management brings expertise and a fresh perspective.
- *Adaptability and innovation*: The ability to adapt to changing market conditions, embrace innovation, and incorporate modern business practices and technologies. Startups need to remain agile and open to change. Embracing innovation and technology allows them to stay competitive and meet evolving customer demands.

- *Strategic planning and business development*: Developing a clear business strategy, setting long-term goals, and continuously seeking opportunities for growth. Strategic planning helps family-owned startups define their path and make informed decisions. Identifying growth opportunities is vital for expanding market presence.
- *Strong financial management*: Maintaining sound financial practices, including budgeting, cash flow management, and prudent investment decisions. Effective financial management ensures the company's financial stability, allowing it to weather economic downturns and invest in growth opportunities.
- *Talent management and human resources*: Attracting, retaining, and developing top talent, both within the family and from external sources. Skilled and motivated employees are essential for a startup's success. Effective talent management helps in building a capable team.
- *Market research and customer focus*: Conducting thorough market research to understand customer needs and preferences and tailoring products or services accordingly. Customer-centricity is a key to building a loyal customer base and sustaining demand for products or services.
- *Ethical values and corporate social responsibility*: Upholding strong ethical values, promoting transparency, and engaging in corporate social responsibility initiatives. Demonstrating ethical behavior and a commitment to social responsibility enhances the company's reputation and fosters trust among stakeholders.
- *Networking and industry connections*: Building a strong network of industry contacts, partners, and mentors. Networking can provide valuable insights, opportunities for collaboration, and access to resources that can contribute to the startup's success.

5.2. *Outcomes: Generations of Success*

5.2.1. The Resilience and Longevity of Family Firms

The concept of business continuity is closely linked to longevity and is seen as a key measure of business success. Van Praag (2003) posits that the longer a business remains operational, the higher its chances of achieving success. This is particularly pertinent in the context of family firms, where longevity represents not only commercial success but also the preservation of family legacy and values.

In emerging economies like India, South Korea, Hong Kong, and the Gulf region, longevity in family firms is influenced by a variety of factors. Jahmurataj et al. (2023) identified three key factors that impact the longevity of family firms: the quality of relationships among family members, the effective transfer of knowledge from the founder to the successor, and the adherence to family's cultural practices. Interestingly, they noted that factors such as the education or professional training of the founder, succession planning, and the preparation of successors do not significantly affect the long-term survival of these businesses. This insight suggests that the interpersonal and cultural aspects of family firms are crucial determinants of their endurance.

However, the longevity of family firms can vary widely (Fig. 2.1). Al-Barghouthi (2016) reveals that family firms in the Gulf region typically have a short average

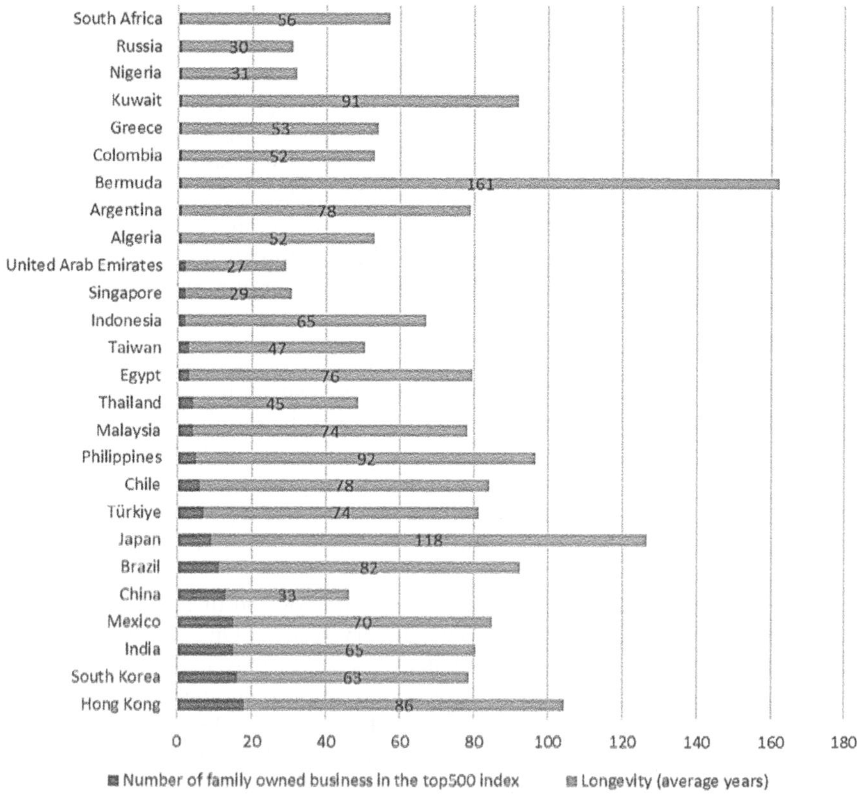

Fig. 2.1. Emerging Economies' Family Firms and Longevity. *Source*: Family Business Index (2023).

lifespan of 23 years. In stark contrast, some of the world's oldest family firms, like the Japanese hotels Nishiyama Onsen Keiunkan and the Hoshi Ryokan, which have been operational since 705 AD and 718 AD, respectively, demonstrate remarkable endurance. Managed by their 46th-generation founding families (O'Hara & Mandel, 2003), these businesses exemplify the potential for extraordinary longevity in family firms. In comparison, Daepp et al. (2015) found that the average survival of 25,000 publicly traded companies from 1950 to 2009 was only 15 years. This discrepancy underscores the unique resilience of family firms, as noted by Baron and Lachenauer (2021), who suggest that these businesses are willing to invest significant resources and effort to ensure their long-term sustainability.

The global significance of family firms is further highlighted by a report from "The Economist" (April, 2015), which states that they constitute more than 90% of all active companies worldwide. This staggering figure underscores the immense influence of family firms on the global business stage. The 2023 Family Business Index corroborates this, showing that despite global economic challenges, the top 500 family firms generated $8.02 trillion in revenue, a 10% increase since 2021, which is a testament to their resilience and longevity.

The enduring and impactful role of family firms in the global business landscape is exemplified in emerging economies. For instance, India has seen its family firms thrive, with 15 companies making it to the top 10 largest family firms for the first time in the 2023 Index. This achievement highlights their growing importance in India's economy and their potential for long-term success, boasting an average longevity of 65 years. Similarly, Hong Kong and South Korea demonstrate the robust presence of family firms, with Hong Kong hosting 18 businesses averaging 86 years of operation, and South Korea's 16 companies contributing a substantial portion of the region's revenue. These examples illustrate the significant and sustained contributions of family firms in emerging economies.

5.2.2. The Dynamics of Innovation in Family Firms

It is widely accepted that family involvement in ownership, management, and governance significantly influences innovation within family firms (Chrisman et al., 2015). This influence is particularly pronounced in family firms, where governance choices are often shaped by a high concentration of ownership. In such firms, members of the controlling families typically occupy top positions in the hierarchy, resulting in their direct and predominant involvement in governance decisions (Di Toma, 2012).

The literature on the relationship between family-owned firms and innovation presents a complex and somewhat contradictory picture. On one hand, there is evidence suggesting that family-dominated businesses may exhibit lower levels of innovation, particularly in terms of research and development (R&D) investments. China's Family Business Health Index Report (2014) highlights a trend of lower R&D intensity in domestic family firms compared to other Chinese private companies (Chen, 2015). This could be attributed to family firms prioritizing non-economic objectives, such as social and emotional wealth, which might discourage them from engaging in high-risk R&D investments. A similar pattern is observed in Gulf Cooperation Council family firms, which are noted for their limited contribution to the knowledge economy, research, and innovation (Ramadani et al., 2022).

Conversely, there is a contrasting perspective that suggests family-managed businesses can foster innovation-friendly environments. For instance, in Indonesia, where a substantial majority of businesses are family-owned, these enterprises actively prioritize innovation alongside profitability and talent attraction and retention. Unlike non-family firms, which often rely on formal control mechanisms that may hinder innovation, family firms tend to maintain open communication channels, make decisions informally, and emphasize process flexibility. These characteristics create an atmosphere conducive to innovation, with strong family ties positively influencing business innovation.

In conclusion, the relationship between family-owned firms and innovation is not straightforward and can vary depending on contextual factors and specific business practices. While some evidence points to lower R&D intensity and limited innovation in certain family firms, others highlight the potential for innovation-friendly environments within family-managed enterprises. The key lies in understanding how different family firms operate and the extent to which they prioritize innovation as part of their strategic objectives.

6. Growth Framework of Family Firms in Emerging Economies

After identifying the opportunities and challenges faced by family firms in emerging economies, we can develop a comprehensive framework (Fig. 2.2) that emphasizes the results of addressing challenges and merging opportunities with critical success factors. The goal is to optimize business growth, longevity, adaptability, and stakeholder satisfaction.

The framework elucidates a conceptual model that delineates diverse factors that have the potential to influence family firms. The following is an analysis of the constituent elements comprising this conceptual framework:

- *Drivers and opportunities*: The growth and performance of family firms can be influenced by various factors. These include economic conditions, the legal and political contexts, the mindset and education of entrepreneurs, and the availability of human resources.
- *Critical success factors* refer to the essential components that play a pivotal role in determining the success of a family-owned firm. The key factors encompassed in this context are deemed to be efficacious succession planning, robust governance and management practices, adaptability and innovation, strategic planning and business development, proficient financial management, talent management and human resources, comprehensive market research and customer-centric approach, ethical values and corporate social responsibility, as well as networking and industry connections.
- *Challenges*: These are the potential hurdles that may be encountered by family firms. The obstacles identified encompass a range of elements, including environmental considerations, sustainability and succession concerns, disputes within family dynamics, challenges related to governance and management, and resistance toward embracing change and adapting to new circumstances.
- *Outcomes* refer to the intended achievements or objectives of a family-owned firm. The ultimate results of skillfully handling the drivers/opportunities, important success elements, and challenges are represented. The identified outcomes encompass business growth, the sustained existence of the business, stakeholder contentment, and the capacity for innovation and adaptability.

The proposed framework posits that via the prioritization of important success criteria and the adept management of problems, a family-owned business can harness the drives and opportunities available to attain advantageous outcomes, including growth, longevity, stakeholder satisfaction, and the capacity to innovate and adapt.

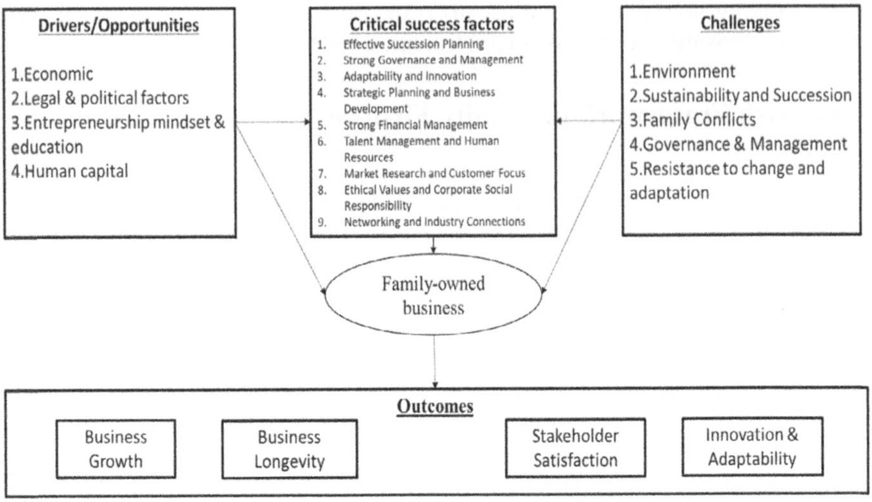

Fig. 2.2. Family Firm Growth Framework. *Source*: Authors.

7. Best Practices and Lessons from the Failure of Family Firms in Emerging Economies

7.1. Success Stories

Start-up family firms in emerging nations might offer insightful information about the particular problems and possibilities they encounter. For instance, "Patanjali Ayurved" stands out as a success story in India. Baba Ramdev and Acharya Balkrishna started this family firm, which has since disrupted the conventional fast-moving consumer goods sector by emphasizing ayurvedic items and promoting a strong "Swadeshi" (Made in India) story. Its explosive growth and increases in market share demonstrate how family-driven innovation can prosper in a developing country.

Another prime example of family-owned business success in India's growing economy is the Tata Group, founded by Jamsetji Tata in 1868. This conglomerate has diversified across multiple sectors, such as telecommunications, information technology, steel, and automobiles, amassing a revenue that exceeded $100 billion in 2020 (Tata Group, 2021). The Tata family's enduring commitment to ethical and socially responsible principles, innovative strategies, and diversification is evident. Their influence extends to strategic decisions, as seen in acquisitions like Tetley Tea and Jaguar Land Rover, which expanded the group's global footprint.

The Philippine family firm beginning "Jollibee Foods Corporation" is another success story. Since 1978, Tony Tan Caktiong and his family have evolved Jollibee from a modest ice cream parlor to one of Southeast Asia's largest and most successful fast-food businesses. Jollibee is a model family firm that responded to shifting market conditions. Tony Tan Caktiong turned his ice cream shop into a fast-food restaurant providing burgers and fried chicken after seeing its popularity. Jollibee's menu includes Filipino-friendly dishes like Chickenjoy, crispy fried chicken, and Jolly Spaghetti, sweet spaghetti.

Jollibee grew due to the family's commitment to quality, customer service, and savvy business decisions. They also understood local tastes and preferences, which helped Jollibee beat McDonald's in the Philippines. Another factor in Jollibee's success is expansion. Under the Tan family, the corporation aggressively expanded domestically and globally. Jollibee Foods Corporation has thousands of outlets in Vietnam, the USA, and Canada. Jollibee Foods Corporation shows how a family firm steeped in local culture and values can expand and become a national symbol of entrepreneurial success in an emerging economy (Gutierrez, 2021).

Another example of a company's trajectory that reflects the potential of family firms to evolve over generations is presented by Alghanim Industries, founded by the prolific entrepreneur Yusuf Alghanim in 1932, which has grown to become Kuwait's largest family firm with a presence in 40 countries. With diverse operations spanning the automotive to services sectors, its legacy stands tall. As of April 2021, the Alghanim family proudly owns 32.75% of Gulf Bank shares valued at $713 million (Ramadani et al., 2022). The success story derives from combining visionary leadership, excellence, strategic diversification, and an inherent sense of responsibility toward its stakeholders.

The success of Patanjali Ayurveda, Tata Group, Jollibee Foods Corporation, and Alghanim Industries highlights the importance of family firms in emerging economies, which are guided by the enduring values and ideals of the families who run them. These qualities, such as ethics, creativity, and long-term vision, are critical to their amazing successes, highlighting the relevance of family values as a driving force behind their long-term success.

7.2. Failure Stories

The Daewoo Group's rise and fall provide valuable insights into family firm dynamics. Founded by Kim Woo-Jung in 1967, family ties initially played a pivotal role in its success, offering financial support and mentorship (Chua et al., 1999). However, as the company expanded rapidly, the intertwining of family and corporate interests led to governance challenges (Faccio et al., 2001). The founder's ambitious global endeavors and personal financial issues further strained the company's stability (Roth, 2003), eventually culminating in its collapse due to mounting debts and a lack of transparency (Chang, 2004). Daewoo's story underscores the delicate balance between family involvement and corporate success. While family connections can drive early achievements, their entanglement in business decisions, along with inadequate governance, can contribute to a company's downfall (Gedajlovic et al., 2012). This narrative underscores the critical importance of robust governance frameworks and the effective separation of family and corporate interests for sustained business stability.

Odebrecht, a well-known Brazilian construction corporation created by the Odebrecht family, went through a major crisis that offers interesting perspectives. Odebrecht's quick worldwide growth and borrowing practices undermined its financial stability, highlighting the significance of prudent expansion and avoiding excessive debt. For family firms, strong governance and adherence to legal and regulatory standards are critical (Smith, 2018). The implications of Odebrecht's governance flaws and failure to comply with anti-corruption laws were severe.

The challenges associated with the family leadership transition, intensified by the deficiency in succession planning, had adverse consequences for Odebrecht. This case revolves around the perils of corruption and the critical role of ethical conduct in business, highlighting the critical significance of ethics, prudent growth, governance, compliance, and effective succession planning in guaranteeing the success as well as longevity of family firms in emerging economies.

In a similar vein, Indian family firm venture Kingfisher Airlines failed. Founded in 2005 by Vijay Mallya, it was an ambitious attempt by the United Breweries Group, a beverage industry giant. Kingfisher Airlines was founded to provide a premium Indian airline experience. The airline grew quickly and was known for great service. However, the venture soon encountered major obstacles. Debt-fueled airline growth was unsustainable. Kingfisher Airlines struggled due to high operational expenses, severe rivalry, and a difficult Indian aviation environment. The global financial crisis raised fuel prices and depreciated the rupee, worsening the airline's finances. Despite restructuring and cost cuts, the airline's indebtedness grew. Kingfisher Airlines had over $1 billion in debt by 2012, resulting in grounded aircraft, underpaid salaries, and angry creditors.

Kingfisher Airlines' bankruptcy underscores numerous key challenges with family firm starts, especially in emerging economies. Overambitious expansion without a viable business plan or risk assessment was a problem. Debt finance and inability to respond to market changes also contributed to its demise. The failure of Kingfisher Airlines warns family firms about over-leverage, quick development without strategic planning, and adaptability in volatile markets. It emphasizes the necessity of sound financial management and market-responsive methods in emerging economy family firm success and longevity (Panigrahi et al., 2019).

8. Conclusion and Implications

Commencing a new business venture unfolds as a multifaceted journey, intricately shaped by the geographical, cultural, and economic milieu wherein entrepreneurs operate. Family firms, in particular, encounter a diverse array of challenges, compelling the need for judicious and innovative resolutions to secure enduring triumph. This section offers key implications for academia and industry arising from these challenges. By addressing these implications, academia and industry can collectively contribute to the growth, resilience, and sustainable success of family-owned startups in emerging economies.

- Understanding the dynamics of traditional family structures, funding mechanisms, succession planning, and demographic considerations can inform tailored strategies to support the growth and sustainability of such enterprises. Industry players can leverage these insights to create targeted support systems and investment opportunities.
- The critical success factors for family-owned startups in emerging economies such as succession and governance, adaptability, strategic planning, financial stability, talent management, customer focus, and ethical values ensure long-term viability and prosperity. Policymakers should recognize their importance in supporting the growth and sustainability of these businesses.

- In academia, a deeper analysis of the entrepreneurial environments in emerging nations becomes imperative through investigating the intricate interplay of factors that foster entrepreneurship, such as political dynamics, familial bonds, international connections, and financial infrastructure. Concurrently, recognize and address the impediments that deter graduate entrepreneurs, including limited capital access, cumbersome banking systems, trust issues, technological deficits, corruption, and competition from imports. Industry stakeholders should consider fostering supportive ecosystems that mitigate these challenges, fostering a conducive environment for emerging entrepreneurs.
- Researchers should delve into the distinctive challenges faced by entrepreneurs in emerging economies, offering insights into motivation, resource accessibility, and the overall entrepreneurial ecosystem. Industry players should collaborate with educational institutions to devise context-specific training programs, mentorship initiatives, and funding avenues, addressing the unique needs of startups in these regions.
- Emphasizing the role of sustainability and governance in family firms suggests the development of educational modules and training programs that address succession planning, corporate governance, and strategic foresight, vital for the longevity of these enterprises. Industry associations and business consultants can collaborate with academic institutions to offer practical guidance and mentoring, aiding family-owned startups in navigating these complexities.
- Exploring the nuanced management dynamics within family-owned startups, particularly the potential conflicts arising from the familial overlap between ownership and management is important for family firms to improve management adaptability and conflict resolution. Educational institutions can offer courses and resources on conflict resolution and management in family firms. Industry experts should advocate for the adoption of best practices in governance, promoting transparency and establishing clear conflict resolution mechanisms.

Furthermore, understanding the prevalent reasons for family firms' failures offers valuable insights for academia and industry:

- Academia can incorporate training in a variety of topics into entrepreneurship programs, emphasizing its critical role in family-owned startups. These include conflict resolution among family members and effective succession planning. Educational institutions should promote adaptability and change management in family-owned startups. Furthermore, they can facilitate workshops and seminars on the adoption of modern business practices and technologies, helping firms stay competitive.
- Industry associations should advocate for the importance of succession planning and provide guidelines for effective transitions. In this line, Buckman et al. (2020) introduced a comprehensive six-stage succession process model for family firms. This non-linear journey can span up to 20 years and adapts as needed.
- Industry stakeholders should invest in digitalization initiatives and collaborate with startups to facilitate their digital transformation journey. On the other

side, academic institutions should introduce digital entrepreneurship programs that equip family firms with the skills to navigate the digital age. For family firms embarking on the complex succession journey, success is not guaranteed, and many may encounter obstacles that necessitate revisiting earlier stages or reevaluating their strategies. As Khan et al. (2022) advocate, entrepreneurs and employers in these family firms should prioritize the integration of digital technologies into their business plans, aligning their operations with evolving market demands. These technologies offer a cost-effective means to foster innovation, access valuable information, and diversify product offerings, with VR technology standing out as a particularly advantageous tool in the digital age (as depicted in Table 2.2). Family firms are increasingly exploring diverse business models that underscore innovation, research and development, and rigorous capital assessment. Moreover, policymakers hold a pivotal role in this context, as they should actively support businesses in their adoption of these new technologies. This support involves creating an enabling environment for digital entrepreneurship, disseminating critical information, and promoting awareness among businesses, ultimately facilitating resource adaptation for digitalization (Khan et al., 2022).

9. Future Research Agenda

The future research agenda for delving into the start-up dynamics and hurdles encountered by family firms in emerging nations can encompass the subsequent avenues of inquiry:

- Conducting in-depth studies comparing the experiences and challenges faced by family-owned startups in various emerging economies can help identify commonalities and differences and provide valuable insights into the impact of cultural, economic, and regulatory factors.
- Researchers are recommended to examine the distinct challenges associated with succession planning that family-owned startups grapple with within emerging economies. Investigate innovative strategies that facilitate seamless generational transitions while ensuring the uninterrupted flow of business operations.
- Assessing the approach of integration of new product development, technology adoption, and the embracement of e-commerce on family-owned startups in emerging economies is another area of research that would support probing the role of innovation in augmenting their competitive edge and market outreach.
- Researchers should delve into the financial constraints confronted by family-owned startups in emerging nations and explore inventive approaches to financing. Analyze the contributions of microfinance, venture capital, and governmental initiatives in supporting these enterprises.
- Institutional support is a key to family start-up success. Evaluating the efficacy of government policies, business incubators, and entrepreneurship ecosystems

in nurturing family-owned startups can provide insights into the tangible benefits of these support systems in fostering growth and long-term viability.
- This chapter emphasizes the socio-cultural dynamics impact: further investigation of the ramifications of cultural norms, societal expectations, and familial dynamics on the management and functioning of family-owned startups can explore how these factors influence decision-making processes.
- Family firm start-up success is related to the extent they embrace sustainability and social responsibility. Therefore, assessing the role of family-owned startups in promoting sustainability and corporate social responsibility in emerging economies and examining their contributions to local communities and environmental initiatives is a significant part of the research agenda.
- Investigating the enduring performance and survival rates of family-owned startups in emerging economies can create a better picture of the determinants that contribute to their sustained prosperity or challenges leading to adversity.
- As highlighted in this study the importance of human resource management, family firms in emerging economies would benefit from the knowledge acquired from exploring the human resource practices and talent management strategies adopted by family-owned startups. Analyze their methods for talent acquisition, retention, and development, especially in the context of generational transitions.
- Another research avenue is studying the influence of family firm associations and networks in offering guidance, knowledge sharing, and best practices for family-owned startups. Researchers are recommended to analyze the impact of these networks on business expansion and resilience.
- Showcasing examples and sharing the best practices from flourishing family-owned startups across diverse emerging economies would disseminate insights and actionable strategies to inspire prospective entrepreneurs.

By addressing these research areas, scholars can contribute to a deeper understanding of the dynamics, challenges, and opportunities faced by family-owned startups in emerging economies, ultimately aiding policymakers, entrepreneurs, and academics in supporting the growth of these enterprises. Ultimately, such endeavors will offer valuable guidance to policymakers, aspiring entrepreneurs, and the academic community, bolstering the growth of these enterprises.

References

Agarwal, R., Kumar, A., & D'Souza, K. (2016). Issues in career choices of successors in family businesses: Perspective from literature review. *Journal of Applied Management and Investments*, *5*(1), 1–19.

Aguilera, R. V., Castro, L. R. K., Lee, J. H., & You, J. (2011). *Corporate governance in emerging markets*. Oxford University.

Al-Barghouthi, S. (2016). Passing the torch, family business succession, case study, Bahrain. *International Journal of Business and Management*, *5*(1), 279–294.

Al-Habshan, K. S. (2017). The current rights of minority shareholders in Saudi Arabia. *International Law Research*, *6*(1), 185–204.

Alkaabi, K., Ramadani, V., & Zeqiri, J. (2023). Universities, entrepreneurial ecosystem, and family business performance: Evidence from the United Arab Emirates. *Journal of the Knowledge Economy*. https://doi.org/10.1007/s13132-023-01384-9

Alkahtani, A., Nordin, N., & Khan, R. U. (2020). Does government support enhance the relation between networking structure and sustainable competitive performance among SMEs? *Journal of Innovation and Entrepreneurship*, *9*(1), 1–16.

Alkahtani, A. W. (2016). Corporate governance standards in Saudi financial sector: Achievements and challenges. *International Journal of Business and Social Science*, *7*(12), 124–138.

Alkahtani, A. W. (2021). Family-owned businesses in Saudi Arabia: Challenges and solutions from a legal perspective. *International Journal of Contemporary Management and Information Technology (IJCMIT)*, *1*(2), 16–22.

Alsharif, D. T. (2019). *In Saudi Arabia, business runs in the family*. https://www.arabnews.com/node/1579676

Al-Sheikh, A. A. (2013). Capital market authority warns the family businesses from the future problems. *Middle East Newspaper*.

Amann, B., & Jaussaud, J. (2012). Family and non-family business resilience in an economic downturn. *Asia Pacific Business Review*, *18*(2), 203–223.

Arruda, C., Nogueira, V. S., Cozzi, A., & Costa, V. (2015). The Brazilian entrepreneurial ecosystem of startups: An analysis of entrepreneurship determinants in Brazil as seen from the OECD pillars. *Journal of Entrepreneurship and Innovation Management*, *2*(3), 17–57.

Baltazar, J., Fernandes, C., Ramadani, V., & Hughes, M. (2023). Family business succession and innovation: A systematic literature review. *Review of Managerial Science*, *17*(8), 2897–2920.

Banki, M. B., & Ismail, H. N. (2015). Understanding the characteristics of family-owned tourism micro businesses in mountain destinations in developing countries: Evidence from Nigeria. *Tourism Management Perspectives*, *13*(1), 18–32.

Baron, J., & Lachenauer, R. (2021). Do most family businesses really fail by the third generation? *Harvard Business Review*. https://hbr.org/2021/07/do-most-family-businesses-really-fail-by-the-third-generation

Basco, R. (2013). The family's effect on family firm performance: A model testing the demographic and essence approaches. *Journal of Family Business Strategy*, *4*(1), 42–66.

Baù, M., Pittino, D., Sieger, P., & Eddleston, K. A. (2020). Careers in family business: New avenues for careers and family business research in the 21st century. *Journal of Family Business Strategy*, *11*(3), 1–15.

Birdthistle, N., & Hales, R. (2023). The meaning of being a family business in the 21st century. In N. Birdthistle & R. Hales (Eds.), *Attaining the 2030 sustainable development goal of responsible consumption and production* (pp. 11–20). Emerald Publishing Limited.

Blank, S. G. (2013). *The startup owner's manual: The step-by-step guide for building a great company*. K & S Ranch.

Brazeau, G. (2013). Entrepreneurial spirit in pharmacy. *American Journal of Pharmaceutical Education*, *77*(5), 1–10.

Buckman, J., Jones, P., & Buame, S. (2020). Passing on the baton: A succession planning framework for family-owned businesses in Ghana. *Journal of Entrepreneurship in Emerging Economies*, *12*(2), 259–278.

Casanova, L., & Miroux, A. (2022). *Emerging market report 2022*. Cornell University Library. https://doi.org/10.7298/9j27-ng36. hdl: 1813/112770.

Cascino, S., Pugliese, A., Mussolino, D., & Sansone, C. (2010). The influence of family ownership on the quality of accounting information. *Family Business Review*, *23*(3), 246–265.

Chandra, Y., & Mathur, K. (2017). Strategic entrepreneurship within family owned firms vs. corporate decision makers: Opportunities and challenges. *Nirma University Journal of Business and Management Studies*, *12*(01–02), 85–102.

Chang, S. J. (2004). Convergence and path-dependency in corporate governance: A comparative study of South Korea and Japan. *Organization Science*, *15*(1), 87–101.

Chen, L. (2015). *2014 Chinese family business health index* (Chinese ed.). Zhejiang University Press. ISBN-10: 7308143244.

Chrisman, J. J., Chua, J. H., & Steier, L. (2005). Sources and consequences of distinctive familiness: An introduction. *Entrepreneurship Theory and Practice*, *29*(3), 237–247.

Chrisman, J. J., Fang, H., Kotlar, J., & De Massis, A. (2015). A note on family influence and the adoption of discontinuous technologies in family firms. *Journal of Product Innovation Management*, *32*(3), 384–388.

Chua, J. H., Chrisman, J. J., & Bergiel, E. B. (2003). An agency theoretic analysis of the professionalized family firm. *Entrepreneurship Theory and Practice*, *27*(4), 361–376.

Chua, J. H., Chrisman, J. J., & Sharma, P. (1999). Defining the family business by behavior. *Entrepreneurship Theory and Practice*, *23*(4), 19–39.

Coşkun, R., Kryeziu, L., & Krasniqi, B. A. (2022). Institutions and competition: Does internationalization provide advantages for the family firms in a transition economy? *Journal of Entrepreneurship and Public Policy*, *11*(2/3), 253–272.

Crunchbase. (2020). *Global venture capital report*. https://www.crunchbase.com/organization/2020

Daepp, M. I. G., Hamilton, M. J., West, G. B., & Bettencourt, L. M. A. (2015). The mortality of companies. *Journal of the Royal Society Interface*, *12*(120), 20150120. https://doi.org/10.1098/rsif.2015.0120

Di Toma, P. (2012). Dalle risorse al know-how esclusivo: il ruolo della corporate governance nello sviluppo di un'impresa familiare. *Piccola Impresa/Small Business*, *1*. https://doi.org/10.14596/pisb.21

Doing Business. (2020). *Doing business report*. World Bank.

Ernest & Young (EY) and University of St. Gallen. (2023). *Family Business Index*. https://familybusinessindex.com/

Faccio, M., Lang, L. H., & Young, L. (2001). Dividends and expropriation. *The American Economic Review*, *93*(1), 173–192.

Fernandez, V. (2023). Family entrepreneurship around the world. *International Review of Financial Analysis*, *89*(1), 102808.

Ferraro, O., & Cristiano, E. (2021). Family business in the digital age: The state of the art and the impact of change in the estimate of economic value. *Journal of Risk and Financial Management*, *14*(2), 301–312.

FTSE. (2014). *Advanced and Secondary Emerging Markets listed at: "FTSE Annual Country Classification Review" (PDF)*. FTSE Group.

Gallo, M. Á., Tàpies, J., & Cappuyns, K. (2004). Comparison of family and nonfamily business: Financial logic and personal preferences. *Family Business Review*, *17*(4), 303–318.

Gedajlovic, E., Carney, M., Chrisman, J. J., & Kellermanns, F. W. (2012). The adolescence of family firm research: Taking stock and planning for the future. *Journal of Management*, *38*(4), 1010–1037.

Gimmon, E., & Levie, J. (2010). Founders' human capital and the performance of UK new technology-based firms. *Strategic Management Journal*, *31*(10), 1064–1086.

Global Entrepreneurship Monitor. (2020). *Global report*. GEM.

Gutierrez, B. P. B. (2021). *Jollibee foods corporation*. https://jollibeegroup.com/

Hofstede, G. (2011). Dimensionalizing cultures: The hofstede model in context. *Online Readings in Psychology and Culture*, *2*(1), 1–20.

Howells, J. (1996). Tacit knowledge. *Technology Analysis & Strategic Management*, *8*(2), 91–106.

IMF. (2015). *World economic outlook*. Retrieved October 15, 2023, from http://www.imf.org/external/pubs/ft/weo/2015/02/pdf/text.pdf

IMF. (2020). *World economic outlook*. IMF.

Jahmurataj, V., Ramadani, V., Bexheti, A., Rexhepi, G., Abazi-Alili, H., & Krasniqi, B. A. (2023). Unveiling the determining factors of family business longevity: Evidence from Kosovo. *Journal of Business Research*, *159*(11), 113745.

Jalal, A., Al Mubarak, M., & Durani, F. (2023). Financial technology (fintech). In A. Hamdan & E. S. Aldhaen (Eds.), *Artificial intelligence and transforming digital marketing* (pp. 525–536). Springer Nature Switzerland.

Katz, J. A. (2003). The chronology and intellectual trajectory of American Entrepreneurship Education: 1876–1999. *Journal of Business Venturing*, *18*(2), 283–300.

Khan, R. U., Abbasi, M. A., Amran, A., & Fawad, A. (2022). *The innovative business model for family-owned firms in the era of digital entrepreneurship: Evidence from emerging economy*. IntechOpen. 10.5772/intechopen.102459

Klein, S., & Blondel, C. (2002). *Ownership structure of the 205 largest listed companies in Germany* [Working papers]. INSEAD.

Kraus, S., Clauss, T., & Kallmuenzer, A. (2023). Introduction to the research handbook on entrepreneurship and innovation in family firms. In S. Kraus, T. Clauss, & A. Kallmuenzer (Eds.), *Research handbook on entrepreneurship and innovation in family firms* (pp. 1–12). Edward Elgar Publishing.

Kraus, S., Harms, R., & Fink, M. (2011). Family firm research: Sketching a research field. *International Journal of Entrepreneurship and Innovation Management*, *13*(1), 32–47.

La Porta, R., Lopez-de-Silanes, F., & Shleifer, A. (1999). Corporate ownership around the world. *The Journal of Finance*, *54*(2), 471–517.

Lin, C., Lin, P., & Song, F. (2010). Property rights protection and corporate R&D: Evidence from China. *Journal of Development Economics*, *93*(1), 49–62.

McKinsey & Company. (2019). The rise of digital consumers in developing economies. *McKinsey Global Institute*. Retrieved from https://www.mckinsey.com/business-functions/mckinsey-digital/our-insights/how-digital-finance-could-boost-growth-in-emerging-economies

Merchant, P., Kumar, A., & Mallik, D. (2018). Factors influencing family business continuity in Indian small and medium enterprises (SMEs). *Journal of Family and Economic Issues*, *39*(2), 177–190.

Mwasalwiba, E. S. (2012). *University entrepreneurship education in Tanzania: Teaching context, students' profiles, expectations and outcomes* [PhD thesis – Research and graduation internal]. Vrije Universiteit Amsterdam.

Nordqvist, M., & Melin, L. (2010). The promise of the strategy as practice perspective for family business strategy research. *Journal of Family Business Strategy*, *1*(1), 15–25.

OECD. (2021). *Economic surveys*. https://www.oecd.org/en/topics/sub-issues/economic-surveys.html

O'Hara, W., & Mandel, P. (2003). *The world's oldest family companies*. Family Business: The Guide for Family Companies. https://www.griequity.com/resources/industry-andissues/familybusiness/oldestinworld.html

Oudah, M., Jabeen, F., & Dixon, C. (2018). Determinants linked to family business sustainability in the UAE: An AHP approach. *Sustainability*, *10*, 246.

Oukil, M. S., & Al-Khalifah, H. (2012). Managerial weaknesses and features of family businesses in the eastern region of Saudi Arabia. *International Conference on Economics, Business and Marketing Management*, *29*(1), 49–54.

Palaiologos, G. (2017). Growing the Arab family business (1): Hybrid organizational arrangements. *Journal of Entrepreneurship and Business Innovation*, *4*(1), 25.

Panigrahi, C. M. A., Sinha, A., Garg, A., & Mehta, A. (2019). A case study on the downfall of kingfisher airlines. *Journal of Management Research and Analysis*, *6*(2), 81–84.

Paun, D. (2019). Tax competition and factors influencing the gross domestic product and foreign direct investments of CEE countries. *Economic Research-Ekonomska Istraživanja*, *32*(1), 876–893.

Pieper, T. M., Astrachan, J. H., & Manners, G. E. (2013). Conflict in family business: Common metaphors and suggestions for intervention. *Family Relations*, *62*(3), 490–500.

Pittino, D., Chirico, F., Baù, M., Villasana, M., Naranjo-Priego, E. E., & Barron, E. (2020). Starting a family business as a career option: The role of the family household in Mexico. *Journal of Family Business Strategy*, *11*(2), 100338.

Poza, E. J. (2013). *Family business* (4th ed.). Cengage Learning.

Ramadani, V., Dzenopoljac, V., Zainal, M., & Dzenopoljac, A. (2022). Family business in Kuwait. In V. Ramadani (Ed.), *Family business in Gulf Cooperation Council countries* (pp. 33–51). Springer International Publishing.

Ramadani, V., Hisrich, R. D., Dana, L.-P., Palalic, R., & Panthi, L. (2019). Beekeeping as a family artisan entrepreneurship business. *International Journal of Entrepreneurial Behavior & Research*, *25*(4), 717–730.

Ramadani, V., & Hoy, F. (2015). Context and uniqueness of family businesses. In L.-P. Dana & V. Ramadani (Eds.), *Family businesses in transition economies* (pp. 9–37). Springer International Publishing.

Ramadani, V., Ilioska, A., Rexhepi, G., & Abazi-Alili, H. (2017). Family business management challenges. In V. Ratten et al. (Eds.), *Gender and family entrepreneurship* (p. 11). Routledge.

Renz, A., & Hilbig, R. (2020). Prerequisites for artificial intelligence in further education: Identification of drivers, barriers, and business models of educational technology companies. *International Journal of Educational Technology in Higher Education*, *17*(1), 1–21.

Rexhepi, G., Bexheti, A., Ibraimi, S., & Kurtishi-Kastrati, S. (2018). The importance of intellectual capital in the selection of global marketing strategies: Evidence from family businesses in Macedonia. *International Journal of Transitions and Innovation Systems*, *6*(2), 108–117.

Rodrigues, A. O. A., Marques, C. S., & Ramadani, V. (2023). Artisan entrepreneurship, resilience and sustainable development: The quintuple helix innovation model in the low-density and cross-border territories. *Journal of Enterprise Information Management*. Ahead of printing. https://doi.org/10.1108/JEIM-02-2023-0066

Roth, K. (2003). As Asia Economy Sank, a company's rise and fall. *The New York Times*. https://www.nytimes.com/2003/07/13/business/asia-economy-sank-a-company-s-rise-and-fall.html

Rovelli, P., Ferasso, M., De Massis, A., & Kraus, S. (2022). Thirty years of research in family business journals: Status quo and future directions. *Journal of Family Business Strategy*, *13*(3), 100422.

Sergieh, A., & Abdelhamid, M. (2022). *Major legal development – New UAE family business law*. Hadef & Partners LLC. https://www.hadefpartners.com/News/594/Major-Legal-Development--New-UAE-Family-Business-Law

Smith, J. (2018). Corporate failures and lessons learned. *Business Review*, *45*(3), 231–245.

Soares, G. G., Braga, V. L., Marques, C. S., & Ratten, V. (2021). Corporate entrepreneurship education's impact on family business sustainability: A case study in Brazil. *The International Journal of Management Education*, *19*(1), 100424.

Tata Group. (2021). *Tata group annual report 2020–21*. https://www.tata.com/docs/default-source/sustainability/annual-report-2020-21.pdf

The Economist. (2015). *To have and to hold*. Retrieved October 15, 2023, from https://www.economist.com/special-report/2015/04/16/to-have-and-to-hold

Transparency International. (2020). *Corruption perceptions index*. Retrieved October 15, 2023, from https://www.transparency.org/en/cpi/2020

Troilo, M. (2010). The role of trust in new SME creation: Differences in motivations and opportunities. *The International Journal of Entrepreneurship and Innovation*, *11*(2), 129–139.

Umans, I., Lybaert, N., Steijvers, T., & Voordeckers, W. (2020). Succession planning in family firms: Family governance practices, board of directors, and emotions. *Small Business Economics*, *54*(1), 189–207.

UNCTAD. (2019). *Digital economy report*. Retrieved on October 15, 2023, from https://unctad.org/publication/digital-economy-report-2019

UNESCO. (2021). *Global education monitoring report*. Retrieved October 15, 2023, from https://en.unesco.org/gem-report/taxonomy/term/238

Van Praag, C. (2003). Business survival and success of young small business owners. *Small Business Economics*, *21*(1), 1–17.

Williams, C. (2019). *Top 10 things a minority shareholder should look out for in a shareholder's agreement. B.Sc., LL.B*. Retrieved October 15, 2023, from https://smallbusiness.chron.com/top-10-things-minority-shareholder-should-look-out-shareholders-agreement-40307.html

World Bank. (2021). *World development indicators*. Retrieved October 15, 2023, from https://databank.worldbank.org/source/world-development-indicators

World Economic Forum. (2020). *The future of jobs report*. Retrieved October 15, 2023, from https://www.weforum.org/reports/the-future-of-jobs-report-2020/

Zephyr. (2021). *Venture capital activity in emerging markets*. Retrieved October 15, 2023, from https://www.zephyrpeacock.com/

Appendix: Emerging Economies Classified

No	Country	No	Country
1	Argentina	21	Nigeria
2	Bangladesh	22	Oman
3	Brazil	23	Pakistan
4	Bulgaria	24	Peru
5	Chile	25	The Philippines
6	China	26	Poland
7	Colombia	27	Qatar
8	The Czech Republic	28	Romania
9	Egypt	29	Russia
10	Greece	30	Saudi Arabia
11	Hungary	31	South Africa
12	India	32	South Korea
13	Indonesia	33	Taiwan
14	Iran	34	Thailand
15	Israel	35	Turkiye
16	Kuwait	36	Ukraine
17	Malaysia	37	The United Arab Emirates
18	Mauritius	38	Venezuela
19	Mexico	39	Vietnam
20	Morocco		

Source: FTSE (2014), IMF (2015), and Casanova and Miroux (2022).

Chapter 3

Family Start-up in Oman: Entrepreneurship Ecosystem Perspective

Hafiz Wasim Akram[a], *Léo-Paul Dana*[b,c], *Haidar Abbas*[d] *and Md. Daoud Ciddikie*[e]

[a]*Dhofar University, Oman*
[b]*Lappeenranta University of Technology, Finland*
[c]*ICD Business School, France*
[d]*University of Technology and Applied Sciences, Oman*
[e]*Sharda University, India*

Abstract

Family startups are essential to a nation's development because they foster creativity, economic expansion, and job creation. They introduce novel concepts, game-changing technologies, and innovative business approaches to the market. Family startups also help a country be more competitive abroad by luring capital, encouraging entrepreneurship, and diversifying the economy beyond its core industries. Additionally, family startups operate as agents of social change by addressing societal problems and providing answers that benefit communities. Therefore, fostering a thriving start-up ecosystem is crucial for a nation's long-term sustainable development and prosperity. Against this background, this book chapter examines the potential and difficulties that family startups in Oman's developing entrepreneurial environment confront. The chapter explores the challenges faced by entrepreneurs as well as the opportunities for growth and innovation in this dynamic market to illuminate the distinctive dynamics of the Omani start-up scene.

Keywords: Economic development; ecosystem; entrepreneurial behaviour; family firm; family startups; government financial support Oman; Omani entrepreneurs; startup

---

Entrepreneurial Behaviour of Family Firms:
Perspectives on Emerging Economies, 43–58

Published under exclusive licence by Emerald Publishing Limited
doi:10.1108/978-1-83753-934-520241003

1. Introduction

A startup is defined as a business enterprise that has been newly founded to provide innovative solutions, services, or products that meet the needs of consumers (Baltazar et al., 2023; Kraus et al., 2023). Katila et al. (2012) define it as 'a company/project undertaken by an entrepreneur to seek, develop, and validate a scalable business model'. Dissimilar to conventional enterprises, the sectors in which startups generally conduct their operations are dynamic, and they adopt agile business models and disruptive technologies. Such ventures are inherently unpredictable, have the potential to grow rapidly, and concentrate on scalability. Startups are frequently confronted with complex issues, including sourcing finance, establishing a base of customers, and dealing with regulatory frameworks (Sreenivasan & Suresh, 2022). Nevertheless, they also offer considerable potential to develop the economy and influence society. As implied by the name, family startups comprise ventures whose establishment and operations are conducted by individuals belonging to the same family (Kammerlander, 2022). Examples of such businesses can be observed throughout history, and they have made a valuable contribution to developing the economies of countries around the world. Family ventures comprise a large proportion of the global economy, playing a role in creating employment opportunities, generating wealth, and developing communities (Kraus et al., 2011; Rovelli et al., 2022). Such ventures take various guises, including small family-owned independent businesses as well as giant multinationals.

The importance of the role of family startups is based on several different factors (Agarwal et al., 2023; Dana & Sharma, 2023; Nziku et al., 2023; Shahzad et al., 2021). Firstly, they provide employment opportunities and facilitate the growth of the economy. Through the establishment and expansion of their ventures, family entrepreneurs can create jobs for both, themselves and other people, thus boosting economic activities within the region and lowering the rate of unemployment. Furthermore, it is generally the case that family startups adopt long-term perspectives, concentrating on growing in a sustainable manner as opposed to gains made in the short term. By becoming stable and focussing on continuity, they can withstand economic crises and play a role in making the economy more resilient in general.

Oman, a country whose history is notable with a burgeoning culture of entrepreneurialism, acknowledges the important role that family startups play in the development of the economy (Arslan et al., 2023). There are various reasons why family startups have specific importance for Oman. (1) Such ventures in Oman play a role in preserving and promoting the customs, crafts, and culture of the country. The cultural heritage of Oman is rich, and these ventures are critical for the preservation of traditional activities. Family startups operating in areas including tourism, cuisine, and handicrafts boost the distinctive identity of the country and draw tourists, thus enhancing this sector of the economy and promoting the rich heritage of Oman. (2) Family startups are important for creating employment opportunities in Oman (Muthuraman & Al Haziazi, 2019). As the population continues to expand, more employment opportunities are required. Family startups are ideally positioned to meet the evolving needs of the labour market and offer employment. It is not only family members who can benefit from employment as jobs are also provided for the broader labour market, thus reducing the number of those unemployed and creating a stable economy. (3) Family startups are potentially capable of contributing to the diversification of the Omani economy. The country is endeavouring to reduce the dominance of the oil and gas industry by diversifying the economy. As a result of their ability to innovate, agility, and willingness to take risks, family startups can expand into different sectors including technology, renewable energy, agriculture, and tourism. By exploring these industries, family startups can play an important role in Oman's plans to diversify the economy, thus assisting with building an economy with increased resilience and sustainability. The culture of entrepreneurialism in Oman is burgeoning (Alalawi, 2020), and family startups make an important contribution to promoting this culture among young people. Through the promotion of entrepreneurship (Bağış et al., 2023; Li et al., 2023; Mahmutaj & Krasniqi, 2019; Yana Mbena et al., 2023; Zayadin et al., 2023) and giving the chance to members of the family to gain knowledge of and participate in business practices, family startups facilitate the process of developing the business leaders and innovators of the future (Tajpour et al., 2022). Such a culture of entrepreneurialism is critical if the economy of Oman is to grow sustainability in the long term and become competitive globally.

2. Overview of Oman's Family Start-up Ecosystem

Oman, a country recognised for its breathtaking scenery and vast cultural history, offers a dynamic and unique family start-up environment in which the characteristics of entrepreneurialism, resilience, and tradition are intertwined. Family ventures have prospered in this environment, making a significant impact on the economic landscape of the country. Such businesses are not merely enterprises; they perfectly represent the values of Omani society, where family connections, respect, trust, and loyalty come together in business pursuits. This thorough review conducts an in-depth exploration of the pervasiveness and importance of family enterprises within Oman, their intrinsic strengths, the difficulties they encounter, the governmental support they are provided, and their future potential as they attempt to navigate the contemporary business environment while still retaining their historical cultural values.

Omani family firms comprise more than merely economic ventures (Razzak et al., 2022); they are institutions that have retained their significance across extended periods, frequently being passed down between generations. Such businesses are characterised by their focus on tradition and continuity, where multiple generations of the family successively take on ownership and management. It is not uncommon for multiple members of the same family to actively participate in operating an individual enterprise, which is a reflection of the deep significance of familial bonds in Omani culture. Respect, loyalty, and family ties have vast significance in Omani society, and such cultural values naturally permeate throughout the business world. Therefore, the operations of family enterprises are not disconnected from society but are profoundly embedded in the sense of community in Oman. Such enterprises promote the traditions and values of Oman, ensuring that they are preserved and propagated to future generations. The strength, stability, and resilience of such enterprises are grounded on the interplay of cultural values.

While the family start-up environment in Oman has an extensive cultural heritage, it also possesses various intrinsic strengths that play a role in making it robust and adaptable. Numerous family enterprises have established significant knowledge regarding domestic markets, customer tastes, and cultural differences. This profound understanding of the local market enables them to offer services and products that satisfy the unique demands and preferences of customers within Oman. Moreover, family enterprises are generally able to benefit from internal capital sources, such as family savings, investments, and combined resources (Mzid et al., 2019). As a result of being financially stable, they have a robust basis that allows them to withstand economic crises and confidently endeavour to expand their businesses and reinvest. Omani family firms are characterised by their stability and long-term perspective (Samara, 2021). Such enterprises are renowned for being capable of weathering short-term market downturns, preferring to place priority on establishing a legacy that can be transferred between generations. Such a long-term vision generally differentiates them from other businesses that are purely focussed on quarterly results. The ability to engage with the community is a further noteworthy strength of Omani family firms. Numerous such businesses are actively engaged in community development efforts by offering employment opportunities and conducting philanthropic works. Such engagement promotes goodwill, loyalty, and beneficial community relations, thus adding to their social capital. Family firms within Oman are also characterised by their ability to be adaptable as they have effectively navigated changes in the market throughout their history. By innovating, evolving, and embracing state-of-the-art business practices, they have continued to remain relevant and competitive.

Nevertheless, despite their strengths, Omani family enterprises are also confronted by a number of issues (Abd El Basset et al., 2022), particularly succession planning. It can be difficult to ensure that leadership and ownership smoothly transition between generations, and if succession planning is not effective, it can result in conflicts, a lack of stability, and a possible decline in the family's wealth. It can be challenging to balance the interests of the family with achieving business goals. The growth of the family firm generally necessitates management to be professionalised and a modern system of governance must be adopted to ensure that the business remains competitive faced with global competition. Transitioning in this way involves an intricate and delicate process.

Although the priority of family enterprises may be to employ members of the family, it is becoming increasingly necessary to recruit externally to benefit from others' expertise in order to innovate, grow, and diversify. Attempting to navigate this continually evolving talent environment while ensuring that the family values are respected can be challenging. A further important challenge involves market competition. The competitors of family enterprises are not only other businesses in the areas but also multinational corporations who are also increasingly operating in their markets (Ramadani et al., 2022). Faced with the continually evolving global business conditions, family firms need to focus on adaptability and differentiating themselves to remain competitive. Furthermore, the regulator conditions create a unique group of issues. It can be difficult to navigate regulatory and compliance regulations, specifically for family firms in the transition from business structures that are informal to those that are more formalised.

Acknowledging that family firms play a key role in developing the Omani economy, the government has implemented several policies and initiatives aimed at facilitating their growth and sustainability (Al Shukaili et al., 2023). Governmental organisations including the Oman Chamber of Commerce and Industry (OCCI) and the Oman Investment Authority (OIA) offer beneficial guidance in terms of registering businesses, permits, licences, market access, thus making the process more efficient for family firms. Family firms can take advantage of financial incentives like low-interest loans, subsidies, and grants, particularly such businesses engaged in strategic industries like technology, manufacturing, and tourism. Such incentives are critical for supporting their efforts to grow and develop. Training programmes covering topics including entrepreneurship, marketing, finance, and management are offered to family firms to enhance their capabilities and skills. Investing in human capital in this way increases the competitiveness and resilience of family firms. Additionally, the government enables local business to access both domestic and global markets via trade agreements, participating in trade fairs, and exhibitions (Alqassabi, 2020). Such initiatives make family firms more visible and expand their reach, thus creating new opportunities to grow and collaborate. A number of Omani chambers of commerce and business associations are actively engaged in promoting collaboration and networking in the family firm community (Dana et al., 2021). This culture of collaboration promotes the sharing of knowledge, the potential for partnerships, and mutual support between family firms. Therefore, the family start-up ecosystem in Oman is a dynamic environment in which innovation is intertwined with tradition, where cultural values are preserved while simultaneously adopting contemporary business practices (Al Baimani et al., 2021). Such family firms, which are profoundly embedded within the society of Oman, comprise more than mere economic entities; they perfectly represent the heritage of the country. The strengths of such businesses, including their local knowledge, financial stability, long-term perspective, engagement with the community, and ability to adapt, mean that they make a valuable contribution to forming the entrepreneurial culture of the country. Nonetheless, they are also confronted by a number of issues, such as succession planning, governance, acquiring new talent, remaining competitive in the market, and regulatory compliance. The government of Oman has intervened in this situation to overcome such problems by offering different types of support, acknowledging the significant role that family firms play in promoting economic growth and sustainability. As Oman persists on its journey towards diversifying the economy (Matar & Kadri, 2023) and becoming globally competitive, family firms will retain their importance in this process, driven by tradition as well as their dedication to conserving cultural heritage while, at the same time, welcoming the opportunity to exploit the potential of the contemporary business environment. The fact that they are resilient, adaptable, and enduring demonstrates their importance for the entrepreneurial environment in Oman as well as their opportunities for further growth and success going forward.

3. Challenges for Family Startups in Oman

Although they are prospering and deeply embedded in the country's economic landscape, Omani family firms are confronted by a distinctive set of difficulties that must be carefully navigated with strategic plans (Akram, 2023; Palalić et al., 2019). Such issues, which include succession planning, governance, market competition, and regulatory compliance, are critical factors that determine the durability and sustainability of family startups in the country. Succession planning constitutes a key challenge facing Omani family firms. In many family businesses, it is traditional for parents to pass management and ownership to their children across generations. Although such continuity can strengthen these businesses, it can also have negative consequences. Smoothly transitioning ownership and leadership between generations can be a complicated endeavour that can present possible risks. If succession plans are not adequately prepared, family conflicts can occur, the stability of the business can diminish, and potentially even the generational wealth accumulated by the family can be eroded. Resultantly, investments must be made by family firms in terms of time and effort to comprehensively develop succession plans that deal with not only how ownership is transferred, but also the values, knowledge, and leadership skills.

A further challenge confronting Omani family startups involves how family interests can be balanced with business goals. With the continued expansion and development of such businesses, professionalisation has become increasingly necessary (Costa et al., 2022). To compete in an economic environment shaped by globalisation, modern governance frameworks, performance metrics, and strategic decision-making processes are frequently required. This necessitates a balance to be struck between the family traditions and values, while simultaneously adopting the practices and professionalism needed to achieve growth sustainably. The transition process has the potential to disrupt the togetherness and harmony of the business and family.

An issue that is increasingly impacting Omani family firms is the availability of talent. Although these businesses generally prefer to hire members of the family, the dynamic business environment necessitates the recruitment of talent and expertise outside this circle, specifically in distinctive sectors like finance, marketing, and technology. Family firms must acknowledge the significance of integrating the distinct attributes of members of the family with the competencies and acumen of external talent (Rothwell & Prescott, 2022). Nevertheless, this process of integration presents certain challenges, as possible conflicts must be managed, and the values and culture of the family must be maintained in the face of a diversifying workforce. Family firms must also deal with other competitors in the market, not only domestically but also internationally. To ensure their competitiveness, they must exhibit adaptability to navigate the changing market environment, customer demands, and developing technologies (Aloulou, 2022; Handoyo et al., 2023). Being adaptable in this way necessitates an innovative mindset as well as the agility to react rapidly to market changes. Family firms must also be willing to make R&D investments, adopt new technologies, and cultivate novel business models. It can be challenging to effectively navigate this environment while maintaining their distinctive identity and customer loyalty.

Additionally, as a result of the growth of such businesses, it is frequently necessary for their operations to shift from an informal business structure to one that is more formalised. Dealing with the complex nature of compliance, licencing and reporting can be a complicated process that consumes significant resources. Businesses must be focussed on remaining up-to-date with regulation changes, making appropriate investments in financial and legal experts, and ensuring that robust internal controls are implemented. If such actions are not taken, family enterprises may be exposed to financial and legal risks that threaten their long-term future. To overcome such problems, family firms must behave proactively, prepare exhaustive succession plans, professionalise their management, and recruit external expertise. Additionally, they must promote an innovative and agile environment while addressing regulatory challenges. If such challenges can be successfully overcome, family firms will not only become resilient and sustainable, but they will also become more competitive internationally. The ability to balance tradition with modernisation, as well as family values with business, needs suitably positions Omani family startups to develop and play a key role in developing the country's economy and wealth in the future.

4. Opportunities and Growth Drivers for Family Firms in Oman

Omani family firms are suitably placed to exploit several opportunities and take advantage of various drivers of growth in the continually evolving Omani business environment. As the process of economic diversification and innovation adoption continues in Oman (Saboori et al., 2022), family startups can make a key contribution to driving the growth of the Omani economy. In this discussion, the different opportunities and drivers of growth that can be exploited by Omani family firms to facilitate sustainable growth and success will be explored. An opportunity that has particular significance for Omani family firms is related to the country's strategic focus on diversifying the economy. Despite its historical dependence on revenues from oil and gas, Oman has now realised the necessity to lessen such reliance on hydrocarbons and develop the resilience of the economy, making it more balanced (Khan & Al-Ghamdi, 2023; Sim, 2023). As part of this process of diversification, family firms can expand into different industries and sectors including renewable energy, technology, manufacturing, and tourism. Such industries present ideal opportunities to grow, innovate, and become sustainable in the long term. By investing in such developing sectors, family firms can play a role in transforming the Omani economy while also ensuring their own long-term futures.

The tourism industry within Oman offers significant potential for family enterprises (Salem et al., 2023; Tripathi & Al Shahri, 2023). The magnificent scenery, extensive cultural heritage, and hospitable environment of Oman make it particularly appealing to international tourists. Investments made by the government in tourism infrastructure, such as cultural sites, hotels, and airports, have produced conditions suitable for the development of family-owned businesses in industries like entertainment, travel, and hospitality. Family firms can make a valuable contribution to boosting the tourism experience and drawing more international tourists in various ways, such as boutique hotels, tour operators, and artisanal craft shops. A further notable driver of growth for Omani family firms is that the government has shown it is committed to promoting entrepreneurship and innovation. Approaches like the 'National Innovation Strategy' emphasise the extent to which Oman is dedicated to forming a knowledge-based economy that fosters technological developments and promotes the growth of small businesses and startups. As a result of their agility and knowledge of the local market, family startups are suitably placed to take advantage of this innovation ecosystem. They can expand into technology-based industries such as IT, e-commerce, and digital services. By focussing on innovation and digital transformation, family firms can become more competitive and relevant in the contemporary business environment.

As Oman is strategically located on global trade routes (El-Rayyes, 2023), such as the Strait of Hormuz, it is well-positioned to act as a global logistics centre. As ports like Salalah and Sohar have been developed to global standards, along with the creation of industrial areas and free zones, family firms can now potentially benefit from trade, transportation, and logistics opportunities. Family-owned logistics businesses can take advantage of the expanding preference for supply chain solutions with increased efficiency and reliability, acting as key actors in supporting trade between Europe, Africa, and Asia. Such a strategic advantage conforms with the wider vision of Oman to become a centre of logistics and trade, meaning that family firms now have the ideal opportunity to expand into these industries. Furthermore, Omani family firms can exploit their extensive knowledge of domestic markets, traditions, and consumer needs to gain a competitive edge (Albimani, 2022). They are suitably placed to act as reliable partners for international businesses seeking to gain a foothold in the market in Oman. Through the establishment of joint ventures and strategic partnerships with international corporations, family firms will be able to benefit from state-of-the-art technologies, resources, and expertise. Such interdependent relationships can promote growth, boost competitiveness, and enable family firms to expand internationally. Moreover, Oman's dedication to foster entrepreneurship can be clearly observed in its attempt to establish conditions that are conducive to the growth of small businesses and startups (Anwar et al., 2023). Initiatives implemented by the government, such as the technology incubators, research parks, and innovation centres, allow family firms to take advantage of funding, mentorship, and beneficial resources. Such initiatives are intended to encourage young people in Oman to become more innovative and creative, promoting an entrepreneurial environment. Family firms can become active participants in such programmes, not only by taking advantage of the available resources but also by imparting their own knowledge and experience to support and mentor future entrepreneurs.

Another example demonstrating how committed the government is to diversify the economy, innovating, and entrepreneurialism is the fact that it has signed free trade agreements with a number of nations and regional blocs, including the United States and member countries of the Gulf Cooperation Council. Such agreements enable trade and investment (Akram, 2020; Kashif & Akram, 2021; Laget et al., 2020), which offers family firms the potential to grow both within the region and further afield. By entering different markets and developing strategic partnerships, family firms can take advantage of larger customer markets and achieve revenue diversification, thus boosting their growth potential. By exploiting such potential and acting in conformity with the vision of the government, family firms can focus on growing sustainably, playing a key role in transforming the Omani economy, and continuing to prosper in competitive international markets.

5. Support Ecosystem and Resources

Omani family startups are key components of the economic ecosystem of Oman, embodying the extensive history of entrepreneurialism and cultural heritage of the country (Khan et al., 2021). To enable such businesses to grow and be sustainable, a supportive environment has been established in Oman, in which businesses are provided access to critical resources that facilitate their success and prosperity. In this discussion, the different components of the supportive ecosystem along with the resources provided that are critical in enabling the success of Oman family startups have been comprehensively reviewed.

5.1. General Support and Initiatives

The government of Oman has demonstrated that it is strongly committed to promoting entrepreneurship and providing support to family firms via a series of policies and initiatives. For example: (1) government bodies like the OIA and the OCCI are key actors in offering guidance for registering businesses, permits, licences, and compliance requirements. Their work facilitates the establishment and operation of family firms, thus mitigating administrative obstacles and impediments; (2) the government of Oman offers financial incentives to allow businesses to expand and invest (Al Shukaili et al., 2023). Such incentives, which take the form of low-interest loans, subsidies, and grants, are specifically beneficial for family firms whose business operations occur in sectors like technology, manufacturing, and tourism, which have strategic significance. Through the critical financial support they provide, businesses are able to grow and develop; (3) in terms of training and development, Omani government institutions and agencies arrange a broad variety of training programmes, workshops, and seminars to improve the expertise and understanding of family firm owners and entrepreneurs (Balushi, 2023). The topics covered by such programmes are varied and can include entrepreneurship, finance, and management. They provide family entrepreneurs with the required insight and knowledge to make educated decisions and engage in effective business operations. In addition to the factors described above, the government of Oman endeavours to enable businesses to compete both domestically and internationally. Via initiatives such as trade agreements, attendance at trade fairs and exhibitions, and work to develop markets, it is possible for family firms to increase their potential customer base and benefit from export potential, thus achieving customer diversification. Business associations and chambers of commerce within Oman can catalyse collaboration and networking among family enterprises. Such platforms offer the potential to share knowledge, develop partnerships, and give mutual support. They facilitate the development of an entrepreneurial community, allowing them to acquire knowledge from the experiences of others and collectively overcome problems.

5.2. Financial Resources

In order for family startups to grow and become sustainable, they need to be able to access financial resources. Consequently, Oman ensures that family firms can access different funding sources, thus providing them with capital when required (Saberi & Hamdan, 2019). For example: (1) the banking industry in Oman provides a variety of financing alternatives customised to the particular needs of family firms. Such options could be loans, overdraft facilities, or lines of credit, which businesses can use as working capital, acquiring assets, and expansion projects; (2) subsidies and grants are often offered by the government as incentives for family firms, which are used to support particular initiatives or projects. Grants like this can considerably alleviate the financial pressures related to specific investments; and (3) support in terms of private equity and venture capital can also be accessed. The transforming entrepreneurial ecosystem in Oman has led to the appearance of venture capital businesses and private equity investors who are actively engaged in searching for opportunities to make investments in family startups that show potential. Such investors not only deliver capital but also offer beneficial knowledge and networks.

5.3. Access to Talent and Expertise

Acknowledging the necessity to recruit from an external talent pool to supplement their own abilities, Omani family firms are endeavouring to seek resources in this area. An increasing number of educational institutions in Oman are providing specialised programmes covering entrepreneurship, technology, management, and business (Al Shabibi, 2020). Family firms have the opportunity to leverage this pool of talent through the recruitment of interns and graduates, thus allowing new ideas and skills to be continually added. Specialised expertise is provided by a number of different consultants and business advisory services within Oman in domains including digital transformation, marketing, finance, and strategy. Employing the services of such professionals can assist family firms with making educated decisions and effectively navigating complicated issues. Mentorship schemes as well as networks allow family startups to engage with both established entrepreneurs and business leaders. Consequently, they can benefit from indispensable guidance, counselling, and a reliable resource for evaluating strategies and ideas. Several technology incubators and accelerators have emerged in Oman (Al Baimani et al., 2021), which offer startups, including those operated by families, access to innovation centres, resources, and mentorship. Such platforms make a key contribution to promoting innovation and the process of developing state-of-the-art solutions. Grants and incentives provided by the government generally incorporate support for R&D efforts. This promotes investments in innovation and technological developments among family firms, making them more competitive in dynamic markets.

5.4. Legal and Regulatory Assistance

For family firms to be successful, they must be able to navigate the legal and regulatory conditions. Oman offers resources for this purpose. For example, legal practices within Oman provide counselling on registering businesses, contracting, compliance, and the protection of intellectual property. Taking advantage of the services of legal experts allows family firms to conduct business operations legally, avoiding legal penalties. Family firms have the opportunity to obtain support and guidance from government bodies tasked with the regulation of particular industries. Such bodies clarify regulations pertaining to specific sectors and compliance criteria, enabling family firms to function in line with industry standards. Therefore, Omani family startups can take advantage of the wide-ranging support provided in the ecosystem and the availability of a variety of different resources facilitating their flourishment and success. As a result of support from the government, financial resources, talent availability, technology, and innovation guidance, as well as legal and regulatory assistance, family firms can overcome the issues generated by entrepreneurship and exploit the potential for growth and sustainability (Fattah et al., 2021). Such resources not only play a key role in making family firms more successful but are also critical for the process of developing and diversifying the Omani economy.

6. Future Outlook

Family firms in Oman can look to the future positively considering the possibilities that lie in front of them. The focus of the country on diversifying the economy is resolute, with investments continuing to be made in industries like renewable energy, technology, manufacturing, and tourism. By diversifying in this way, it is possible to create new opportunities for the expansion and innovation of family firms, playing a role in transforming the Omani economy. The tourism industry specifically constitutes an opportunity for growth for family startups (Razzak et al., 2022). The captivating scenery, extensive cultural heritage, and warm hospitality mean that international tourists continue to visit. With continued governmental investments in tourism infrastructure, family-run enterprises operating in the entertainment, travel, and hospitality industries can potentially flourish, thus allowing tourists to benefit from distinctive, genuine experiences.

Furthermore, the strategic position of Oman on global trade routes situates the nation as a possible global logistics centre. The establishment of high-quality ports, free zones, and industrial areas offers the potential for family firms to expand in terms of trade, transportation, and logistics, allowing them to be key actors in enabling trade between Europe, Africa, and Asia. Moreover, the extent to which Oman is committed to promoting innovation and entrepreneurship is exemplified by the different initiatives it has implemented, including the National Innovation Strategy. Such commitment to the formation of a knowledge-based economy promotes the development of technology and facilitates the advancement of small businesses and startups. As a result of their agility and knowledge of local markets, family startups are suitably positioned to flourish in such an ecosystem driven by innovation. Government initiatives aimed at promoting entrepreneurship via educational institutions, mentorship schemes, and the availability of financial resources are also beneficial for family enterprises. Such initiatives create a basis for future entrepreneurs and generate an environment that can facilitate the flourishment of family startups. Despite the potential, Omani family startups are confronted by several issues that must be carefully considered and addressed with strategic plans. A challenge that is increasingly drawing attention is the ability to access talent. Although such businesses generally prefer to hire members of the family, the dynamic business environment means that they must be able to access outside talent and expertise, particularly those operating in specialised industries. Balancing the integration of external professionals while ensuring that the culture and values of the family are preserved can be challenging. To ensure competitiveness, they must be capable of adapting to the changing market environment, consumer preferences, and technological developments. In order to adapt in this way, businesses must be committed to innovation and exhibit the necessary agility to react rapidly to market changes.

7. Conclusion

To conclude this exhaustive review of family startups in the context of Oman, it is clear that such businesses play a critical role in the economic and social tapestry of the nation. Their distinctive combination of resilience, innovation, and tradition not only exemplifies the extensive cultural heritage of Oman but also emphasises their significant potential to contribute to the country's efforts to diversify the economy. In exploring the complexities and potential inherent to the family firm ecosystem in Oman, various key themes have been identified, each of which elucidates the future in different ways. Similar to startups in other countries, those in Oman experience problems with the process of succession planning. Seamlessly transitioning between generations is a key challenge, as it is not only ownership and wealth that must be transferred, but the values and legacy of the family must also be preserved. Dealing with this complex issue requires a painstaking and frequently emotional process in which professional guidance and open dialogue are critical. In the process of preparing for such leadership changes, they must balance the need to preserve their heritage with the adoption of contemporary governance structures and practices.

In the preceding chapter, it has been discussed that the diversification of the economy in Oman offers a range of different opportunities for family startups.

The country's strategic dedication to lessening its dependence on oil and gas while diversifying into industries like manufacturing, technology, and tourism emphasises the productive environment in which such businesses can thrive. By expanding into such fields, family startups not only have the opportunity to facilitate their long-term survival but can also play an important role in achieving Oman's efforts to diversify and increase the resilience of its economy in the future.

A specific aspect of the entrepreneurial environment of Oman that has exhibited superior performance is the tourism industry. As a result of the captivating scenery, extensive cultural heritage, and focus on sustainable tourism, Oman is highly appealing to international tourists who desire to take advantage of distinctive and genuine experiences. Family-owned industries operating in the entertainment, travel, and hospitality industries are suitably placed to exemplify the fundamental nature of Omani hospitality and offer tourists an experience of the country's welcoming environment and culture. However, there are also complex issues obstructing progress in this regard. As global business conditions are continually evolving, family startups need to address the problems of new competitors in the market, rapid shifts in customer demands, and the need to embrace technological developments. To flourish under such dynamic conditions, they must be willing to adopt innovation and become more agile. This necessitates a progressive vision, R&D investments, and the readiness to adapt quickly to changing conditions.

A key theme that emerged was the ability to access external talent and expertise. Although family firms generally take pride in their internal cohesion and tradition, there is a growing recognition that the integration of outside professionals into their operations is necessary. This would ensure the competitiveness of the business in specialised industries, promote innovation, and allow a balance to be struck between preserving tradition and welcoming progress.

Omani family firms are well-positioned to make an important contribution to achieving the country's objective of becoming a global logistics centre. The strategic position of the country, strengthened by its high-quality ports and transportation facilities, provides family startups operating in the fields of logistics and transportation the unparalleled opportunity to facilitate international trade. As Oman is repositioned as a critical connection between Europe, Africa, and Asia, family firms can play an important role in this process of transformation. In terms of entrepreneurship, Oman's dedication to innovation and the formation of a knowledge-based economy are exemplified by the different initiatives and support mechanisms it has implemented. Family startups are suitably positioned to exploit this ecosystem, taking advantage of their agility and knowledge of the local market to drive technological development and generate value in emerging industries. Looking forward, Omani family startups must confront such challenges and take advantage of future opportunities. Succession planning, professionalisation, adaptation to the market, availability of external talent, and compliance with changing regulations all constitute key components of this process. They can become more resilient and grow by collaborating and networking with other entrepreneurs, along with ongoing learning and adaptation.

References

Abd El Basset, F., Bell, R., & Al Kharusi, B. (2022). Reducing barriers to female entrepreneurship in Oman: Does family matter?. *Journal of Enterprising Communities: People and Places in the Global Economy*. Vol. ahead-of-print No. ahead-of-print. https://doi.org/10.1108/JEC-01-2022-0009

Agarwal, S., Ramadani, V., Agrawal, V., & Dixit, J. K. (2023). Guest editorial: Gender, entrepreneurship and family business. *Journal of Family Business Management*, *13*(3), 546–551.

Akram, H. W. (2020). Trade within South Asia: Unrealistic expectations. *South Asia Research*, *40*(3), 381–396.

Akram, H. W. (2023). Current issues in entrepreneurship in Oman. In V. Ratten (Ed.), *Entrepreneurship business debates: Multidimensional perspectives across geo-political frontiers* (pp. 51–65). Springer Nature Singapore. https://doi.org/10.1007/978-981-99-1071-7_4

Al Baimani, N., Clifton, N., Jones, E., & Pugh, R. (2021). Applying the ecosystem model in a new context? The case of business incubation in Oman. *Growth and Change*, *52*(2), 663–686.

Al Shabibi, I. (2020). *Planning for entrepreneurialism in a rentier state economy: Entrepreneurship education for economic diversification in Oman* [Doctoral dissertation]. Cardiff University.

Al Shukaili, A. M., Al Kindi, K., Kassim, N. M., Ahmed, Z., & Al Hosni, K. (2023). Can government financial support enhance job creations: Insights from Oman. *Journal of Science and Technology Policy Management*, *14*(5), 807–829.

Albimani, N. M. (2022). *The impact of dynamic capabilities on small and medium-sized enterprises (SMES) performance in Oman* [Doctoral dissertation]. University of South Alabama.

Aloulou, W. J. (2022). Family business in Gulf Cooperation Council countries (GCC): Toward the future. In *Family business in Gulf Cooperation Council countries* (pp. 143–156). Springer International Publishing.

Alqassabi, M. A. (2020). Insights on sustainability of small and medium enterprises in Oman: A conceptual framework. *International Journal of Economics and Financial Issues*, *10*(1), 209–218.

Anwar, I., Ahmad, A., Saleem, I., & Yasin, N. (2023). Role of entrepreneurship education, passion and motivation in augmenting Omani students' entrepreneurial intention: A stimulus-organism-response approach. *The International Journal of Management Education*, *21*(3), 100842.

Arslan, A., Al Kharusi, S., Hussain, S. M., & Alo, O. (2023). Sustainable entrepreneurship development in Oman: A multi-stakeholder qualitative study. *International Journal of Organizational Analysis*, *31*(8), 35–59.

Bağış, M., Kryeziu, L., Kurutkan, M. N., Krasniqi, B. A., Hernik, J., Karagüzel, E. S., & Ateş, Ç. (2023). Youth entrepreneurial intentions: A cross-cultural comparison. *Journal of Enterprising Communities: People and Places in the Global Economy*, *17*(4), 769–792.

Baltazar, J., Fernandes, C., Ramadani, V., & Hughes, M. (2023). Family business succession and innovation: A systematic literature review. *Review of Managerial Science*, *17*(8), 2897–2920.

Balushi, A. (2023). *The SME sector is poised to have a better outlook in 2023 compared to 2022 as per plan outlay of the authority for small and medium enterprises development*. Retrieved December 01, 2023, from https://www.omanobserver.om/article/1132325/oman/asmed-launches-programmes-to-hone-entrepreneurial-skills

Costa, A. D., Zen, A. C., & Spindler, E. D. S. (2022). Family succession, professionalization and internationalization: A study of Brazilian family businesses. *Journal of Family Business Management*, *12*(4), 1065–1080.

Dana, L. P., Palalic, R., & Ramadani, V. (2021). *Entrepreneurship in the Gulf Cooperation Council region: Evolution and future perspectives*. World Scientific.

Dana, L. P., & Sharma, N. (2023). SMEs and start-ups: The growth engine of India. In L. P. Dana, O. Gautam, A. Gupta, & N. Sharma (Eds.), *Indian SMEs and start-ups: Growth through innovation and leadership* (pp. 1–18). World Scientific.

El-Rayyes, R. N. (2023). Oman's role in the gulf co-operation council and the region. In B. R. Pridham (Ed.), *Oman: Economic, social and strategic developments* (pp. 195–208). Routledge.

Fattah, A. M. A., Al Halbusi, H., Dahleez, K. A., Al Sinawi, S., & Al Wahibi, G. (2021). An investigation of components deriving entrepreneurial activities in Duqm city: A special economic zone in Oman. *International Journal of Entrepreneurship*, *25*, 1–14.

Handoyo, S., Suharman, H., Ghani, E. K., & Soedarsono, S. (2023). A business strategy, operational efficiency, ownership structure, and manufacturing performance: The moderating role of market uncertainty and competition intensity and its implication on open innovation. *Journal of Open Innovation: Technology, Market, and Complexity*, *9*(2), 100039.

Kammerlander, N. (2022). Family business and business family questions in the 21st century: Who develops SEW, how do family members create value, and who belongs to the family?. *Journal of Family Business Strategy*, *13*(2), 100470.

Kashif, M., & Akram, H. W. (2021). Trade creation, trade diversion and consumer surplus in Asean-India free trade agreement: A single market partial equilibrium approach. *Academy of Strategic Management Journal*, *20*, 1–10.

Katila, R., Chen, E. L., & Piezunka, H. (2012). All the right moves: How entrepreneurial firms compete effectively. *Strategic Entrepreneurship Journal*, *6*(2), 116–132.

Khan, G. M., Al Abri, S., & Rahman, S. A. (2021). Entrepreneurship in Oman. In *Entrepreneurship in the Gulf Cooperation Council region: Evolution and future perspectives* (pp. 45–77).

Khan, M. I., & Al-Ghamdi, S. G. (2023). Hydrogen economy for sustainable development in GCC countries: A SWOT analysis considering current situation, challenges, and prospects. *International Journal of Hydrogen Energy*, *48*(28), 10315–10344.

Kraus, S., Clauss, T., & Kallmuenzer, A. (2023). Introduction to the research handbook on entrepreneurship and innovation in family firms. In S. Kraus, T. Clauss, & A. Kallmuenzer (Eds.), *Research handbook on entrepreneurship and innovation in family firms* (pp. 1–12). Edward Elgar Publishing.

Kraus, S., Harms, R., & Fink, M. (2011). Family firm research: Sketching a research field. *International Journal of Entrepreneurship and Innovation Management*, *13*(1), 32–47.

Laget, E., Osnago, A., Rocha, N., & Ruta, M. (2020). Deep trade agreements and global value chains. *Review of Industrial Organization*, *57*, 379–410.

Li, H., Kang, Q., Calabrò, A., Kraus, S., & Jones, P. (2023). International entrepreneurship: Analysing the current state of research. *European Journal of International Management*, *21*(1), 96–120.

Mahmutaj, L. R., & Krasniqi, B. (2019). Open innovation in a start-up firm. In G. Rexhepi, R. D. Hisrich, & V. Ramadani (Eds.), *Open innovation and entrepreneurship: Impetus of growth and competitive advantages* (pp. 109–126). Springer.

Matar, L., & Kadri, A. (2023). China against US imperialism in the Arabian Sea: The case of Oman. *Middle East Critique*, *32*(2), 285–303.

Muthuraman, S., & Al Haziazi, M. (2019). Entrepreneurial growth: Challenges to young Omani entrepreneurs. *International Journal of Business and Applied Social Science*, *5*(7), 98–114.

Mzid, I., Khachlouf, N., & Soparnot, R. (2019). How does family capital influence the resilience of family firms?. *Journal of International Entrepreneurship*, *17*(2), 249–277.

Nziku, D. M., Dana, L. P., Balslev, H., & Salamzadeh, A. (Eds.). (2023). *Women entrepreneurs in the Middle East: Context, ecosystems, and future perspectives for the region*. World Scientific Publishing Company.

Palalić, R., Dana, L. P., & Ramadani, V. (2019). Refugee entrepreneurship: A case study from the Sultanate of Oman. In S. Heilbrunn, J. Freiling, & A. Harima, (Eds.), *Refugee entrepreneurship: A case-based topography* (pp. 207–219). Edward Elgar.

Ramadani, V., Dzenopoljac, V., Zainal, M., & Dzenopoljac, A. (2022). Family business in Kuwait. In V. Ramadani, W.J. Aloulou, & M. Zainal, (Eds.), *Family business in Gulf Cooperation Council countries* (pp. 33–51). Springer International Publishing.

Razzak, M. R., Palalić, R., & Al-Riyami, S. (2022). Family business in Oman. In V. Ramadani, W. J. Aloulou, & M. Zainal (Eds.), *Family business in Gulf Cooperation Council countries* (pp. 67–90). Springer International Publishing.

Rothwell, W. J. & Prescott, R. K. (Eds.). (2022). *Succession planning for small and family businesses: Navigating successful transitions*. CRC Press.

Rovelli, P., Ferasso, M., De Massis, A., & Kraus, S. (2022). Thirty years of research in family business journals: Status quo and future directions. *Journal of Family Business Strategy*, *13*(3), 100422.

Saberi, M., & Hamdan, A. (2019). The moderating role of governmental support in the relationship between entrepreneurship and economic growth: A study on the GCC countries. *Journal of Entrepreneurship in Emerging Economies*, *11*(2), 200–216.

Saboori, B., Zaibet, L., & Boughanmi, H. (2022). Export diversification, energy consumption, economic growth and environmental degradation: Evidence from Oman. *International Journal of Ambient Energy*, *43*(1), 8486–8504.

Salem, I. E., Abbas, H., Akram, H. W., & Elbaz, A. M. (2023). Contemporary sustainability themes in tourism and hospitality during and post COVID-19: Critical review and a step strategies forward for post the pandemic. *Sustainable Development*, *31*(5), 3946–3964.

Samara, G. (2021). Family businesses in the Arab Middle East: What do we know and where should we go?. *Journal of Family Business Strategy*, *12*(3), 100359.

Shahzad, M. F., Khan, K. I., Saleem, S., & Rashid, T. (2021). What factors affect the entrepreneurial intention to start-ups? The role of entrepreneurial skills, propensity to take risks, and innovativeness in open business models. *Journal of Open Innovation: Technology, Market, and Complexity*, *7*(3), 173.

Sim, L. C. (2023). Renewable energy and governance resilience in the Gulf. *Energies*, *16*(7), 3225.

Sreenivasan, A., & Suresh, M. (2022). Modeling the enablers of sourcing risks faced by startups in COVID-19 era. *Journal of Global Operations and Strategic Sourcing*, *15*(2), 151–171.

Tajpour, M., Salamzadeh, A., Ramadani, V., Palalić, R., & Hosseini, E. (2022). Knowledge sharing and achieving competitive advantage in international environments: The case of Iranian digital start-ups. In V. Jafari-Sadeghi & L. P. Dana (Eds.), *International entrepreneurship in emerging markets* (pp. 206–224). Routledge.

Tripathi, S., & Al Shahri, M. S. T. (2023). Paradigm shift from traditional to communication and technology acceptance models for the survival of family businesses in Oman. In H. Siringoringo & R. Kuruppuge (Eds.), *Perspectives and strategies of family business resiliency in unprecedented times* (pp. 39–63). IGI Global.

Yana Mbena, J., Durst, S., Kraus, S., & Viala, C. (2023). Investigating the impact of the dynamics of entrepreneurial intentions on ventures' formalization. *Journal of Entrepreneurship in Emerging Economies*, Vol. ahead-of-print No. ahead-of-print. https://doi.org/10.1108/JEEE-01-2023-0007.

Zayadin, R., Zucchella, A., Anand, A., Jones, P., & Ameen, N. (2023). Entrepreneurs' decisions in perceived environmental uncertainty. *British Journal of Management*, *34*(2), 831–848.

Chapter 4

Entrepreneurial Orientation and Firm Growth in Tunisian Family Firms: The Moderating Role of Generational Involvement

Rim Gafsi

Sousse University, Tunisia

Abstract

In family firms, growth is intricately linked not only to strategic business decisions but also to the dynamics of generational involvement and entrepreneurial orientation (EO). While previous research has explored the connection between family firm growth and EO, it often overlooks the moderating role that generational involvement could play in this relationship. To address this gap in the literature and investigate its potential impact, this study aims to examine how generational involvement shapes the effects of EO on growth. Based on a quantitative study involving 150 Tunisian family firms and employing a questionnaire-based approach along with structural equation modeling using SPSS 22 and AMOS software, the findings reveal that not all dimensions of EO equally contribute to growth. Specifically, proactiveness, competitive aggressiveness, and autonomy influence growth directly and in the presence of generational involvement as moderators. The effectiveness of these dimensions in driving growth is contingent upon the active and collaborative participation of diverse family generations in the entrepreneurial activities of the family firm. This research pinpoints the importance of family firms that wish to ensure long-term EO when multiple generations are involved. It also reaffirms the importance of these notions within family firms for sustaining long-term EO. Furthermore, this study advocates for additional empirical research

Entrepreneurial Behaviour of Family Firms:
Perspectives on Emerging Economies, 59–85

Published under exclusive licence by Emerald Publishing Limited
doi:10.1108/978-1-83753-934-520241004

on the potential role of generational involvement in establishing professionalization and family governance mechanisms. It seeks to explore their impact on the sustainability of entrepreneurial family firms.

Keywords: Entrepreneurial orientation; firm growth; generational involvement; family firm; Tunisia

1. Introduction

Entrepreneurship is vital for economic growth as it involves creating businesses and jobs, and family firms play a key role in this process (Ramadani & Hoy, 2015). However, understanding entrepreneurial attitudes in family firms is limited. EO serves as a vital concept in this context, representing performance-boosting entrepreneurial attitudes (Wales et al., 2013). Numerous references have influenced the development of EO, with its interpretation evolving Miller and Friesen (1982), Covin and Slevin (1989), Lumpkin and Dess (1996), Wiklund and Shepherd (2005), Covin et al. (2006), Miller and Whitney (1999), Rauch et al. (2009), Covin and Lumpkin (2011), and Covin and Miller (2014). While consensus on EO dimensions is lacking, Miller's (1983) framework and Lumpkin and Dess's (1996) proposals remain widely acknowledged benchmarks. Yazdanpanah et al. (2023) and Zellweger and Sieger (2012) define EO with five dimensions: innovativeness, proactiveness, risk-taking (Miller, 1983), autonomy, and competitive aggressiveness (Lumpkin & Dess, 1996). Applied increasingly in family firms, EO in this context is influenced by family-related factors, such as a focus on positive image, societal reputation, and a transgenerational mindset (Chirico & Nordqvist, 2010; Kraus et al., 2012; Zellweger & Sieger, 2012). Family firms, exclusively owned and operated by founding family members, aim to pass the business to the next generation (Chrisman et al., 2005).

EO is recognized as a catalyst for firm growth and strong performance (Campopiano et al., 2019; Lomberg et al., 2017; Pittino et al., 2017). It is a valuable predictor of firm success during economic instability and environmental turbulence (Kraus et al., 2012). Many studies show a strong link between EO and firm performance. A high level of EO is correlated with the company consistently outperforming others over an extended period (Arzubiaga et al., 2018; Covin & Slevin, 1989, 1991; Gupta & Batra, 2016; Wiklund, 1999; Wiklund & Shepherd, 2005; Zehir et al., 2015). The environmental context shapes an organization's EO (Lumpkin & Dess, 1996; Van Doorn et al., 2013; Wiklund & Shepherd, 2005; Zahra & Covin, 1995), but research indicates a negative correlation in uncertain and turbulent economic environments (Hemmert et al., 2023). Some studies suggest a non-linear EO-performance relationship (Kreiser et al., 2013), and certain EO dimensions may selectively influence growth (Lisboa et al., 2016; Wales et al., 2013, 2020). These findings underscore the need for further research in different economic contexts. Maintaining a transgenerational EO is essential for the perpetuation of family firms (Kellermanns et al., 2008; Naldi et al., 2007).

Agca and Kizildag (2013) define generational involvement as the presence of multiple family generations in top management at the same time. It can enhance EO when family members collaborate effectively, sharing diverse skills and perspectives that lead to increased innovation, risk-taking, and proactive behaviors. However, conflicts or differences in entrepreneurial attitudes between generations can stifle EO. The influence of EO in family firms evolves across generations. In first-generation firms, the founder plays a crucial role in driving EO. In second-generation family firms, the CEO's interpretations of the competitive environment become more influential. By the third generation and beyond, access to non-family managerial and financial resources becomes a key driver of EO. The shifting dynamics highlight the changing factors that contribute to entrepreneurial attitudes in different stages of a family firm's life cycle (Cruz & Nordqvist, 2007). However, the intersection of family and business dimensions in family firms creates specific sets of resources and capabilities that could either ease or hinder entrepreneurial activities. Therefore, it is necessary to explore how EO impacts growth in the context of family firms. How does family firms' EO influences their growth, and what factors facilitate or impede this relationship? These questions are essential to understanding the specific challenges and opportunities that family firms face in their pursuit of growth and sustainability. In this paper, we will explore the literature that addresses the impact of EO on a family firm's growth. Despite the significant contribution of family firms to economic growth, the topic is not given serious attention in emerging countries (Zainol & Ayadurai, 2011). According to the authors, EO research has been done primarily in the context of the United States or other developed countries and has scarcely been conducted in emerging economies (ibid.).

In Tunisia, family firms emerged post-independence in 1956 and became key players in the new open economy during the early 1970s. After almost five decades, a second generational transition occurred. International pressures and changes in codes and structures are influencing the shift in governance from stable "insider" relations to a more flexible "outsider" model. In other words, the shift implies a move away from traditional, rigid governance practices to more dynamic and responsive models that consider external influences. Despite the evolving business landscape, family influence remains strong in major private enterprises, with family-owned small- and medium-sized enterprises (SMEs) playing a pivotal role in contributing 70% to Tunisia's GDP (Ellouze & Mnasri, 2020). Understanding the governance of these family firms is crucial for establishing effective systems that safeguard shareholder interests in this dynamic market. In Tunisia's economy, family-owned enterprises, especially in emerging markets, are integral. A significant majority of small and medium enterprises are family-owned, and a noteworthy portion of large firms is family-controlled. According to Ellouze and Mnasri (2020), 110 out of the top 200 Tunisian firms and 42 out of 79 listed on the Tunisian stock exchange were family-controlled. Recognized for their productivity, these family firms can generate substantial long-term value (ibid.).

Addressing these issues, this chapter aims to enhance our comprehension of the correlation between EO and the growth of family firms. The study is based on data obtained from a questionnaire of 150 owner-managers of SME family firms in Tunisia. The research hypotheses were assessed using a quantitative method, employing a structural equation modeling (SEM) approach. The chapter is structured as follows: first, it presents the theoretical background. Second, it displays the research design and outlines sample characteristics. Third, the study presents the results from SEM. Fourth, the results are discussed and interpreted. To conclude, theoretical and practical implications are developed, and the limitations of the study are stated.

2. Literature Review and Research Hypothesis

In family-owned businesses, the significance of EO is amplified due to the intertwining of family and business, creating a distinctive environment (Casillas & Moreno, 2010; Dessi et al., 2023). In this context, EO pertains to the strategic decision-making processes and styles employed by these firms when engaging in entrepreneurial activities (Lumpkin & Dess, 1996, 2001).

2.1. EO as a Catalyst for Family Firm's Growth

Entrepreneurial behavior, guided by the founder, is closely linked to EO, which significantly impacts business performance (Rezaei & Ortt, 2018). EO has evolved, with different interpretations and dimensions proposed (Covin & Slevin, 1989; Lumpkin & Dess, 1996; Miller, 1983). Miller's three-dimensional model and Lumpkin-Dess's five-dimensional model are two prominent approaches. Miller's model combines its dimensions into a single indicator of EO, while Lumpkin-Dess's approach allows for independent variation among the dimensions, offering more flexibility for different contexts. This chapter adopts the definition proposed by Alvarez-Torres et al. (2019), which includes five dimensions: calculated risk-taking, innovation, proactivity, competitiveness, and autonomy. These dimensions collectively represent an organization's capacity and management style.

In recent years, there has been a significant focus on researching the growth of family firms. The growth of these businesses is closely tied to the generation currently in charge and the process of succession and generational transition (Stenholm et al., 2016; Zahra, 2003). Family firm managers are known to have extended time horizons for their businesses, driven by the desire to preserve them for future generations. This long-term perspective contrasts with short-term profit-focused strategies, as family firms prioritize conditions that support long-term growth. This emphasis on long-term growth over short-term profits helps family firms avoid a "quarterly earnings mentality" (Miroshnychenko et al., 2021; Zapata-Cantu et al., 2023). Some family members are committed to ensuring the ongoing strength of the business by investing in its future, improving relationships with employees through training and better working conditions (De Massis et al., 2018), and building lasting connections with external stakeholders like suppliers and customers. Moreover, they may allocate resources generously to innovate the business by introducing new products and expanding into new markets.

2.2. Exploring the Relationships Between EO and Family Firms' Growth

The relationship between a firm's EO and its performance has been extensively studied both theoretically and empirically (Dessi et al., 2023). EO is considered a finite resource, and firms excelling in EO tend to outperform those that do not possess this resource, aligning with the resource-based view of firms (Barney, 1991; Miller, 2011). Prior research has shown a clear positive link between EO and firm performance, especially in family firms, where EO positively influences growth and performance, particularly in later generations (Arzubiaga et al., 2018; Casillas et al., 2011; Moreno-Menéndez & Casillas, 2021; Rauch et al., 2009; Stenholm et al., 2016). Adopting an EO strategy can be beneficial for companies aspiring for business growth (Eggers et al., 2013). However, some studies have noted a negative correlation between EO and family firm growth in uncertain and turbulent economic environments (Hemmert et al., 2023). There is also evidence of a non-linear relationship between EO and performance (Kreiser et al., 2013). Additionally, different dimensions of EO can impact growth differently, and not all dimensions of EO may positively affect business performance, depending on the firm's circumstances (Lisboa et al., 2016; Lumpkin & Dess, 1996; Wales et al., 2013, 2020). Lumpkin and Dess (1996) established that EO can be seen as a multidimensional construct, with independent variables, leading to a need to assess the individual impact of each dimension separately for a comprehensive understanding of EO.

2.2.1. Innovativeness and Firm Growth

Semrau et al. (2016) define innovativeness as a willingness to engage in new ideas and processes that can lead to product, process, or technological advancements. It's vital for distinguishing successful organizations, enhancing performance, and gaining a competitive edge. While family firms often exhibit lower innovativeness levels, there's evidence that innovation positively impacts their growth due to their long-term orientation and goal of passing a thriving business to the next generation (Baltazar et al., 2023; Hernández-Linares et al., 2021; Stenholm et al., 2016). However, other empirical studies found no significant association between innovativeness and family firm growth (Kallmuenzer et al., 2018). In family firms, innovation is essential for long-term sustainability and alignment with the company's vision. Single owners tend to be more innovative and show a stronger EO (Miller et al., 2011). Governance within family firms plays a crucial role in influencing innovation decisions and improving company performance (Chrisman et al., 2015; Rezaei & Ortt, 2018). These firms often invest more in research and development, driven by their entrepreneurial tendencies and the need to introduce innovations in products, processes, or markets to prepare for future generations (Naldi et al., 2007). Allocating resources to innovation is a key strategy for enhancing firm performance and fostering growth, with positive factors related to product innovation contributing to the overall firm success (Kraus et al., 2012). Therefore, our hypothesis arises:

> *H1a.* There is a significant relationship between innovativeness and family firm growth.

2.2.2. Proactiveness and Firm Growth

Proactiveness represents a forward-thinking business strategy aimed at anticipating and addressing opportunities and threats (Hughes & Morgan, 2007). It involves the capacity to anticipate future demands and proactively shape the business environment. While innovativeness focuses on pursuing potential opportunities, proactiveness revolves around identifying and seizing those opportunities (Hernández-Linares et al., 2021). Proactiveness goes beyond merely responding to external pressures; it actively engages in molding the business environment (Rauch et al., 2009). In the context of family firms, proactiveness is particularly crucial because they often exhibit lower bureaucracy and greater flexibility, allowing them to make swift decisions and respond promptly to emerging opportunities. The long-term orientation of family firms contributes to their proactiveness and ultimately enhances their performance (Stenholm et al., 2016). Numerous empirical studies support the idea that proactiveness is a vital driver of sustained growth and performance in family firms (Casillas & Moreno, 2010; Kallmuenzer et al., 2018; Stenholm et al., 2016). Thus, the second hypothesis arises:

> *H2a.* There is a significant relationship between proactiveness and family firm growth.

2.2.3. Risk-taking and Firm Growth

Risk-taking signifies a firm's willingness to invest resources in uncertain projects, emphasizing measured and well-considered risk-taking. This dimension encourages firms to embrace uncertainty, as excessive risk aversion can hinder the exploration of new opportunities and disrupt the current business landscape, impacting overall performance positively (Rauch et al., 2009; Short et al., 2009). The impact of risk-taking on family firm performance shows various findings. Some studies have found no significant effect of risk-taking on family firm performance (Casillas & Moreno, 2010; Casillas et al., 2011; Kallmuenzer et al., 2018; Stenholm et al., 2016), while others argue that the alignment of interests between owners and managers in family firms results in less formal control and monitoring systems, allowing managers more decision-making autonomy, which may negatively impact performance (Naldi et al., 2007). Preferences for low-risk strategies in family firms could hinder their adaptability in dynamic and uncertain environments (Stenholm et al., 2016). Therefore, our third hypothesis will be formulated as follows:

> *H3a.* There is a significant relationship between risk-taking and family firm growth.

2.2.4. Competitive Aggressiveness and Firm Growth

To gain a deeper insight into the link between EO and a company's performance, the researchers turned their attention to competitive aggressiveness, which serves as an indicator of a firm's competitive nature (Aldabbas & Oberholzer, 2023; Al-Harthi et al., 2023; Al-Mamary & Alshallaqi, 2022; Blok, 2018; Hughes-Morgan et al., 2018; Shajrawi & Aburub, 2023; Thomran et al., 2022). It reflects a company's willingness to engage in direct and vigorous competition to improve its market position. Competitive aggressiveness is associated with being highly responsive and open to innovative approaches, allowing a business to assertively protect or enhance its market position (Lumpkin & Dess, 2001). While previous research generally suggests that a competitive and assertive approach is linked to better performance, there are conflicting findings. Some studies (e.g., Nadkarni et al., 2016) support the idea that aggressive competition leads to better results, while others, like Hughes and Morgan (2007) and Lumpkin and Dess (2001), present opposing results. In the context of family firms, there is limited research on competitive aggressiveness (Hernández-Linares et al., 2021; Hernández-Linares & López-Fernández, 2018), indicating that this aspect of OE may not significantly impact the growth (Casillas & Moreno, 2010) or performance (Kallmuenzer et al., 2018) of family firms. Family firms often prioritize maintaining a positive family reputation and image (Zellweger & Sieger, 2012), leading them to avoid aggressive actions against competitors that could result in negative consequences, such as financial losses. Instead, family firms tend to adopt a defensive approach focused on survival rather than an offensive strategy for maximizing financial returns (Short et al., 2009). Thus, we proposed the fourth hypothesis:

> *H4a.* There is a significant relationship between competitive aggressiveness and family firm growth.

2.2.5. Autonomy and Firm Growth

Autonomy, defined as the capacity for individuals or teams to independently conceive and execute an idea or vision, plays a vital role in fostering an entrepreneurial environment (Lumpkin & Dess, 1996). It goes beyond mere team organization, representing a strategic orientation that enables the development and execution of entrepreneurial initiatives. However, despite its significance, autonomy has received relatively limited theoretical and empirical attention in its relationship to firm performance, as highlighted by Rauch et al. (2009). Existing research on the role of autonomy within EO presents mixed findings. Some scholars, such as Hughes and Morgan (2007), fail to establish a significant connection between autonomy and firm performance, while others, like Lechner and Gudmundsson (2014), suggest that autonomy can impact firm differentiation, subsequently affecting performance. In the context of family firms, the investigation of the autonomy dimension of EO is even more limited. Some studies, like Casillas and Moreno (2010), do not confirm a positive link between autonomy and family firm growth, whereas Kallmuenzer et al. (2018) report a somewhat significant and positive relationship. Additionally, Zellweger and Sieger (2012) examined the EO of long-surviving family firms and emphasized the importance of "internal autonomy," which relates to the autonomy of employees or teams, aligning with the perspective presented by Nordqvist et al. (2008). Our fifth hypothesis will be formulated as follows:

> *H5a.* There is a significant relationship between autonomy and family firm growth.

2.2.6. The Moderating Effect of Generational Involvement

Generational involvement, defined as the participation of multiple family generations in a business's management, plays a significant role in a family firm's EO and performance (Chirico et al., 2011). Martin and Lumpkin (2003) suggest that when younger generations take the direction of a family firm, it tends to become more innovative and entrepreneurial due to their fresh ideas and willingness to take risks. In contrast, first-generation family firms, as indicated by Kellermanns and Eddleston (2006), are generally less open to corporate entrepreneurship and risk-taking. Many scholars argue that involving different generations in a family firm leads to increased entrepreneurial behavior, challenging the prevailing notion that family firms are typically risk-averse and resistant to change. Chirico et al. (2011) propose that higher levels of generational involvement may negatively moderate the relationship between EO and firm performance, with generational involvement affecting EO in various ways, either linearly, curvilinearly, or through moderating influences. Second-generation family firms, according to Casillas et al. (2010), tend to exhibit higher levels of EO compared to their first-generation counterparts. However, the impact of generational involvement on how EO influences a company's growth is complex and influenced by various factors, including the business's structure, external influences, and the direction of entrepreneurial behavior aimed at achieving growth objectives.

- *Innovativeness/generational involvement/firm growth*

According to Cruz and Nordqvist (2007), first-generation family firms emphasize internal leadership, while second-generation businesses prioritize external factors. The different orientations of first- and second-generation businesses have various effects on how innovativeness influences their growth. Second-generation businesses, with their greater external focus, are more likely to identify competitive opportunities that can be leveraged through new products, services, and processes, which boost growth. They tend to have more formalization and professionalization, leading to strategic planning and management that drive growth through innovation. Second-generation businesses are more open to recruiting non-family members who can bring fresh perspectives and identify opportunities for change. Furthermore, innovations introduced by subsequent generations often prioritize expansion as their primary goal, aligning with their strong focus on growth (Kellermanns & Eddleston, 2006; Kellermanns et al., 2008). Hence, we propose,

> *H1b.* Generational involvement will moderate the relationship between innovativeness and growth in family firms in such a way that a firm's innovativeness will have a more intense influence on growth in second-generation than in first-generation family firms.

- ***Proactiveness/generational involvement/firm growth***

Second- or subsequent-generation businesses anticipate that proactive behavior, supported by formalization, planning, and a growth-oriented mindset, will lead to more significant growth compared to first-generation family firms (Casillas et al., 2010; Sadiku-Dushi & Ramadani, 2020). Indeed, the structured environment in second-generation businesses facilitates proactive actions, making them more effective in accessing resources and capabilities founder (Kellermanns et al., 2008). Furthermore, the inherent growth orientation of second-generation businesses places a premium on proactive actions aimed at boosting sales, contributing to their overall growth (Kellermanns & Eddleston, 2006).

> *H2b.* Generational involvement will moderate the relationship between proactiveness and growth in family firms in such a way that a firm's proactiveness will have a more intense influence on growth in second-generation than in first-generation family firms.

- ***Risk-taking/generational involvement/firm growth***

Generational involvement significantly moderates the relationship between risk-taking and business growth. In businesses with non-family members in managerial roles and more formalized decision-making, risk management becomes less reliant on the founder's singular vision (Cruz & Nordqvist, 2007; Kellermanns et al., 2008; Naldi et al., 2007; Zahra, 2005). In first-generation businesses, two extremes can occur: excessive risk-taking with minimal control due to the founder's sole decision-making, or excessive caution driven by a desire to protect family wealth, resulting in slow, incremental changes and less overall growth.

> *H3b.* Generational involvement will moderate the relationship between risk-taking and growth in family firms in such a way that a firm's risk-taking will have a more intense influence on growth in second-generation than in first-generation family firms.

- ***Competitive aggressiveness/generational involvement/firm growth***

Generational involvement significantly shapes the relationship between competitive aggressiveness and the growth of family-owned businesses (Martin & Lumpkin, 2003). In first-generation firms, founders' caution moderates the influence of competitive aggressiveness on growth. In contrast, second-generation firms, driven by successors with fresh perspectives and a greater appetite for risk, embrace competitive aggressiveness more readily. Generational involvement intensifies the impact of competitive strategies on growth in second-generation firms, where successors are more ambitious and competitive, balancing tradition and innovation while ensuring family cohesion and business prosperity.

> *H4b.* Generational involvement will moderate the relationship between competitive aggressiveness and growth in family firms in such a way that a firm's competitive aggressiveness will have a more intense influence on growth in second-generation than in first-generation family firms.

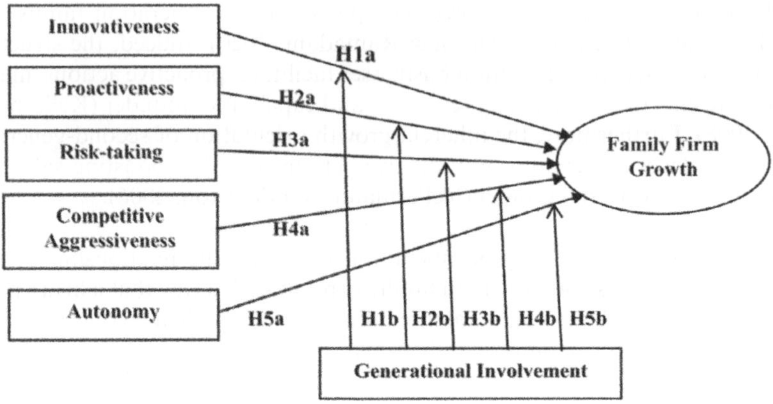

Fig. 4.1. Conceptual Model and Hypotheses. *Source*: Author construction.

- ***Autonomy/generational involvement/firm growth***

Generational involvement in family firms moderates the relationship between autonomy and growth (Eddleston et al., 2008). In first-generation firms, the founder's influence restricts autonomy, aligning growth with their vision. In contrast, second-generation firms involve multiple family members, leading to more decentralized decision-making and increased autonomy. Autonomy has a more significant impact on growth in second-generation businesses, as they are more flexible and adaptable in their decision-making. This highlights the evolving nature of family firms during generational transitions.

> *H5b*. Generational involvement will moderate the relationship between autonomy and growth in family firms in such a way that a firm's autonomy will have a more intense influence on growth in second-generation than in first-generation family firms.

Fig. 4.1 presents the different hypotheses proposed based on the review of the literature.

3. Methodology

3.1. Sample and Data Collection

We undertook this research on Tunisian family firms selected from the agency for the promotion of industry and innovation database, which serves as an exclusive resource offering insights into companies. After a refinement process that involved excluding entries lacking mailing addresses and those with inconsistent data or exceptionally high growth rates, the number of businesses reached 410 SME firms. Subsequently, a questionnaire was sent via the Internet to the CEOs of these businesses. To boost their response rates, we have opted to use telephone communication. In the end, we received 180 questionnaires, but unfortunately, 30 of them had to be excluded due to incomplete or incorrect information. This leaves us with a total of 150 valid responses, constituting a response rate of 36.58%. While various criteria have been proposed to define the concept of family firm (Dyer, 2003), we have chosen to use two specific criteria: companies in which both ownership and management are consolidated within one or more families, with these owning families possessing over 50% of the shares and involving at least two family members actively participating in the firm's operations.

3.2. Data Analysis

The demographic characteristics of respondents will be processed using IBM SPSS 22.

In this study, we employ the two-stage approach outlined by Anderson and Gerbing (1988) to conduct SEM. In the first stage, the research model uses confirmatory factor analysis with IBM SPSS 22 to assess the reliability and validity of the measurement model. In the second stage, this study employs SEM using IBM AMOS to test the research hypotheses. This involves examining both the direct influence between variables and the impact of moderating variables. Notably, we use SPSS for preliminary analysis and AMOS for inferential analysis especially the measurement model and structural model (Ramadani et al., 2022). According to Kline (2016), SEM analysis offers greater flexibility in its rules and allows for fewer measurement errors in the inclusion of multiple construct indicators.

To assess the impact of generational involvement as a moderating variable, the study utilized the Ping method. This involved testing the significance of the indirect effect of the independent variable on the dependent variable through the moderating variable.

3.3. Measures

3.3.1. Dependent Variable: Firm Growth

Firm growth was assessed by calculating the percentage growth in sales over four years. This method of using sales as a growth indicator is well-established in the literature. It's considered appropriate for two reasons:

1. *Theoretical*: Sales are a suitable indicator when the goal is to measure increased business activity rather than merely tracking fixed assets or employee numbers, which primarily reflect input increases (Davidsson & Wiklund, 1999).
2. *Empirical*: It's chosen because of a strong correlation among different measurements (Delmar et al., 2003).

Considering both theoretical and empirical factors, the study selected the percentage growth in sales between 2015 and 2019 as a single indicator of increased business activity. This measure has been widely employed in prior research, including family firm studies (Schulze et al., 2001).

3.3.2. Independent Variables: EO Dimensions

As mentioned above, EO is a multidimensional, latent construct. Consistent with Shan's et al. (2016) research, EO was measured using Hughes and Morgan's (2007) 18-item measure, and a 5-point Likert-type scale scored from 1 "strongly agree" to 5 "strongly disagree." We use Hughes and Morgan's (2007) scale because Lumpkin and Dess (1996) theoretically proposed five EO dimensions and later proposed scales for competitive aggressiveness and autonomy (Lumpkin & Dess, 2001), but they did not propose a scale for all EO dimensions. To remedy this, Hughes and Morgan (2007) used Lumpkin and Dess's work as a guide in developing scales for all EO dimensions and mostly sourced the items from previous studies (Hornsby et al., 2002; Hult & Ketchen, 2001; Lumpkin & Dess, 2001).

Cronbach's alpha test was performed to evaluate the internal consistency of the variables measured by multiple items. As can be gleaned from Table 4.2, all variables showed values above the minimum threshold value of 0.7 (Yi et al., 2021). The Cronbach's alpha reached satisfying levels for innovativeness ($\alpha = 0.72$), proactiveness ($\alpha = 0.7$), risk-taking ($\alpha = 0.83$), competitive aggressiveness ($\alpha = 0.74$), and autonomy ($\alpha = 0.75$).

3.3.3. Moderating Variable

To measure generational involvement, a single-item question was presented to the respondents to report the number of generations (one, two, three, or more than three) involved in the management of the firm (Kellermanns & Eddleston, 2006). Moderating variables are variables that can strengthen or weaken the relationship between the independent and dependent variables.

4. Results

4.1. Descriptive Statistics

As can be seen in the descriptive statistics in Table 4.1. On average, responding firms are 30 years old. Young firms (Anderson & Reeb, 2004) dominate the sample (<50). Moreover, in all firms, the CEO is a member of the board.

4.2. Model Testing

Following the guidelines from Hair et al. (2011) and Gotz et al. (2010), a three-step process was employed to assess the measurement model, which includes examining individual item reliability, convergent validity, and discriminant validity. As recommended by Hair et al. (2014) and Hair et al. (2011), it was stipulated that indicator loadings (factor loadings) should exceed the threshold of 0.70 to be considered significant. Based on these recommendations, this study established a cutoff value of 0.70 for factor loadings as indicative of significance. As demonstrated in Table 4.2, all item loadings fell within the range of 0.70 to 0.51 for their respective constructs.

The study assessed the convergent validity of each construct, which examines how effectively an item accurately represents the intended latent construct and

Table 4.1. Sample Characteristics.

	No. of Respondents (150)	Percentage
Gender of respondents		
Male	112	74.66
Female	38	25.33
Size of firm		
Small (10–50 employees)	102	68
Medium (51–250 employees)	48	32
Age		
<50 years	123	82
≥50 years	27	18
Type of business		
Industry (manufacturing)	90	60
Services	60	40
CEO duality	138	92
Age of respondents (mean)	*43.4*	
Generation		
Second generation	72	48
Third generation	*78*	*52*

Source: Author construction.

how it correlates with other measurements of the same latent construct (Hair et al., 2011; Valerie, 2012). To evaluate convergent validity, two criteria were considered: the average variance extracted (AVE) and the composite reliability (CR), both set at a threshold of 0.70 (ibid.). An AVE exceeding 0.5 and a CR of 0.7 or higher are acceptable. As indicated in Table 4.2, all factor loadings exceeded 0.5, and the AVE values met the criterion. Additionally, the CR values were all above 0.7. Consequently, it can be confidently concluded that convergent validity has been successfully established.

The subsequent step encompassed the evaluation of discriminant validity following Hair et al. (2011). Discriminant validity requires that each latent construct's AVE should exceed the highest squared correlation between that construct and any other latent construct (Fornell & Larcker, 1981). Additionally, the factor loadings of each construct's indicators should be greater than their cross-loadings with other constructs. Table 4.3 shows that the discriminant validity is satisfied because the AVE's square root of every construct is superior to the correlation among other constructs in the structural model.

After identifying an appropriate measurement model, we employed the SEM approach to test the hypotheses of the structural model and assess whether the

Table 4.2. The Quality and Reliability of Measurement Scales and Constructs.

Scale Composition	Loading	CR	Cronbach's α	AVE
INNOV1: We actively introduce improvements and innovations in our business	0.770	0.832	0.740	0.700
INNOV2: Our business is creative in its methods of operation	0.821			
INNOV3: Our business seeks out new ways to do things	0.700			
PROA1: We always try to take the initiative in every situation (e.g., against competitors, in projects and when working with others)	0.879	0.801	0.788	0.738
PROA2: We excel at identifying opportunities	0.772			
PROA3: We initiate actions to which other organizations respond	0.899			
RISK1: The term 'risk taker' is considered a positive attribute for people in our business	0.854			
RISK2: People in our business are encouraged to take calculated risks with new ideas	0.871	0.86	0.83	0.757
RISK3: Our business emphasizes both exploration and experimentation for opportunities	0.709			
COMP1: Our business is intensely competitive	0.751			
COMP2: In general, our business takes a bold or aggressive approach when competing	0.880	0.79	0.74	0.726
COMP3: We try to undo and out-maneuver the competition as best as we can	0.700			
AUT1: Employees are permitted to act and think without interference	0.930			

Table 4.2. (*continued*)

Scale Composition	Loading	CR	Cronbach's α	AVE
AUT2: Employees perform jobs that allow them to make and instigate changes in the way they perform their work tasks	0.784			
AUT3: Employees are given freedom and independence to decide on their own how to go about doing their work	0.950	0.882	0.75	0.770
AUT4: Employees are given freedom to communicate without interference	0.769			
AUT5: Employees are given authority and responsibility to act alone if they think it to be in the best interests of the business	0.840			
AUT6: Employees have access to all vital information	0.700			

Source: Author construction.

Table 4.3. Discriminant Validity of Construct.

Construct	INNOV	PROAC	RISK	COMP	AUTO
INNOV	0.833				
PROAC	−0.145	0.750			
RISK	0.269	−0.094	0.761		
COMP	0.702	−0.056	0.237	0.850	
AUTO	−0.654	0.253	0.49	−0.452	0.854

The diagonal represents the square root of the average variance extracted while the other entries represent squared correlations.

Source: Author construction.

proposed research model fits the real data best. Table 4.4 links the required and actual fit indices, demonstrating that the structural model adequately fits the data (Kline, 2016). Indeed, the chi-square ratio is equal to 1.80. According to Hooper et al. (2008), the root mean square residual (RMSEA) is a highly informative criterion, and it is generally recommended that the best RMSEA values ideally equal or are less than 0.07 (Steiger, 2007). Our analysis met this criterion, as the RMSEA value was 0.04. The comparative fit index (CFI)

Table 4.4. Evaluation of Model Fitting Indices.

		Measurement Model		
Fit Indices	**Criterion**	**Initial Model**	**Respecified Model**	**Structural Model**
χ^2/d.f.	<3.00	1.92	1.85	1.8
GFI	>0.9	0.93	0.94	0.93
NFI	>0.9	0.97	0.94	0.95
TLI	>0.95	0.96	0.95	0.97
CFI	>0.95	0.90	0.95	0.96
RMSEA	<0.07	0.05	0.04	0.04

The study hypothesizes that EO dimensions influenced family firm growth. In addition, generational involvement is supposed to moderate this relationship. Table 4.5 recapitulates all results and analysis of the structural model.

Source: Author construction.

should exceed the threshold of 0.95 for a model to be considered well-fitting. Our model achieved a CFI of 0.96. Goodness of fit index (GFI) values are expected to exceed 0.90 (Byrne, 1994), and our GFI value stood at 0.93. Similarly, the normed fit index (NFI) is ideally expected to be above 0.90 (Byrne, 1994), and our analysis yielded an NFI value of 0.95. The Tucker–Lewis index (TLI), also referred to as the non-normed fit index (NNFI), should surpass 0.95, and in our case, the TLI/NNFI was calculated to be 0.97. Table 4.4 presents the model fit indices.

4.3. Hypothesis Testing

4.3.1. Hypothesis Testing the Direct Effects Between Variables

Once a structural model is deemed suitable, the subsequent step involves assessing the extent of influence between the independent variable and the dependent variable. To assess this hypothesis, the examination is carried out by analyzing the research model's estimated outcomes. Decision-making criteria, as outlined by Hair et al. (2011), involve scrutinizing the CR value, which should exceed 1.96, and the *p*-value, which should be less than 0.05. When these conditions are met, the hypothesis is supported, indicating that the variable exerts a significant impact. Conversely, if the CR value falls below 1.96 and the *p*-value exceeds 0.05, the hypothesis is rejected, signifying that the variable does not have an effect. The model's estimation results are detailed in Table 4.5. *H2a*, *H4a*, and *H5a* are supported. This is because the CR values are 5.03, 6.42, and 10.02, respectively (CR ≥ 1.96), and the effect is significant because the probability values are less than 0.05. However, *H1a* and *H3a* are not supported because both the CR value and the probability value are not significant.

Table 4.5. Findings of Hypothesis Testing.

Hyp	Relation	CR	*p*-Value	Results of Hyp
H1a	INNOV → GROW	0.43	0.10	Not supported
H2a	PROA → GROW	5.03	0.02	Supported
H3a	RISK → GROW	−7.63	0.10	Not supported
H4a	COMP → GROW	6.42	0.00	Supported
H5a	AUTO → GROW	10.02	0.00	Supported

Source: Author construction.

Table 4.6. Findings of Hypothesis Testing/Interaction Variable Between EO Dimensions and Generational Involvement.

Hyp	Relation	CR	*p*-Value	Results of Hyp
H1a	INNOV * GEN INVO → GROW	1.43	0.09	Not supported
H2a	PROA * GEN INVO → GROW	3.82	0.00	Supported
H3a	RISK * GEN INVO → GROW	0.63	0.15	Not supported
H4a	COMP* GEN ONVO → GROW	2.67	0.00	Supported
H5a	AUTO * GEN INVO → GROW	4.56	0.00	Supported

Source: Author construction.

4.4. Hypothesis Testing the Effects of the Moderating Variable

In SEM, there are various ways to check for moderating effects. Ping (1996) introduced one simple approach known as the Ping method. According to this method, you use a single indicator to represent a moderating variable. In the moderation analysis, data are inputted from the variables related to the moderation interaction, namely, EO dimensions, generational involvement, and family firm growth. The subsequent step involves constructing the moderation interaction model, wherein the generational involvement variable serves as the moderator influencing the relationship between EO dimensions and family firm growth.

From the findings presented in Table 4.6, the interaction variable between EO dimensions and generational involvement does not have an identical significant effect on family firm growth ($p < 0.05$ and CR > 1.96). Only *H2b*, *H4b*, and *H5b* are supported. Therefore, it can be inferred that generational involvement acts as a moderator, influencing the relationship between EO and family firm growth.

5. Discussion

This research aims to explore the impact of EO on family firms' growth by elucidating the role of generational involvement. The SEM technique was applied to examine survey data collected from a Tunisian family firm. Our results reinforce the idea that in family firms, the influence on firm growth is not similar across all five EO dimensions, emphasizing the importance of distinguishing between these dimensions (Casillas & Moreno, 2010; Hernández-Linares et al., 2021; Hughes & Morgan, 2007; Lumpkin & Dess, 1996). Additionally, we discovered a connection between generational involvement and some EO dimensions.

Among the dimensions considered, it's important to note that risk-taking and innovativeness did not demonstrate any statistically significant direct or indirect influence on the growth of family firms. The analysis conducted suggests that there is no meaningful correlation between the level of risk-taking behavior within these firms. One potential explanation for this finding could be the effective risk diversification strategies that family firms employ. These firms often balance riskier ventures with conservative approaches, which may mitigate the overall impact of risk on growth. Additionally, family firms tend to implement robust risk management practices, further reducing the negative consequences of risk-taking. Furthermore, some family-owned enterprises prioritize stability and long-term sustainability over rapid growth, deliberately opting for more conservative strategies. While this might limit short-term growth potential, it can lead to steady, sustainable, and resilient business outcomes in the long term. Regarding innovativeness, the absence of a significant association with firm performance aligns with the results found by Kallmuenzer et al. (2018). However, this outcome stands in contrast to most existing studies in the field (Casillas & Moreno, 2010; Casillas et al., 2010; Craig et al., 2014; Hatak et al., 2016; Hernández-Linares et al., 2021; Kellermanns et al., 2012; Naldi et al., 2007; Stenholm et al., 2016). Hernández-Linares et al. (2021) suggest that the reason for these differing results could be that, in a prolonged economic crisis, being innovative is crucial for staying afloat, but it may not be enough by itself to guarantee growth or improved performance. We also hypothesized that proactiveness would have a favorable impact on the growth of family firms. Our findings indicate that within the Tunisian family firm context, a proactive inclination equips firms with the capacity to foresee changes or emerging needs in the market, enabling them to leverage opportunities arising from their business environment (Covin & Slevin, 1989; Hughes & Morgan, 2007; Wiklund & Shepherd, 2005). This reaffirms the positive influence of proactiveness on firm growth, highlighting the imperative for family enterprises to take proactive measures to outpace competitors through the introduction of innovative ideas, products, or services (Casillas & Moreno, 2010; Casillas et al., 2010; Kallmuenzer et al., 2018; Stenholm et al., 2016). Competitive aggressiveness was hypothesized to have a significant effect on the growth of the family. This finding is in line with the study of Hernández-Linares et al. (2021) who argue that within the domain of family firms, those that consistently and promptly act in their market environment are often successful in seizing business opportunities and gaining the benefits of being a first mover. This dimension, frequently neglected by numerous researchers, carries substantial significance and merits further investigation. The significant relationship between autonomy and firm growth can be succinctly explained as follows: when employees and teams are granted a degree of autonomy within a company, they gain the ability to make decisions and take actions independently. This autonomy often fosters a culture of innovation, quick response to market changes, and efficient problem-solving. In the context of family firms, where a strong desire for survival is prevalent, autonomy empowers the organization to adapt swiftly and capitalize on emerging opportunities. As a result, the firm can expand its market presence, introduce new products or services, and effectively navigate challenges. In essence, autonomy fuels growth by enabling a more agile and proactive approach to business operations, which, in turn, leads to improved performance and expansion. Regarding the moderating role of generational involvement in the relationships between the EO dimensions and family firm growth, not all the hypotheses were supported. Generational involvement did appear to significantly moderate the relationship between proactiveness, competitive aggressiveness, autonomy, and firm growth within the context of family firms.

6. Conclusion, Limitations, Implications, and Further Research

Our research examined and tested the effect of EO and the moderation of generational involvement on firm growth. Even though we found empirical support for the hypotheses, this line of inquiry also opens an opportunity for theory building regarding which dimension of EO is more appropriate concerning newly founded enterprises in emerging market settings. This study has a few limitations that should be considered. First, it cannot be used to draw nationwide conclusions about family firms due to its reliance on convenience sampling and its confined sampling scope within Tunisia. From a statistical perspective, the sample might not possess the ability to be representative and, therefore, may not be appropriate for making broad inferences about the general population. Consequently, the study's findings may not be definitive for the broader context of family firms. Second, our sample, specific to our country, could possess distinct attributes that do not necessarily mirror the situations of family firms in other emerging nations. Finally, this study did not assess control variables relevant to family firm aspects that could offer valuable theoretical and empirical insights. A key suggestion for future research on generational involvement is to explore the potential impact of contextual family variables. An intriguing avenue for examination could involve prominent family variables, such as CEO tenure. CEO tenure significantly affects the development and endurance of EO, showing a pattern of an upside-down U relationship (Boling et al., 2016).

Despite these limitations, this study has important implications for academics. From a research perspective, it advances our understanding of the relationship between EO, generational involvement, and firm growth concerning emerging economies or markets. Previous studies have explored fragmented results (weak, significant, or insignificant relationship) between EO and firm growth. However, our research finds that generational involvement is a significant moderator factor between EO dimensions and firm growth in emerging economies. In other words, higher levels of EO are associated with increased engagement and participation of different generations within the business. It also provides empirical evidence that family firms can maintain and develop a long-term EO. At the same time, further research is needed to examine whether or not there are other additional family firm moderators to influence the relationship between EO, generational stage, and growth. For instance, it would be interesting to examine organizational culture as a moderating variable since it is embedded in and nurtured by family and business. For practitioners in family firms, understanding the distinct roles of proactiveness, competitive aggressiveness, and autonomy can enhance the development of sustainable entrepreneurial family firms. Long-term EO is a more complex phenomenon than the sum of multiple generations' efforts. It involves a synergy of perspectives between old and young generations, emphasizing effective and efficient coordination and collaboration among different generations within the firm. Previous studies have asserted that the involvement of a young generation on the company's board and its collaboration with the older generation is expected to be a source of open-minded initiatives (e.g., Bannò & Sgobbi, 2016). Managers in family firms should prioritize cultivating a culture of proactiveness, competitive aggressiveness, and autonomy to maintain a strong level of EO and consequently foster growth. Managers of new ventures in both emerging and developed markets should promote or employ entrepreneurial activities to exploit new opportunities as a means of sustaining performance. An enduring entrepreneurial culture can be a more viable growth strategy as compared to investment in other activities (Anwar & Shah, 2020). This is even more important for new and small ventures in emerging economies with significant resource constraints (Cai et al., 2016).

Future research should explore the longitudinal dynamics of EO dimensions in family firms, examining how these relationships evolve over time and respond to external factors. Understanding how generational involvement influences the connection between EO and growth can help with effective management. Additionally, exploring how EO interacts with cultural influences and adapts to trends like digital transformation and sustainability provides valuable guidance for family firms in the changing business landscape. Furthermore, conducting meaningful cross-country comparisons, especially in the context of family firm succession studies, would contribute to the existing knowledge base. Finally, this study advocates for more empirical research to examine how generational involvement impacts the creation of professionalization and family governance mechanisms. The aim is to understand how these mechanisms influence the sustainability of entrepreneurial family firms.

References

Agca, V., & Kizildag, D. (2013). Linking generational involvement to intrapreneurship activities in Turkish family firms: An empirical study. *Business Management Dynamics*, *2*(12), 47–57.

Aldabbas, H., & Oberholzer, N. (2023). The influence of transformational and learning through R&D capabilities on the competitive advantage of firms. *Arab Gulf Journal of Scientific Research, 42*(1), 85–102. https://doi.org/10.1108/AGJSR-08-2022-0141

Al-Harthi, S., Anatolievich-Bachkirov, A., Al-Riyami, S., & Al-Jahwari, M. (2023). Entrepreneurial orientation and competitive aggressiveness: A need for conceptual refinement and contextualization. *Arab Gulf Journal of Scientific Research*. https://doi.org/10.1108/AGJSR-04-2023-0161

Al-Mamary, Y. H., & Alshallaqi, M. (2022). Impact of autonomy, innovativeness, risk-taking, proactiveness, and competitive aggressiveness on students' intention to start a new venture. *Journal of Innovation & Knowledge*, *7*(4), 100239. https://doi.org/10.1016/j.jik.2022.100239

Alvarez-Torres, F. J., Lopez-Torres, G. C., & Schiuma, G. (2019). Linking entrepreneurial orientation to SMEs' performance: Implications for entrepreneurship universities. *Management Decision*, *57*(12), 3364–3386. https://doi.org/10.1108/MD-11-2018-1234

Anderson, J. C., & Gerbing, D. W. (1988). Structural equation modeling in practice: A review and recommended two-step approach. *Psychological Bulletin*, *103*(3), 411–423. https://doi.org/10.1037/0033-2909.103.3.411

Anderson, R. C., & Reeb D. M. (2004). Board composition: Balancing family influence in S&P 500 firms. *Administrative Science Quarterly*, *49*(2), 209–237. http://www.jstor.org/stable/4131472

Anwar, M., & Shah, S. Z. (2020). Entrepreneurial orientation and generic competitive strategies for Journal of Management emerging SMEs: Financial, and non-financial performance perspective. *Journal of Public Affairs*, *21*(1), e2125. https://doi.org/10.1002/pa.2125

Arzubiaga, U., Iturralde, T., Maseda, A., & Kotlar, J. (2018). Entrepreneurial orientation and firm performance in family SMEs: The moderating effects of family, women, and strategic involvement in the board of directors. *International Entrepreneurship and Management Journal*, *14*, 217–244. https://doi.org/10.1007/s11365-017-0473-4

Baltazar, J., Fernandes, C., Ramadani, V., & Hughes, M. (2023). Family business succession and innovation: A systematic literature review. *Review of Managerial Science*, *17*(8), 2897–2920.

Bannò, M., & Sgobbi, F. (2016). Family business characteristics and the approach to HRM in overseas ventures. *Journal of Small Business Management*, *54*(2), 640–658. https://doi.org/10.1111/jsbm.12162

Barney, J. (1991). Firm resources and sustained competitive advantage. *Journey of Management*, *17*(1), 99–120. https://doi.org/10.1177/014920639101700108

Boling, J. R., Pieper, T. M., & Covin, J. G. (2016). CEO tenure and entrepreneurial orientation within family and nonfamily firms. *Entrepreneurship Theory and Practice*, *40*(4), 891–913. https://doi.org/10.1111/etap.12150

Blok, V. (2018). Philosophy of innovation: A research agenda: Guest editorial. *Philosophy of Management*, *17*(1), 1–5. https://doi.org/10.1007/s40926-017-0080-z

Byrne, B. M. (1994). *Structural equation modeling with EQS and EQS/Windows: Basic concepts, applications and programming*. Sage.

Cai, L., Chen, J., Peng, X., & Chen, B. (2016). The effect of symbiosis strategy on opportunity creation: Case study of new ventures in China. *International Journal of Technology Management*, *72*(1–3), 171–191. https://doi.org/10.1504/IJTM.2016.080550

Campopiano, G., Brumana, M., Minola, T., & Cassia, L. (2019). Does growth represent chimera or bellerophon for a family business? The role of entrepreneurial orientation and family influence nuances. *European Management Review*, *17*(3), 765–783. https://doi.org/10.1111/emre.12351

Casillas, J. C., & Moreno, A. M. (2010). The relationship between entrepreneurial orientation and growth: The moderation role of family involvement. *Entrepreneurship & Regional Development*, *22*(3–4), 265–291. https://doi.org/10.1080/08985621003726135

Casillas, J. C., Moreno, A. M., & Barbero, J. L. (2010). A configurational approach of the relationship between entrepreneurial orientation and growth of family firms. *Family Business Review*, *23*(1), 27–44. https://doi.org/10.1177/0894486509345159

Casillas, J. C., Moreno, A. M., & Barbero, J. L. (2011). Entrepreneurial orientation of family firms: Family and environmental dimensions. *Journal of Family Business Strategy*, *2*(2), 90–100. https://doi.org/10.1016/j.jfbs.2011.03.002

Chirico, F., & Nordqvist, M. (2010). Dynamic capabilities and transgenerational value creation in family firms: The role of organizational culture. *International Small Business Journal*, *28*(5), 487–504. https://doi.org/10.1177/0266242610370402

Chirico, F., Sirmon, D., Sciascia, S., & Mazzola, P. (2011). Resource orchestration in family firms: Investigating how entrepreneurial orientation, generational involvement, and participative strategy affect performance. *Strategic Entrepreneurship Journal*, *5*(2), 307–326. https://ssrn.com/abstract=2177317

Chrisman, J. J., Chua, J. H., & Sharma, P. (2005). Trends and directions in the development of a strategic management theory of the family firm. *Entrepreneurship Theory and Practice*, *29*(5), 555–575. https://doi.org/10.1111/j.1540-6520.2005.00098.x

Chrisman, J., Chua, J., De Massis, A., Frattini, F., & Wright, M. (2015). The ability and willingness paradox in family firm innovation. *Journal of Product Innovation Management*, *32*(3), 310–318. https://doi.org/10.1111/jpim.12207

Covin, J. G., Green, K. M., & Slevin, D. P. (2006). Strategic process effects on the entrepreneurial orientation–sales growth rate relationship. *Entrepreneurship Theory and Practice*, *30*(1), 57–81. https://doi.org/10.1111/j.1540-6520.2006.00110.x

Covin, J. G., & Slevin, D. P. (1989). Strategic management of small firms in hostile and benign environments. *Strategic Management Journal*, *10*(1), 75–87. https://doi.org/10.1002/smj.4250100107

Covin, J. G., & Slevin, D. P. (1991). A conceptual model of entrepreneurship as firm behavior. *Entrepreneurship Theory and Practice*, *16*(1), 7–26. https://doi.org/10.1177/104225879101600102

Covin, J. G., & Miller, D. (2014). International entrepreneurial orientation: Conceptual considerations, research themes, measurement issues, and future research directions. *Entrepreneurship Theory and Practice*, *38*(1), 11–44. https://doi.org/10.1111/etap.12027

Covin, J. G., & Lumpkin, G. T. (2011). Entrepreneurial orientation theory and research: Reflections on a needed construct. *Entrepreneurship Theory and Practice*, *35*(5), 855–872. https://doi.org/10.1111/j.1540-6520.2011.00482.x

Craig, J. B., Dibrell, C., & Garrett, R. (2014). Examining relationships among family influence, family culture, flexible planning systems, innovativeness and firm performance. *Journal of Family Business Strategy*, *5*(3), 229–238. https://doi.org/10.1016/j.jfbs.2013.09.002

Cruz, C., & Nordqvist, M. (2007). Entrepreneurial orientation in family businesses: A generational perspective [*8th Annual international family enterprise research academy conference*]. Nyenroede, Netherlands.

Davidsson, P., & Wiklund, J. (1999). *Conceptual and empirical challenges in the study of firm growth* [Paper presented at the state of the art in entrepreneurship conference]. Fort Lauderdale, FL.

Delmar, F., Davidsson, P., & Gartner, W. B. (2003). Arriving at the high-growth firm. *Journal of Business Venturing*, *18*(2), 189–216. https://doi.org/10.1016/S0883-9026(02)00080-0

De Massis, A., Kotlar, J., Mazzola, P., Minola, T., & Sciascia, S. (2018). Conflicting selves: Family owners' multiple goals and self-control agency problems in private firms. *Entrepreneurship Theory and Practice*, *42*(3), 362–389. https://doi.org/10.1111/etap.12257

Dessi, C., Dettori, A., & Floris, M. (2023). Exploring different configurations of entrepreneurial orientation in small artisan family firms: A multi-case study. *Journal of Family Business Strategy*, *14*(3), 100503. https://doi.org/10.1016/j.jfbs.2022.100503

Dyer, W. G., Jr. (2003). The family: The missing variable in organizational research. *Entrepreneurship Theory and Practice*, *27*(4), 401–416. https://doi.org/10.1111/1540-8520.00018

Eddleston, K. A., Kellermanns, F. W., & Sarathy, R. (2008). Resource configuration in family firms: Linking resources, strategic planning and technological opportunities to performance. *Journal of Management Studies*, *45*(1), 26–50. https://doi.org/10.1111/j.1467-6486.2007.00717.x

Eggers, F., Kraus, S., Hughes, M., Laraway, S., & Snycerski, S. (2013). Implications of customer and entrepreneurial orientations for SME growth. *Management Decision*, *51*(3), 524–546. https://doi.org/10.1108/00251741311309643

Ellouze, D., & Mnasri, K. (2020). Risking-taking behaviour of family firms: Evidence from Tunisie. *International Journal of Entrepreneurship and Small Business*, *39*(1/2), 192–221. https://doi.org/10.1504/ijesb.2020.10025931

Fornell, C., & Larcker, D. F. (1981). Evaluating structural equation models with unobservable variables and measurement error. *Journal of Marketing Research*, *18*(1), 39–50. https://doi.org/10.2307/3151312

Gotz, O., Liehr-Gobbers, K., & Krafft, M. (2010). Evaluation of structural equation models using the partial least squares (PLS) approach. In V. E. Vinzi, W. W. Chin, J. Henseler, & H. Wang (Eds.), *Handbook of partial least squares: Concepts, methods and applications* (pp. 691–711). Springer. https://doi.org/10.1007/978-3-540-32827-8_30

Gupta, V. K., & Batra, S. (2016). Entrepreneurial orientation and firm performance in Indian SMEs: Universal and contingency perspectives. *International Small Business Journal*, *34*(5), 660–682. https://doi.org/10.1177/0266242615577708

Hair, J. F., Hult, G. T. M., Ringle, C. M., & Sarstedt, M. (2014). *A primer on partial least squares structural equation modeling (PLS-SEM)*. Sage Publications.

Hair, J. F., Ringle, C. M., & Sarstedt, M. (2011). PLS-SEM: Indeed a silver bullet. *Journal of Marketing Theory and Practice*, *19*(2), 139–152. https://doi.org/10.2753/MTP1069-6679190202

Hatak, I., Kautonen, T., Fink, M., & Kansikas, J. (2016). Innovativeness and family-firm performance: The moderating effect of family commitment. *Technological Forecasting and Social Change*, *102*, 120–131. https://doi.org/10.1016/j.techfore.2015.02.020

Hemmert, M., Cross, A. R., Cheng, Y., Kim, J. J., Kotosaka, M., Waldenberger, F., & Zheng, L. J. (2023). Environmental uncertainty and the entrepreneurial orientation–performance relationship among East Asian new technology-based firms: An institutional perspective. *Asian Business & Management*, *22*, 1683–1711. https://doi.org/10.1057/s41291-023-00227-4

Hernández-Linares, R., & López-Fernández, M. C. (2018). Entrepreneurial orientation and the family firm: Mapping the field and tracing a path for future research. *Family Business Review*, *31*(3), 318–351. https://doi.org/10.1177/0894486518781940

Hernández-Linares, R., Kellermanns, F. W., López-Fernández, M. C., & Sarkar, S. (2021). The effect of socioemotional wealth on the relationship between entrepreneurial orientation and family business performance. *Business Research Quarterly*, *23*(3), 174–192. https://doi.org/10.1177/2340944420941438

Hooper, D., Coughlan, J., & Mullen, M. R. (2008). Structural equation modelling: Guidelines for determining model fit. *Electronic Journal of Business Research Methods*, *6*(1), 53–60. https://doi.org/10.21427/D7CF7R

Hornsby, J. S., Kuratko, D. F., & Zahra, S. A. (2002). Middle managers' perception of the internal environment for corporate entrepreneurship: Assessing a measurement scale. *Journal of Business Venturing*, *17*(3), 253–273. https://doi.org/10.1016/S0883-9026(00)00059-8

Hughes, M., & Morgan, R. (2007). Deconstructing the relationship between entrepreneurial orientation and business performance at the embryonic stage of firm growth. *Industrial Marketing Management*, *36*(5), 651–661. https://doi.org/10.1016/j.indmarman.2006.04.003

Hughes-Morgan, M., Kolev, K., & McNamara, G. (2018). A meta-analytic review of competitive aggressiveness research. *Journal of Business Research*, *85*, 73–82. https://doi.org/10.1016/j.jbusres.2017.10.053

Hult, G. T. M., & Ketchen, D. J., Jr. (2001). Does market orientation matter? A test of the relationship between positional advantage and performance. *Strategic Management Journal*, *22*(9), 899–906. https://doi.org/10.1002/SMJ.197

Kallmuenzer, A., Strobl, A., & Peters, M. (2018). Tweaking the entrepreneurial orientation-performance relationship in family firms: The effect of control mechanisms and family-related goals. *Review of Managerial Science*, *12*(4), 855–883. https://doi.org/10.1007/S11846-017-0231-6

Kellermanns, F. W., & Eddleston, K. A. (2006). Corporate entrepreneurship in family firms: A family perspective. *Entrepreneurship Theory and Practice*, *30*(6), 809–830. https://doi.org/10.1111/j.1540-6520.2006.00153.x

Kellermanns, F. W., Eddleston, K. A., Barnett, T., & Pearson, A. (2008). An exploratory study of family member characteristics and involvement: Effects on entrepreneurial behavior in family firms. *Family Business Review*, *21*(1), 1–14. https://doi.org/10.1111/j.1741-6248.2007.00107.x

Kellermanns, F. W., Eddleston, K. A., & Zellweger, T. M. (2012). Extending the socioemotional wealth perspective: A look at the dark side. *Entrepreneurship Theory and Practice*, *36*(6), 1175–1182. https://doi.org/10.1111/j.1540-6520.2012.00544.x

Kline, R. B. (2016). *Principles and practice of structural equation modelling* (4th ed., p. 326). The Guilford Press.

Kraus, S., Rigtering, J. P. C., Hughes, M., & Hosman, V. (2012). Entrepreneurial orientation and the business performance of SMEs: A quantitative study from the Netherlands. *Review of Managerial Science*, *6*(1), 161–182. https://doi.org/10.1007/s11846-011-0062-9

Kreiser, P. M., Marino, L. D., Kuratko, D. F., & Weaver, K. M. (2013). Disaggregating entrepreneurial orientation: The non-linear impact of innovativeness, proactiveness and risk-taking on SME performance. *Small Business Economics*, *40*(2), 273–291. https://doi.org/10.1007/s11187-012-9460-x

Lechner, C., & Gudmundsson, S. V. (2014). Entrepreneurial orientation, firm strategy and small firm performance. *International Small Business Journal*, *32*(1), 36–60. https://doi.org/10.1177/0266242612455034

Lisboa, A., Skarmeas, D., & Saridakis, C. (2016). Entrepreneurial orientation pathways to performance: A fuzzy-set analysis. *Journal of Business Research*, *69*(4), 1319–1324. https://doi.org/10.1016/j.jbusres.2015.10.099

Lomberg, C., Urbig, D., Stockmann, C., Marino, L. D., & Dickson, P. H. (2017). Entrepreneurial orientation: The dimensions shared effects in explaining firm performance. *Entrepreneurship Theory and Practice*, *41*(6), 973–998. https://doi.org/10.1111/etap.12237

Lumpkin, G. T., & Dess, G. G. (1996). Clarifying the entrepreneurial orientation construct and linking it to performance. *Academy of Management Review*, *21*(1), 135–172. https://doi.org/10.2307/258632

Lumpkin, G. T., & Dess, G. G. (2001). Linking two dimensions of entrepreneurial orientation to firm performance: The moderating role of environment and industry life cycle. *Journal of Business Venturing*, *16*(5), 429–451. https://doi.org/10.1016/S0883-9026(00)00048-3

Martin, W. L., & Lumpkin, G. T. (2003). From entrepreneurial orientation to "family orientation": Generational differences in the management of family businesses [*Paper presented at the 22nd Babson College entrepreneurship research conference*]. Wellesley, MA, USA.

Miller, D., & Friesen, P. H. (1982). Innovation in conservative and entrepreneurial firms: Two models of strategic momentum. *Strategic Management Journal, 3*(1), 1–25. https://doi.org/10.1002/smj.4250030102

Miller, D. (1983). The correlates of entrepreneurship in three types of firms. *Management Science, 29*(7), 757–868. https://doi.org/10.1287/mnsc.29.7.770

Miller, D., & Whitney, J. O. (1999). Beyond strategy: Configuration as a pillar of competitive advantage. *Business Horizons, 42*(3), 5–17. https://doi.org/10.1016/S0007-6813(99)80016-0

Miller, D. (2011). Miller (1983) revisited: A reflection on EO research and some suggestions for the future. *Entrepreneurship Theory and Practice, 35*(5), 873–894. https://doi.org/10.1111/j.1540-6520.2011.00457.x

Miller, D., Le Breton-Miller, I., & Lester, R. H. (2011). Family and lone founder ownership and strategic behavior: Social context, identity, and institutional logics. *Journal of Management Studies, 48*(1), 1–25. https://doi.org/10.1111/j.1467-6486.2009.00896.x

Miroshnychenko, I., De Massis, A., Miller, D., & Barontini, R. (2021). Family business growth around the world. *Entrepreneurship Theory and Practice, 45*(4), 682–708. https://doi.org/10.1177/1042258720913028

Moreno-Menéndez, A. M., & Casillas, J. C. (2021). How do family businesses grow? Differences in growth patterns between family and non-family firms. *Journal of Family Business Strategy, 12*(3), 100420. https://doi.org/10.1016/j.jfbs.2021.100420

Nadkarni, S., Chen, T. X., & Chen, J. H. (2016). The clock is ticking! Executive temporal depth, industry velocity, and competitive aggressiveness. *Strategic Management Journal, 37*(6), 1132–1153. https://doi.org/10.1002/smj.2376

Naldi, L., Nordqvist, M., Sjöberg, K., & Wiklund, J. (2007). Entrepreneurial orientation, risk taking, and performance in family firms. *Family Business Review, 20*(1), 33–47. https://doi.org/10.1111/j.1741-6248.2007.00082.x

Nordqvist, M., Habbershon, T. G., & Melin, L. (2008). Transgenerational entrepreneurship: Exploring entrepreneurial orientation in family firms. In H. Landström, D. Smallbone, H. Crijns, & E. Laveren (Eds.), *Entrepreneurship, sustainable growth and performance: Frontiers in European entrepreneurship research* (pp. 93–116). Edward Elgar.

Ping, R. A. (1996). Latent variable interaction and quadratic effect estimation: A two-step technique using structural equation analysis. *Psychological Bulletin, 119*(1), 166–175. https://doi.org/10.1037/0033-2909.119.1.166

Pittino, D., Francesca, V., & Giancarlo, L. (2017). A configurational analysis of the antecedents of entrepreneurial orientation. *European Management Journal, 35*(2), 224–237. https://doi.org/10.1016/j.emj.2016.07.003

Ramadani, V., & Hoy, F. (2015). Context and uniqueness of family businesses. In L. P. Dana & V. Ramadani (Eds.), *Family Businesses in Transition Economies* (pp. 9–37). Springer. https://ssrn.com/abstract=2559662

Ramadani, V., Rahman, M. D., Salamzadeh, A., Rahaman, M. D. S., & Abazi, H. (2022). Entrepreneurship education and graduates' entrepreneurial intentions: Does gender matter? A multi-group analysis using AMOS. *Technological Forecasting and Social Change, 180*, 121693. https://doi.org/10.1016/j.techfore.2022.121693

Rauch, A., Wiklund, J., Lumpkin, G. T., & Frese, M. (2009). Entrepreneurial orientation and business performance: An assessment of past research and suggestions for the future. *Entrepreneurship Theory and Practice, 33*(3), 761–787. https://doi.org/10.1111/j.1540-6520.2009.00308.x

Rezaei, J., & Ortt R. (2018). Entrepreneurial orientation and firm performance: The mediating role of functional performances. *Management Research Review, 41*(7), 878–900. https://doi.org/10.1108/MRR-03-2017-0092

Sadiku-Dushi, N., & Ramadani, V. (2020). Entrepreneurial marketing mindset: What entrepreneurs should know? In V. Ramadani, R. Palalić, L. P. Dana, N. Krueger, & A. Caputo (Eds.), *Organizational mindset of entrepreneurship* (pp. 181–210). Springer. https://doi.org/10.1007/978-3-030-36951-4_9

Schulze, W. S., Lubatkin, M. H., Dino, R. N., & Buchholtz, A. K. (2001). Agency relationships in family firms: Theory and evidence. *Organization Science*, *12*(2), 99–116. https://www.jstor.org/stable/3086050

Semrau, T., Ambos, T., & Kraus, S. (2016). Entrepreneurial orientation and SME performance across societal cultures: An international study. *Journal of Business Research*, *69*(5), 1928–1932. https://doi.org/10.1016/j.jbusres.2015.10.082

Shajrawi, A., & Aburub, F. (2023). Impact of ERP usage on service differentiation: Role of mediating effect of organizational agility. *Arab Gulf Journal of Scientific Research*, *41*(3), 359–375. https://doi.org/10.1108/AGJSR-06-2022-0085

Shan, P., Song, M., & Ju, X. (2016). Entrepreneurial orientation and performance: Is innovation speed a missing link. *Journal of Business Research*, *69*(2), 683–690. https://doi.org/10.1016/j.jbusres.2015.08.032

Short, J. C., Payne, G. T., Brigham, K. H., & Broberg, J. C. (2009). Family firms and entrepreneurial orientation in publicly traded firms. A comparative analysis of the S&P 500. *Family Business Review*, *22*(1), 9–24. https://doi.org/10.1177/0894486508327823

Steiger, J. H. (2007). Understanding the limitations of global fit assessment in structural equation modeling. *Personality and Individual Differences*, *42*(5), 893–898. https://doi.org/10.1016/j.paid.2006.09.017

Stenholm, P., Pukkinen, T., & Heinonen, J. (2016). Firm growth in family businesses: The role of entrepreneurial orientation and the entrepreneurial activity. *Journal of Small Business Management*, *54*(2), 697–713. https://doi.org/10.1111/jsbm.12166

Thomran, M., Alshallaqi, M., Al-Mamary, Y. H., & Abdulrab, M. (2022). The key enablers of competitive advantage formation in small and medium enterprises: The case of the Ha'il region. *Frontiers in Psychology*, *13*, 1030405. https://doi.org/10.3389/fpsyg.2022.1030405

Valerie, F. (2012). Re-discovering the PLS approach in management science. *Management*, *15*(1), 101–123.

Van Doorn, S., Jansen, J. J., Van den Bosch, F. A., & Volberda, H. W. (2013). Entrepreneurial orientation and firm performance: Drawing attention to the senior team. *Journal of Product Innovation Management*, *30*(5), 821–836. https://doi.org/10.1111/jpim.12032

Wales, W. J., Gupta, V. K., & Mousa, F. T. (2013). Empirical research on entrepreneurial orientation: An assessment and suggestions for future research. *International Small Business Journal*, *31*, 357–383. https://doi.org/10.1177/0266242611418261

Wales, W. J., Covin, J. G., & Monsen, E. (2020). Entrepreneurial orientation: The necessity of a multilevel conceptualization. *Strategic Entrepreneurship Journal*, *14*(4), 639–660. https://doi.org/10.1002/sej.1344

Wiklund, J. (1999). The sustainability of the entrepreneurial orientation performance relationship. *Entrepreneurship Theory and Practice*, *24*(1), 37–48. https://doi.org/10.1177/104225879902400103

Wiklund, J., & Shepherd, D. (2005). Entrepreneurial orientation and small business performance: A configurational approach. *Journal of Business Venturing*, *20*(1), 71–91. https://doi.org/10.1016/j.jbusvent.2004.01.001

Yazdanpanah, Y., Toghraee, M. T., Salamzadeh, A., Scott, J. M., & Palalić, R. (2023). The influence of entrepreneurial culture and organizational learning on entrepreneurial orientation: The case of new technology-based firms in Iran. *International Journal of Entrepreneurial Behavior & Research*, *29*(5), 1181–1203. https://doi.org/10.1108/IJEBR-03-2022-0310

Yi, H. T., Amenuvor, F. E., & Boateng, H. (2021). The impact of entrepreneurial orientation on new product creativity, competitive advantage and new product performance in SMEs: The moderating role of corporate life cycle. *Sustainability*, *13*(6), 3586. https://doi.org/10.3390/su13063586

Zahra, S. A., & Covin, J. G. (1995). Contextual influences on the corporate entrepreneurship-performance relationship: A longitudinal analysis. *Journal of Business Venturing*, *10*(1), 43–58. https://doi.org/10.1016/0883-9026(94)00004-E

Zahra, S. A. (2003). International expansion of U.S. manufacturing family businesses: The effect of ownership and involvement. *Journal of Business Venturing*, *18*(4), 495–512. https://doi.org/10.1016/S0883-9026(03)00057-0

Zahra, S. A. (2005). Entrepreneurial risk taking in family firms. *Family Business Review*, *18*(1), 23–40. https://doi.org/10.1111/j.1741-6248.2005.00028.x

Zainol, F. A., & Ayadurai, S. (2011). Entrepreneurial orientation and firm performance: The role of personality traits in Malay Family Firm in Malaysia, *International Journal of Business and Social Science*, *2*(1), 59–72.

Zapata-Cantu, L., Sanguino R., Barroso, A., & Nicola-Gavrilă, L. (2023). Family business adapting a new digital-based economy: Opportunities and challenges for future research. *Journal of the Knowledge Economy*, *14*, 408–425. https://doi.org/10.1007/s13132-021-00871-1

Zehir, C., Can, E., & Karaboga, T. (2015). Linking entrepreneurial orientation to firm performance: The role of differentiation strategy and innovation performance. *Procedia-Social and Behavioral Sciences*, *210*, 358–367. https://doi.org/10.1016/j.sbspro.2015.11.381

Zellweger, T., & Sieger, P. (2012). Entrepreneurial orientation in long-lived family firms. *Small Business Economics*, *38*, 67–84. https://doi.org/10.1007/s11187-010-9267-6

Chapter 5

Corporate Social Responsibility and (Organizational) Conservatism in Moroccan Family Firms: Insights from a Qualitative Approach

Hamza Nidaazzi and Hind Hourmat Allah

Cadi Ayyad University, Marrakech, Morocco

Abstract

This chapter explores the interplay between organizational conservatism (OC) and corporate social responsibility (CSR) practices within family firms, specifically in Morocco. By exploring the familial dimensions of CSR, the study aims to uncover the impact of OC on CSR strategies, outcomes, and implications. Employing an exploratory qualitative design with multiple case studies, the research examines three Moroccan family firms. Thematic content analysis (TCA) was used to synthesize interview data and extract primary themes. The findings illustrate that OC fosters stable, values-driven, and sustainable CSR initiatives. This is achieved through the alignment of shared values, cautious change management, prudent financial strategies, commitment to legacy, and integration with family values. Moreover, the study underscores the informal nature of CSR practices in the Moroccan context, which are deeply intertwined with cultural, social, and religious norms. The implications of this research shed light on the effectiveness of OC in promoting enduring and meaningful CSR efforts within family firms. This study contributes to a nuanced understanding of the relationship between conservatism, CSR, and familial dimensions, enriching the discourse on responsible business practices.

Keywords: Organizational conservatism; corporate social responsibility; family firm; organizational behavior; Morocco

Entrepreneurial Behaviour of Family Firms:
Perspectives on Emerging Economies, 87–110

doi:10.1108/978-1-83753-934-520241005

1. Introduction

CSR has gained significant attention in business studies due to the increasing recognition of organizations' ethical and societal responsibilities (Wickert, 2021). However, research on the engagement of family firms in CSR is limited (Stock et al., 2023), and most studies have overlooked the influence of conservatism on shaping CSR practices. Family firms are unique organizational entities characterized by strong family values (Parada et al., 2020), a long-term orientation (Vlasic, 2022), and a deep attachment to tradition and stability (Lumpkin et al., 2008). Nevertheless, these traits can lead to OC, resulting in a tendency to maintain the *status quo*. Although this disposition may have negative consequences, it can contribute to CSR in Moroccan family firms.

In Morocco, family firms are attracting increasing interest from management researchers due to their prevalence and impact on socioeconomic growth (Nassiri & Sabbari, 2020). According to Allali (2012), around 12 major families in Morocco alone contribute 25–30% of the national gross domestic product. However, family firms in Morocco go beyond this. Moroccan small- and medium-sized enterprises are primarily based on family structures, accounting for 93% compared to 7% for large enterprises (Haut-Commissariat au Plan, 2019). In the conservative and culturally rich Moroccan milieu, CSR practices are embedded within a complex mosaic of traditions, religious values, and socioeconomic contexts. These elements have a direct impact on family firms' conduct, in which strategy is driven by the family's unique perception, and its idiosyncrasy means that CSR practices are modeled on family values and customs. However, the exact mechanisms by which OC influences CSR adoption, vision, values, and outcomes within Moroccan family firms have yet to be comprehensively studied. This research aims to unravel these connections, shedding light on the impact of OC on CSR initiatives in the Moroccan family firm landscape.

This study follows a qualitative research approach, employing a multiple case study methodology to provide an in-depth exploration of three Moroccan family firms. By delving into the narratives of these firms' leaders, we intend to uncover the multidimensional aspects of OC and its influence on CSR practices. Furthermore, the study explores the familial dimensions inherent to these organizations, investigating how family values, traditions, and legacies interact with the firms' conservative orientations to shape their CSR strategies.

This research addresses the gaps in the existing literature, which has often overlooked the complex interplay between cultural norms, organizational traditions, and CSR practices in family firms operating in conservative environments. The findings of this study hold implications for both theoretical advancements in CSR literature and practical insights for family firms navigating the delicate balance between traditional and contemporary societal expectations.

In the following sections, we present our theoretical background and research methodology. We then delve into the results of our investigation, exploring the manifestations of OC and its impact on CSR vision, values, strategies, and outcomes within the selected family firms. Finally, we discuss the implications of our findings, drawing connections between our research and existing literature, and highlighting the significance of OC as a catalyst for responsible business practices within family firms in the Moroccan context.

2. Theoretical Background

2.1. Family Firm OC

OC within family firms is rooted in a steadfast commitment to maintaining the status quo and fostering harmony in both familial and business relationships. This perspective is often associated with individuals who resist change and uphold established traditions. Mannheim's work (1986) highlights the gradual nature of change influenced by social, cultural, and psychological factors inherent to each family's fundamental ideology. However, this conventional interpretation falls short, as it overlooks the intricate nature of the "family legacy" that warrants deeper scrutiny.

Various definitions converge to elucidate the nuanced dimensions of OC in family firms. It emerges as a principled resistance to change, contrasting with a desire for stability (Conover & Feldman, 1981), embracing dogmatic ideologies (Nisbet, 1952), and embodying the intergenerational preservation of traditions (Gutek, 1997). Jost et al. (2003) characterize it as a belief system rooted in a yearning for order and gradual evolution within existing social norms. The conservative attitude is also psychological, marked by caution and skepticism toward radical ideas (Basly, 2007; Michels, 1962). This multifaceted perspective intertwines with culture (Johnson & Lenartowicz, 1998; Minton & Wruck, 2001) and cognition (Freeden et al., 2013; Nisbet, 1952; Timur, 1988), revealing a comprehensive framework. Cazabat (2014) delves into OC as a societal construct, encompassing a counterbalance to progressivism. These definitions coalesce rather than clash, painting conservatism as an intricate amalgamation of stances.

In family firms, OC takes on a distinct patrimonial dimension. This orientation, marked by unique perceptions of the enterprise and the market, introduces conflicting objectives such as prioritizing emotional connections over rationality. It embodies a dual commitment: preserving the business within the family heritage and seeking immediate financial profits. This equilibrium informs the distinct management approach of family firms, characterized by a gradual and protective strategy. The pursuit of generational continuity underscores this conservative stance, viewing the business as an essential family asset to be safeguarded for long-term income. While conservatism navigates a delicate balance between economic and social purposes, it remains a pervasive and enduring force within the fabric of family firms, driven by an innate desire to safeguard their wealth, influence, and legacy.

2.2. CSR in Family Firms

The field of CSR in family firms has garnered increasing attention in recent years (Mariani et al., 2023). Stock et al. (2023) emphasize the growth of this area, not only acknowledging its potential but also highlighting the need for further exploration.

Family firms are distinct due to their historical lineage and strong corporate identity, which can shape their commitment to CSR (Battisti et al., 2023; Hirigoyen & Poulain-Rehm, 2014; Lamb & Butler, 2018; Zientara, 2017). The literature indicates that family enterprises tend to exhibit a greater dedication to CSR compared to non-family firms, driven by factors such as socioemotional wealth (SEW) preservation and a long-term perspective (Combs et al., 2023; López-González et al., 2019).

These findings are supported by Battisti et al. (2023), who suggest that family firm's communication strategies can impact their CSR performance. Family firms often invest in building their reputation and fostering relationships with stakeholders to ensure the firm's longevity and benefit future generations (Combs et al., 2023). This emphasis on the long term can influence CSR initiatives and reporting practices, as indicated by Ma (2023).

Despite these positive trends, the literature also acknowledges challenges unique to family firms. Lamb et al. (2017) introduce the concept of "concerns," suggesting that family firms may harbor reservations about the potential impact of CSR on their control over the business. This highlights the delicate balance that family firms must strike between CSR initiatives and maintaining their core values and operations. Additionally, López-González et al. (2019) indicate that contingent factors, such as family involvement in management and board positions, can moderate family firms' CSR behavior.

The influence of family ownership and involvement on CSR is further explored by Block and Wagner (2010), who find that family and founder ownership is associated with fewer CSR concerns. Moreover, Uhlaner et al. (2004) note that the family nature of a business often affects relationships with employees, clients, and suppliers. Interestingly, family firms are shown to be more accountable to shareholders than non-family firms when it comes to environmental investments (Abeysekera & Fernando, 2020; Chen & Liu, 2022). This emphasizes the potential for aligning CSR efforts with shareholder interests in family firms.

2.3. OC and CSR in FB

The literature review presents three main theoretical perspectives that examine the impact of OC on CSR within the context of family firms: stewardship, SEW, and resource dependency.

2.3.1. Stewardship

The stewardship approach posits that family firms exhibit a distinct inclination toward CSR due to their long-term orientation and sense of responsibility toward the company, the family, and the community (Dick et al., 2021). This orientation aligns with the stewardship theory's premise that managers within family firms, acting as stewards, prioritize the collective firm interests and exhibit altruistic behavior (Davis et al., 1997). This proactive engagement in CSR is underscored by the family firms' values, continuity preservation, and efforts to cultivate relationships with various stakeholders, including employees, customers, suppliers, and business partners (Miller et al., 2008; Le Breton-Miller & Miller, 2009).

The analysis further reveals that the presence of stewards in family firms, who prioritize long-term sustainability and societal impact, strengthens the family firms' propensity for CSR activities (Lv et al., 2020; Zientara, 2017). This is corroborated by the idea that stewardship behavior is driven by faith-led values, influencing the organizational and leadership practices of family firms (Carradus et al., 2020). The values upheld by family firms also play a pivotal role in determining the extent of their engagement in CSR initiatives (Marques et al., 2014). Collectively, this body of research underscores the significance of the stewardship theory in explaining the positive relationship between OC in family firms and their commitment to CSR activities. The stewardship theory provides a compelling framework that accounts for the alignment of family firms' values, long-term orientation, and the presence of stewards, resulting in a proactive approach to CSR that benefits both the firm and society (Battisti et al., 2023; Francis et al., 2013; Lamb & Butler, 2018).

2.3.2. Socioemotional Wealth

SEW refers to the emotional benefits that result from the achievement of non-economic goals centered on the family in family firms (Berrone et al., 2012; Wu, 2018). Initially conceptualized by Gómez-Mejía et al. (2007) as the non-financial elements of a firm fulfilling the family's emotional needs, like identity, family influence, and legacy continuity, SEW drives decision-making in family firms. Berrone et al. (2012) further delineate five dimensions of SEW that are also entrenched in the conservative posture of family firms: family control and influence, familial identification with the firm, binding social ties, emotional attachment of family members, and renewal of family bonds through succession. These dimensions reflect the intricate interplay of emotions, values, relationships, and long-term commitment that differentiate family firms and underscore the nuanced nature of their decision-making processes.

Several studies shed light on the impact of SEW on CSR strategies within family firms. Combs et al. (2023) reveal that family firm not only preserve SEW but also excel in CSR practices due to SEW motivations. This suggests that family firms leverage their emotional wealth to enhance their CSR efforts. Moreover, Hsueh et al. (2023) explore how different configurations of SEW lead to varied CSR strategies. Family firms with high SEW prioritize CSR initiatives aligned with their values and legacy, while those with low SEW focus on initiatives aligned with financial goals. This highlights the role of SEW in guiding CSR priorities. Additionally, Labelle et al. (2018) indicate that family firms with high SEW prioritize CSR initiatives that align with their values and legacy, focusing on positive external regard rather than solely measurable revenue growth. Hernández-Perlines et al. (2023) emphasize that family firms prioritize SEW protection, even at financial costs, leading them to take risks and engage in CSR initiatives to safeguard their emotional wealth. Nevertheless, the literature also underscores challenges faced by family firms in evaluating the impact of CSR on SEW. Labelle et al. (2018) highlight that measuring and assessing the effects of CSR initiatives on SEW can be intricate. This difficulty in quantifying the impact may hinder the ability of family firms to evaluate the effectiveness of their CSR strategies. Moreover, Andriyani and Rochayatun (2022) reveal that CSR in family firms can be a sustainable means of building reputation, family identity, and competitive advantage, further emphasizing the importance of SEW considerations in driving CSR efforts.

2.3.3. Resource Dependency

Resource dependency theory, as articulated by Radhakrishnan et al. (2018) and Hillman et al. (2009), establishes the foundation for understanding how external resources influence an organization's behavior. This theory underscores that organizations engage in transactions with external actors to acquire necessary resources. Nekhili et al. (2017) highlight the significance of CSR for family firms, as it can enhance their market value and stakeholder relations. Additionally, Songini et al. (2021) emphasize the unique relationship family firms have with their local communities, further motivating their engagement in CSR activities that positively impact their environment.

García-Sánchez et al. (2021) elucidate that family firms are often stakeholder-oriented and prioritize SEW, resulting in a comprehensive consideration of the interests of internal and external stakeholders. Kuttner et al. (2020) underline the dominance of social CSR activities within family firms, particularly in areas concerning employees and the immediate company environment. Furthermore, the study by Combs et al. (2023) suggests that family firms can leverage their distinctive resources, such as the reputation and strong stakeholder relationships, to effectively implement CSR strategies. Lv et al. (2020), in line with resource dependency theory, point out that family firms regard families and social relationships as crucial institutions.

3. Methodology

A qualitative exploratory methodology was selected to examine the relationship between OC and CSR in Moroccan family enterprises. The objective is to deepen our comprehension of how managers perceive CSR practices and what are the main aspects they value most. This approach is fitting for emerging studies in cases where the current theory seems insufficient, as noted by Eisenhardt (1989).

We conducted a detailed analysis to delve into the context of each family firm. We examined also all entities owned by the flatter, scrutinized their governance structures, and engaged in discussions with employees and family members to gain a multifaceted understanding of their personal experiences, operations, and dynamics. Employing an exploratory approach was essential as the literature's contributions may not uniformly apply across all contexts, especially in light of the distinctive conservative cultural aspects inherent to Moroccan context.

To achieve our objective, we conducted semi-structured interviews, allowing for an in-depth collection of data. These in-person conversations were carefully documented and transcribed with precision, culminating in an extensive corpus of approximately 150 pages of rich, detailed verbatim.

This method was selected to capture essential information, leveraging the open-ended format to encourage unrestrained expression among the participants. The semi-structured nature of the interviews provided a dynamic platform to observe and understand the development of the respondents' viewpoints, accommodating the fluidity of their thought processes and any emerging discrepancies in their narratives.

For this inquiry, we engaged with three representatives from Moroccan family firms through semi-structured interviews that incorporated open-ended queries (Table 5.1). The decision to interview this specific number of family firms was due to the achievement of theoretical saturation – a state where subsequent interviews yield no new information, thus providing no further contribution to the analytical depth of the study (Glaser & Strauss, 1967; Pires, 1997). We also respected qualitative principles: homogeneity, balance, and diversity (Yin, 1994).

Our interviews can be classified as semi-structured; they were guided by a broad set of topics pertinent to Moroccan family firms rather than a predetermined list of questions, allowing for considerable flexibility within a structured framework (Kvale, 1996). We utilized an interview guide with the flexibility to pose specific questions or adapt the dialogue in response to the participant's previous statements, even incorporating their exact phrasing when beneficial. Throughout these conversations, we maintained a consistent focus on the central themes of our study, ensuring a coherent progression that was outlined to participants at the outset of each interview.

We selected family firms across different industries, sizes, genders, functions/positions, diverse generations, and varying attributes for our interviews, aiming to dissect the impact of familial context on the perception of CSR. Each session spanned one to two hours, was audio-recorded using a Dictaphone upon obtaining consent, and was later transcribed verbatim. In keeping with the preferences of the participants, anonymity was maintained throughout the process.

For our analysis, we employed TCA, a widely recognized and historically rich method in the field of management sciences. Vaismoradi et al. (2016) define it as "a research technique used in qualitative research to identify, analyze, and report patterns or themes within the data collected from various sources, such as interviews, focus groups, or open-ended survey questions." We adhered to the guidelines set forth by Braun and Clarke (2006), who offer a comprehensive guide to conducting thematic analysis, affirming its suitability for identifying, analyzing, and reporting themes within data.

Table 5.1. Sampled Family Firms.

Index	Firm				Family					Participants			
	Industry	Size	Number of Employees (approx.)	Age	Family Influence	Family Member Count	Relevant Stakeholders	Generation Level	Succession	Function/ Position	Age (approx.)	Gender	Academic and Professional Experiences
Case A	Agriculture Food	Medium-sized business	100	7 years since 2014	Capital majority, managing director	2	The company is co-founded and co-managed by a brother and sister who are part of an older family firm	First generation	–	Co-founder/ co-director	50	Female	Had 20 years' experience in food industry in Italy and started the business with her brother after leaving their father's company after his death
Case B	Manufacturing Construction Chemicals	Conglomerate	500	43 years since 1980	Capital majority, supervisory board	3	The first successor is still the president. His son and daughter collaborate in management	Second and third generations	1991	Head of finance and IT	30	Male	Studied Finance and joined the company just after graduation
Case C	Tourism Hospitality	Holding	300	70 years since 1953	Capital majority, management board	8	The founder died. His sons have chosen their oldest brother to be his successor. The latter has been managing and growing the firm until now	Second generation, preparing the transition to the third generation	1999	CEO	40	Male	Acquired a management education and became part of the company following several professional experiences in banking

4. Results

4.1. Contextualization: Insights from Morocco

The landscape of CSR in the conservative context of Morocco is complex and multifaceted, as revealed by an in-depth analysis of key literature. The legal framework for CSR in Morocco has evolved gradually over time to reflect a commitment to CSR values. Environmental laws have promoted sustainable development since 2003, such as Law 13-03 on air pollution, Law 12-03 on environmental impact assessments, Law 10–95 on water, Law 08.01 on quarry operations, and Law 28-00 on waste management, while the Labor Code of 2004 (Law 65–99) emphasizes fundamental human rights. The Moroccan government's efforts to align domestic legislation with international conventions signal a commitment to responsible business practices.

Over the years, Morocco has created a wide range of organizations specializing in social, economic, and environmental issues. At the same time, several initiatives have been launched, especially since the royal speech of 2005 and the adaptation of legal and institutional frameworks, as shown in Table 5.2.

Maroclear was the first financial market infrastructure to receive the CSR label,[1] awarded in March 2013 and renewed in 2016 by the CGEM Label award committee. Several organizations and companies have since been awarded the label.

The adoption of CSR in Morocco is not without challenges. Ibenrissoul et al. (2022) highlight that Moroccan corporate executives often prioritize compliance with laws and ethical values over a genuine commitment to CSR. This dichotomy underscores the need to bridge the gap between legal compliance and true CSR integration. The economic dimension of CSR, as explored by Abbass et al. (2023), shows the potential to generate consumer-perceived value, hinting at the alignment between societal expectations and business strategies.

El Baz et al. (2016) reveal that Moroccan SMEs often view CSR from a constraint-reducing perspective, using it as a tool to address economic pressures and enhance competitiveness. While this approach reflects the pragmatism of businesses, it also opens avenues for integrating CSR practices into the broader fabric of corporate strategy.

From a family firm perspective, Cruz et al. (2014) underscore that institutional and organizational conditions act as catalysts in the relationship between firm type and CSR. This reflects the interdependence between corporate structure, institutional influences, and CSR practices. Furthermore, the works of Ourdi et al. (2021), Tahri and El Khamlichi (2019), and Touate and Bennouna (2018) converge in emphasizing the increasing concern of companies about their social and environmental dimensions. Elbaz and Laguir (2014) suggest that family structure positively influences the CSR orientation of Moroccan family firms and, thus, enhances their financial performance. Another study by Kammoun et al. (2021) found that the more social enterprises are, the more they achieve better financial results in the Moroccan context.

---

[1]Maroclear, "Our CSR strategy." https://www.maroclear.com/fr/notre-politique-rse.

Table 5.2. Institutionalization of CSR in Morocco.

Organizations			Initiatives		
Year	Original Name	Translation	Year	Original Name	Translation
2007	L'Instance Centrale de Prévention de la Corruption (ICPC)	The Central Authority for the Prevention of Corruption	2005	L'initiative Nationale pour le Développement Humain (INDH)	The National Initiative for Human Development
2009	Le Conseil de la Concurrence (CC)	The Competition Council	2006	La charte de la CGEM	The CGEM Charter
2011	Le Conseil National des Droits de l'Homme (CNDH)	The National Council for Human Rights	2006	« Label RSE » de la CGEM	CGEM "CSR Label"
2017	L'Observatoire de la Responsabilité Sociale au Maroc (ORSEM)	The Observatory of Social Responsibility in Morocco	2010	La Normalisation Marocaine (NM)	Moroccan standardization
2021	Le Conseil Économique Social et Environnemental (CESE)	The Economic, Social, and Environmental Council	2012	« Top performers » de la Vigeo Eiris	"Top performers" by Vigeo Eiris
			2018	Indice « ESG 10 » de la BVC et VE	The "ESG 10" index by BVC and VE
			2019	Circulaire de l'AMMC	AMMC Newsletter

In the Moroccan context, family firms tend to show a stronger CSR orientation compared to non-family firms. A study on Moroccan family firms found that family structure positively influences the CSR orientation of these businesses, which, in turn, enhances their financial performance (Elbaz & Laguir, 2014). This suggests that family firms in Morocco are more inclined to integrate CSR principles into their activities, potentially leading to a higher level of performance compared to non-family firms in terms of CSR orientation. Moreover, Moroccan family owners tend to focus on the long term and invest more in enhancing their company's reputation and building deeper connections with employees, suppliers, and communities. However, Moroccan family firms may report their CSR practices in a manner that is less compliant with national and international standards than non-family firms, as they value their non-economic goals and are more inclined to care for their socioeconomic wealth. These CSR practices often emerge within a philanthropic framework, as highlighted by Ait Mhamed (2020) and El Baz et al. (2016). However, the emergence of CSR in the region is not solely driven by internal motivations. External pressures, such as those exerted by multinational corporations, foreign clients, and international initiatives, play a significant role in fostering CSR adoption (Hattabou & Louitri, 2011).

The relationship between OC and CSR in Morocco is influenced by various industries and contextual factors. The conservative nature of Moroccan society, shaped by religious discourse, tradition, and the state's support, affects the implementation of CSR practices. Cherkaoui (2016, 2020) emphasizes the contextual impact on CSR policies, where companies' engagement varies based on their societal context. The informal and unwritten system of governance observed by Birgach et al. (2020) further underscores the unique cultural and religious factors that shape business practices in Morocco. Islam holds a significant influence on CSR practices in Morocco. The alignment between Islamic values and CSR principles is evident through *Istikhlaf*, *Attaqwa*, and *Zakat*. The integration of these values into business operations highlights the potential for businesses to create positive societal impact while upholding religious principles. *Istikhlaf* highlights the idea of stewardship, viewing property rights as societal ownership and encouraging responsible commercial practices that deter capital concentration and waste. *Attaqwa* guides individuals in business toward conscientious conduct, fostering a balance between material and spiritual values and promoting actions that reflect Quranic teachings. *Zakat*, a fundamental pillar, embodies social responsibility by advocating economic equity through the sharing of wealth with those in need, thereby fostering inclusivity and reducing disparities. These principles rooted in Islam form the foundation of CSR in conservative countries, guiding ethical business practices that contribute to societal well-being and aligning with Islamic values of stewardship, responsible conduct, and social equity.

Additionally, the relationship between OC and CSR is deeply influenced by the industry context. In Morocco, conservative industries like agriculture, crafts, textiles, hospitality, tourism, and construction exhibit a tendency toward traditionalism, which permeates into the CSR strategies of family firms in these sectors. For instance, in agriculture and crafts, CSR might prioritize sustaining local communities and economies, while in tourism, the focus could shift toward environmental and cultural preservation. Governance mechanisms, as per Kammoun et al. (2020), particularly influence CSR in these conservative contexts, where centralized and traditional management might restrict CSR innovation. Industry-specific CSR variations, highlighted by Jamali et al. (2020), suggest that industries that are more exposed to globalization, like processing, align their CSR with international standards, contrasting with more localized industries focusing on addressing domestic socioeconomic issues. The ownership structure in family firms further complicates this relationship, as noted by Elbaz and Laguir (2014), where traditional family values may reinforce conventional CSR approaches in conservative industries, or alternatively, drive a more progressive CSR agenda in sectors more open to change.

4.2. Conservative Organizational Stance

Case A

Case A exhibits OC in its decision-making processes and overall business approach. The co-founder's emphasis on careful risk management is a clear indication of OC. While she acknowledges her expertise in the domain, she often defers to her brother, who has more experience in the Moroccan context and extensive external contacts: "There are decisions, even though I have the expertise, I cannot risk. Mostly, my brother makes the decisions because he lived in Morocco before me. Also, he has several external contacts related to the company." Furthermore, the company's conservative approach is also evident in her preference for working with clients who share the same values and cultural appreciation for their products. By choosing clients who understand their work process and respect their product's quality, the firm seeks to avoid potential challenges that might arise from working with clients unfamiliar with their business practices: "We choose clients with good values and a positive mindset, those who aim to deliver the best to satisfy the end customer, not just those seeking cost savings."

The co-founder's cautious financial management approach also reflects OC. The company's strategy of starting small and gradually investing while avoiding excessive debt aligns with a conservative financial mindset that prioritizes financial stability and minimizes financial risks: "When I finance an activity, I try to start with small steps. Then I invest gradually until we reach our goal. If possible, I avoid taking loans."

Case B

Case B exhibits a degree of OC in its operations and decision-making processes. The firm's owner, the patriarch, appears to be inclined toward traditional methods and is hesitant to embrace significant changes. He values stability and the *status quo*, which can lead to a reluctance to explore new opportunities or adopt innovative approaches. This resistance to change may be observed in the company's long-standing practices and its preference for proven methods "My father is more conservative than we are, we want to make changes, but he has his own way of working and he doesn't want to go too far outside it."

The firm's long-serving employees, particularly those who have been with the company for many years, show little enthusiasm for innovation. They are content with the familiar ways of doing things and are less receptive to modifying existing processes, even when potential improvements are identified: "For example, I found that there were some tasks that were repetitive, so maybe we could change them [...] they resist to such decision because they've been working in the same way for 40 years."

The firm places great emphasis on preserving the family legacy and ensuring the continuity of the business across generations: "It's a heritage that has been passed down from generation to generation. Just as my grandfather passed it on to my father and my father to me, I hope to pass it on to my children, perhaps one day." Overall, the firm's OC is influenced by its founder's vision and its long-serving employees who are resistant to significant changes.

Case C

Case C exhibits a clear sense of OC, as seen in its adherence to traditional practices. They value the practices initiated by their patriarch, which have been successful over time, and are resistant to changing them. This resistance to change is evident in their cautious approach to adopting new technologies and practices, even if they have the potential to enhance efficiency or profitability: "We have some practices that were initiated by our patriarch and we wouldn't want to change them [...] our partners aren't going to agree to change our ways."

The firm's OC is reinforced by its family-oriented decision-making process. The values and visions of family members working in the family group are considered fundamental and guide the firm's actions. The CEO mentions his personal attachment to the founder's vision and how it influences his decision-making: "I'm very attached to the vision of the founding father and I try totally to stick to that vision in my decisions and even in my everyday way of being."

The firm's conservatism is evident in its financial practices, as it prioritizes self-financing and maintaining a high cash flow. The founder's preference for self-financing and cautiousness toward external funding aligns with their conservative values and desire for financial stability: "The boss favors self-financing [...] available funds must first be used up before resorting to other means."

4.3. CSR Vision, Values, and Strategies

Case A

The firm demonstrates a clear CSR vision, values, and strategies that are deeply rooted in its commitment to cultural traditions, employee welfare, and sustainable business practices.

The co-founder emphasizes the importance of preserving the company's culture and tradition. She believes that by protecting and adhering to these values, the business can thrive internally. This strong attachment to cultural heritage reflects the company's CSR vision of preserving local customs and promoting responsible business practices: "It's certain, if we protect our culture and tradition and follow order, everything will be fine internally. Order is essential for success."

The company's CSR approach involves prioritizing the well-being of its employees. The interviewee expresses concern for her employees and ensures they follow strict protocols in handling delicate processes in cheese making. She provides guidance and takes precautions to prevent deviations from the established procedures, emphasizing the significance of experience in maintaining product quality and safety. Moreover, she acknowledges the impact of business decisions on employees and the business itself, highlighting the importance of careful risk management: "If this risk affects my employees or the business, I will not risk venturing into projects in unfamiliar domains [...]."

The company's CSR strategy involves carefully choosing partners and clients who share the same values and cultural appreciation for their product. The codirector emphasizes the importance of working with clients who allow them to explain their work process and who prioritize customer satisfaction over cost savings. This approach demonstrates a commitment to ethical business relationships and ensures that their product is represented and used responsibly by their clients: "We choose clients with good values and a positive mindset, those who aim to deliver the best to satisfy the end customer, not just those seeking cost savings."

The company's CSR strategy also includes giving back to the community through charitable actions. The interviewee mentions that they practice *Sadaqa*,[2] where they donate products or surplus production to those in need. This demonstrates a commitment to supporting and contributing positively to the local community: "we provide our Sadaqa, and we also give away returned or surplus products."

Case B

The firm's CSR vision revolves around making a positive impact on the community. The owner emphasizes the importance of creating jobs, especially for the local population, and being socially responsible by giving back to society. The company's CSR vision aligns with the idea of contributing to the well-being of people and society as a whole. "We made donations for the municipality and the mayor appreciated it. It also helps recruit people and support families and that's very important."

The interviewee highlights several core values that are central to the firm's CSR approach. One of the most prominent values is the sense of responsibility toward employees and the local community. The firm demonstrates care for its employees by offering job opportunities to local residents who were affected by the COVID-19 pandemic, as well as creating a harmonious work environment within the company.

The firm's commitment to CSR is also evident in its philanthropic efforts and positive social impact. It is actively engaged in donating to local associations, participating in charitable activities, and supporting healthcare initiatives: "We've

---

[2]*Sadaqa* is a benevolent act carried out with the intention of assisting others. While *Zakat* is a mandatory practice in Islam, *Sadaqa* is voluntary and not obligatory.

worked with many children's associations and doctors for the approximate caravans in the Atlas Mountains."

The firm's ethical values are deeply rooted in the belief in maintaining a family-centered business and preserving the patrimony for future generations. They prefer to collaborate with family members and believe in the importance of transmitting the business legacy from one generation to the next: "We believe in uniformity, which is why the founder passed on all the assets to his children and why he doesn't collaborate with outsiders."

Case C

The firm appears to have a strong commitment to its core values, which are deeply rooted in the family's traditions and ancestral practices. The CEO expresses a sense of pride in the company's conservative approach and believes it can have beneficial aspects both for the business and its employees. He emphasizes the importance of preserving certain methodologies and practices initiated by their patriarch, which have received positive feedback from partners over time. These values are central to the organization's identity and guide its decision-making processes: "In our family group, we have certain practices that were initiated by our patriarch and that we wouldn't want to change. Even our business partners would not want us to change our ways of doing things."

The firm's CSR strategies appear to be deeply intertwined with its family-oriented structure. The CEO mentions that the values and visions of the family members working in the group are shared by all employees, creating a cohesive organizational culture. In the recruitment process, they place significant importance on identifying candidates who align with the company's core values. This suggests that the firm values continuity and strives to maintain a sense of unity and shared purpose: "We try to recruit people who have and could adopt the same values. The members of the family working in the group, as well as the other employees, share the basic values initiated by the founder."

While the firm displays a strong adherence to its traditional values, it also exhibits a degree of responsiveness to change, albeit cautiously. The CEO acknowledges the need to improve certain aspects of the organization and is open to exploring new technologies and ideas. However, he prefers a gradual and careful approach, seeking evidence of success before fully embracing new practices: "We're always on the lookout in our sector, but that doesn't mean we're going to adopt a new technology straight away. We'll wait for it to prove itself and see how the sector develops with this technology."

The firm also demonstrates a sense of generosity and community involvement, especially through the actions of the founder. The CEO mentions various charitable acts, such as giving *Sadaqa* and supporting employees' pilgrimage to Mecca. This indicates a commitment to giving back to society and fostering a positive impact beyond the company's operations: "The boss is a great patron, he always gives Sadaqa, sends employees on Umrah, gives sheep to employees during Eid al-Adha, and always welcomes everyone [...] During the COVID-19 pandemic, he offered the family group hotels to the regional authorities for medical use."

4.4. CSR Outcomes

4.4.1. Environmental-related CSR

Case A shows a level of environmental responsibility in its operations. While not explicitly mentioned in the interview, the co-founder highlights the importance of adhering to strict processes in cheese-making, such as pasteurization, coagulation, fermentation, and sealing. These processes, when done correctly, can minimize waste and environmental impacts. Additionally, the company's focus on carefully selecting clients who appreciate their product and value sustainable practices suggests a commitment to promoting environmentally responsible consumption.

The *Case B* shows a proactive approach to environmental responsibility, focusing on reducing waste and adopting sustainable practices. They emphasize the importance of preserving resources and minimizing their environmental footprint. For instance, they mention investing in new machinery to improve efficiency and reduce energy consumption: *"We've invested a lot in new machinery, to be more efficient, save more energy, etc."*

For *Case C*, there is limited explicit mention of environmental CSR initiatives. However, we can infer some aspects of their approach. The firm's cautious and conservative nature may have implications for their environmental practices. While they express a willingness to explore new technologies, they prefer to wait and see how these technologies perform in the sector before adopting them. This cautious approach could extend to adopting environmentally sustainable practices, as they may require significant changes in operations.

4.4.2. Economic-related CSR

Case A demonstrates economic-related CSR through its emphasis on internal order and professionalism. By maintaining efficient operations and strict quality control, the company ensures optimal utilization of resources, ultimately contributing to economic sustainability. Moreover, the co-founder's cautious approach toward risk and preference for self-financing over excessive debt indicates a responsible financial management strategy that fosters the company's long-term stability and economic viability.

In terms of economic responsibility, *Case B* plays a significant role in creating job opportunities, particularly for the local population. They recognize the impact of their business on the local economy and aim to provide stability to the community members.

Case C's economic CSR practices appear to be influenced by their family-oriented values and commitment to long-term partnerships. They prioritize maintaining positive relationships with partners and clients, emphasizing mutual trust and respect. Their conservative business approach, especially regarding payment terms, demonstrates stability and reliability in their economic dealings, which can be seen as a form of economic CSR: "We can't make changes to evolve in our environment for the simple reason that our boss, it doesn't fit with his ethics." The firm's dedication to long-term partnerships and financial stability indirectly contributes to economic CSR by fostering sustainable economic relationships within its industry.

4.4.3. Social-related CSR

Case A's social-related CSR efforts are evident in its employee-oriented approach. The co-founder shows genuine concern for the well-being of her employees by providing them with clear guidance, strict protocols, and training to ensure the quality and safety of their products. Furthermore, the firm's commitment to involving family members, particularly her children, in the business to pass it on to future generations, reflects a focus on fostering a sense of family and community within the company.

Case B's CSR efforts extend to social aspects, as they actively engage in philanthropy and support various community initiatives. They collaborate with associations and organizations to give back to society and address the needs of vulnerable populations, such as providing medical assistance and supporting children's programs in underprivileged areas.

Case C's social CSR efforts are evident through their emphasis on family values, employee recruitment based on shared values, and community involvement. The company's strong family orientation extends to its workforce, where members of the family and non-family employees are expected to share and uphold the same values. This inclusive approach in recruitment may foster a positive and cohesive work culture, promoting social responsibility within the organization. Additionally, the firm's founder is depicted as a generous individual who engages in acts of charity, supporting employees during religious holidays. These charitable acts demonstrate a commitment to social responsibility and community well-being.

5. Discussion

The impact of family firm OC on their CSR initiatives can yield positive outcomes in various dimensions. One of the most apparent impacts of OC on CSR is its contribution to stability and long-term commitment. The conservative approach to decision-making and business practices helps create a stable operational environment for the company. This stability, as highlighted by the example of maintaining strict quality control, enables the firm to plan, implement, and sustain CSR initiatives consistently over time. Bolton et al. (2015) suggest that CSR can lead to risk-averse behavior in group decision-making, aligning with the firm's cautious approach to risk management.

The alignment of OC with shared values is instrumental in enhancing CSR efforts. By recruiting employees who share the same values as the firm and fostering a sense of unity among the workforce, the company builds a foundation that promotes CSR practices throughout the organization. This commitment to shared values ensures that CSR initiatives are not only top-down directives but are embraced and advocated by all levels of the organization. The firm's preference for hiring locally and recruiting young individuals from the surrounding areas reflects a focus on community engagement, which positively impacts their CSR efforts. Guo et al. (2020) suggest that companies allocating more resources to CSR programs are likely to employ conservatism to credibly engage in actions aligned with stakeholder interests.

The firm's cautious approach to change, inherent in OC, prevents hasty decisions that might undermine the long-term sustainability of CSR efforts. Furthermore, the firms' conservative financial management approach, as demonstrated by their prudence in taking calculated risks, contributes to the sustainability of their CSR initiatives. The alignment of CSR with family values and the founder's vision, as highlighted in the results section, further underscores the responsible financial management and commitment to the long-term sustainability of CSR efforts.

The commitment to family legacy and values, a central aspect of the firms' OC, extends to their CSR initiatives. This alignment instills a sense of responsibility and pride in contributing positively to society, ensuring that CSR efforts reflect and honor the firm's heritage and SEW. According to Dick et al. (2021), executives who display an abundance of self-assurance generally showcase exceptional performance in CSR. The enduring commitment to employee well-being, community involvement, and ethical partnerships align with the idea of preserving a family legacy, as it demonstrates the values and principles that have been passed down through generations.

The predominant CSR initiatives in Morocco that hold the greatest influence are informal practices deeply ingrained within the fabric of social, cultural, and religious norms. This informality within Morocco's CSR landscape is a result of the potent sway of informal institutionalization, coupled with the intimate connections between family firms and informal CSR establishments (Elbousserghini et al., 2019).

The main explored themes are summarized in Fig. 5.1.

6. Conclusion

This study aims to delve into the intricate relationship between OC and CSR initiatives within family firms in Morocco. Through a qualitative exploration of three family firms (Cases A, B, and C), the study illuminated how OC influences CSR practices across environmental, economic, and social dimensions. The findings revealed that OC plays a pivotal role in shaping CSR initiatives. The stability engendered by conservative decision-making fosters sustainable CSR efforts over time. This alignment with shared values within the organization ensures that CSR becomes an intrinsic part of the company's identity, rather than a mere obligation. The cautious approach to change management inherent in conservatism prevents rash decisions that might undermine CSR sustainability. Moreover, the financial prudence associated with conservatism enhances the economic viability of CSR undertakings. The commitment to family legacy and values underscores the social responsibility inherent in preserving a family's heritage and SEW. The significance of these findings lies in the enriched understanding of how OC affects CSR strategies and outcomes, especially within the unique cultural and business context of Morocco. These insights have practical implications for family firm leaders, as they navigate the delicate balance between tradition and modernity in CSR practices. While the study sheds light on these dynamics, some limitations should be acknowledged. The sample size of three family firms might not capture the full diversity of family firms in Morocco, limiting the generalizability of findings. For future

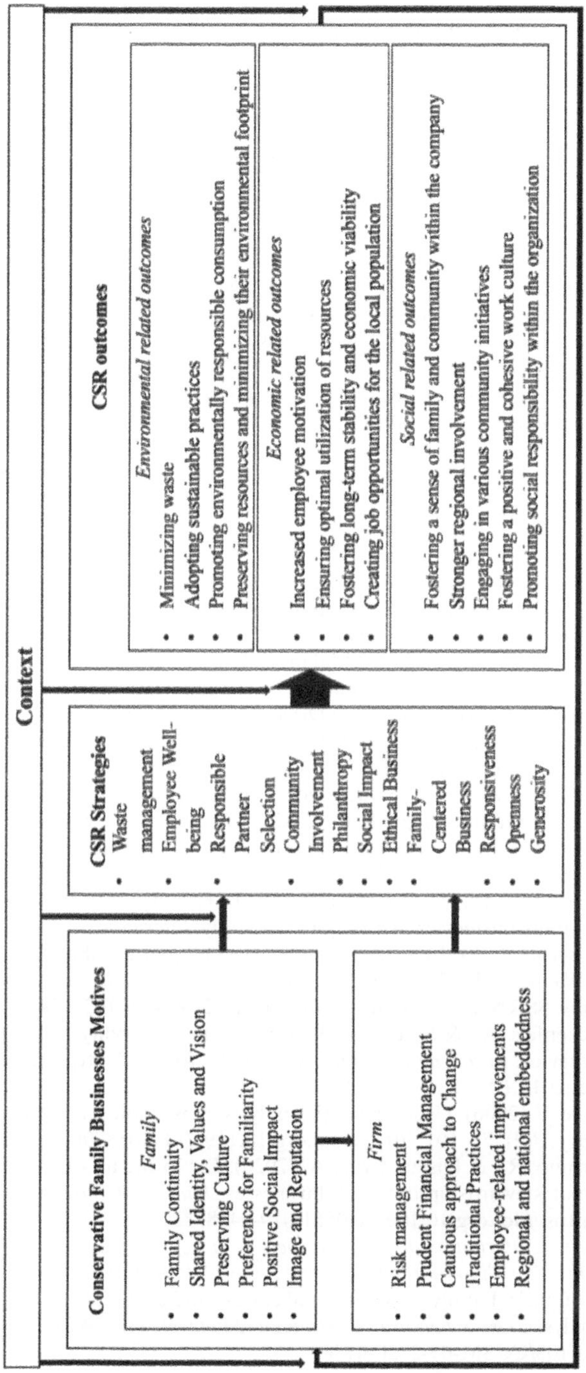

Fig. 5.1. Conceptual Model.

research, a larger and more diverse sample could provide a broader perspective on the interplay between OC and CSR. Quantitative studies could complement the qualitative insights presented here, offering a more comprehensive understanding of the relationship's nuances. Exploring how different industries and contexts influence the OC–CSR relationship could further enrich our understanding.

References

Abbass, Z., Benjelloun Andaloussi, O., & Rais, F. (2023). The role of CSR practices in generating consumer perceived value: Empirical evidence from Moroccan banking sector. *Social Responsibility Journal*, *19*, 1809–1829. https://doi.org/10.1108/SRJ-07-2022-0298

Abeysekera, A. P., & Fernando, C. S. (2020). Corporate social responsibility versus corporate shareholder responsibility: A family firm perspective. *Journal of Corporate Finance*, *61*, 101370. https://doi.org/10.1016/j.jcorpfin.2018.05.003

Ait Mhamed, H. (2020). Corporate social responsibility in Morocco: Are small and medium-sized enterprises (SMEs) socially responsible?. *Al-Uqud: Journal of Islamic Economics*, *4*(2), 174–185. https://doi.org/10.26740/al-uqud.v4n2.p174-185

Allali, B. (2012). *Conférence donnée sur « Contexte général et enjeux des entreprises familiales et des familles en affaires » à Attijariwafabank le 28 juin.*

Andriyani, F., & Rochayatun, S. (2022). Corporate social responsibility in family business: A scoping literature review. *Li Falah: Jurnal Studi Ekonomi dan Bisnis Islam*, *7*(2), 21–32. https://dx.doi.org/10.31332/lifalah.v7i2.4599

Basly, S. (2007). Conservatism: An explanation of the financial choices of the small and medium family enterprise. *Corporate Ownership and Control*, *5*(1), 459–469.

Battisti, E., Nirino, N., Leonidou, E., & Salvi, A. (2023). Corporate social responsibility in family firms: Can corporate communication affect CSR performance?. *Journal of Business Research*, *162*, 113865. https://doi.org/10.1016/j.jbusres.2023.113865

Berrone, P., Cruz, C., & Gomez-Mejia, L. R. (2012). Socioemotional wealth in family firms: Theoretical dimensions, assessment approaches, and agenda for future research. *Family Business Review*, *25*(3), 258–279. https://doi.org/10.1177/0894486511435355

Birgach, H., Berrada El Azizi, T., & Habba, B. (2020). Family governance mechanisms in Moroccan family businesses: An exploratory study. *International Journal of Business and Management*, *15*(8), 14. https://doi.org/10.5539/ijbm.v15n8p101

Block, J. H., & Wagner, M. (2010). *Corporate social responsibility of large family and founder firms*. SSRN 1625674. https://doi.org/10.2139/ssrn.1625674

Bolton, G. E., Ockenfels, A., & Stauf, J. (2015). Social responsibility promotes conservative risk behavior. *European Economic Review*, *74*, 109–127. https://doi.org/10.1016/j.euroecorev.2014.10.002

Braun, V., & Clarke, V. (2006). Using thematic analysis in psychology. *Qualitative Research in Psychology*, *3*(2), 77–101. https://doi.org/10.1191/1478088706qp063oa

Carradus, A., Zozimo, R., & Discua Cruz, A. (2020). Exploring a faith-led open-systems perspective of stewardship in family businesses. *Journal of Business Ethics*, *163*(4), 701–714. https://doi.org/10.1007/s10551-019-04387-2

Cazabat, G. (2014). *L'internationalisation des petites entreprises: une nouvelle représentation, la facilitation d'internationalisation* [Doctoral dissertation]. Paris, CNAM.

Chen, J., & Liu, L. (2022). Family firms, national culture and corporate social performance: A meta-analysis. *Cross Cultural & Strategic Management*, *29*(2), 379–402. https://doi.org/10.1108/CCSM-09-2020-0178

Cherkaoui, A. (2016). Pratiques RSE des PME au Maroc: une analyse perceptuelle auprès des dirigeants casablancais. *Question (s) de Management*, *3*(14), 13–26. https://doi.org/10.3917/qdm.163.0013
Cherkaoui, A. (2020). L'engagement RSE des entreprises comme levier de leur contribution au développement des territoires au Maroc: Illustration par trois études de cas. *Revue des Etudes Multidisciplinaires en Sciences Economiques et Sociales*, *5*(3), 51–68. https://doi.org/10.48375/IMIST.PRSM/remses-v5i3.19820
Combs, J. G., Jaskiewicz, P., Ravi, R., & Walls, J. L. (2023). More bang for their buck: Why (and when) family firms better leverage corporate social responsibility. *Journal of Management*, *49*(2), 575–605. https://doi.org/10.1177/01492063211066057
Conover, P. J., & Feldman, S. (1981). The origins and meaning of liberal/conservative self-identifications. *American Journal of Political Science*, *25*, 617–645.
Cruz, C., Larraza-Kintana, M., Garcés-Galdeano, L., & Berrone, P. (2014). Are family firms really more socially responsible?. *Entrepreneurship Theory and Practice*, *38*(6), 1295–1316. https://doi.org/10.1111/etap.12125
Davis, J. H., Schoorman, F. D., & Donaldson, L. (1997). Toward a stewardship theory of management. *Academy of Management Review*, *22*(1), 20–47. https://doi.org/10.5465/amr.1997.9707180258
Dick, M., Wagner, E., & Pernsteiner, H. (2021). Founder-controlled family firms, overconfidence, and corporate social responsibility engagement: Evidence from survey data. *Family Business Review*, *34*(1), 71–92. https://doi.org/10.1177/0894486520918724
Eisenhardt, K. M. (1989). Building theories from case study research. *Academy of Management Review*, *14*(4), 532–550. https://doi.org/10.5465/amr.1989.4308385
El Baz, J., Laguir, I., Marais, M., & Staglianò, R. (2016). Influence of national institutions on the corporate social responsibility practices of small-and medium-sized enterprises in the food-processing industry: Differences between France and Morocco. *Journal of Business Ethics*, *134*, 117–133. https://doi.org/10.1007/s10551-014-2417-z
Elbaz, J., & Laguir, I. (2014). Family businesses and corporate social responsibility (CSR) orientation: A study of Moroccan family firms. *Journal of Applied Business Research (JABR)*, *30*(3), 671–688. https://doi.org/10.19030/jabr.v30i3.8552
Elbousserghini, J., Berger-Douce, S., & Jamal, Y. (2019). La RSE des PME: l'étude du contexte marocain. *Revue Internationale PME*, *32*(1), 19–40. https://doi.org/10.7202/1059179ar
Francis, R. N., Harrast, S., Mattingly, J., & Olsen, L. (2013). The relation between accounting conservatism and corporate social performance: An empirical investigation. *Business and Society Review*, *118*(2), 193–222. https://doi.org/10.1111/basr.12008
Freeden, M., Sargent, L., & Stears, M. (2013). *The Oxford handbook of political ideologies*. Oxford University Press.
García-Sánchez, I. M., Martín-Moreno, J., Khan, S. A., & Hussain, N. (2021). Socio-emotional wealth and corporate responses to environmental hostility: Are family firms more stakeholder oriented?. *Business Strategy and the Environment*, *30*(2), 1003–1018. https://doi.org/10.1002/bse.2666
Glaser, B., & Strauss, A. (1967). *The discovery of grounded theory: Strategies for qualitative research*. Aldine Pub. Co.
Gómez-Mejía, L. R., Haynes, K. T., Núñez-Nickel, M., Jacobson, K. J., & Moyano-Fuentes, J. (2007). Socioemotional wealth and business risks in family-controlled firms: Evidence from Spanish olive oil mills. *Administrative Science Quarterly*, *52*(1), 106–137. https://doi.org/10.2189/asqu.52.1.106
Guo, J., Huang, P., & Zhang, Y. (2020). Accounting conservatism and corporate social responsibility. *Advances in Accounting*, *51*, 100501. https://doi.org/10.1016/j.adiac.2020.100501
Gutek, G. L. (1997). *Philosophical and Ideological Perspectives on Education* (2nd edn.). Allyn and Bacon.

Hattabou, A., & Louitri, A. (2011). Développement durable et management des PME: une analyse en termes de proximité. Illustration par un cas du secteur Textile-Habillement. *Revue Management et Avenir*, *3*(43), 122–142.

Haut-Commissariat au Plan. (2019). Enquête nationale auprès des entreprises.

Hernández-Perlines, F., Araya-Castillo, L., Millán-Toledo, C., & Cisneros, M. A. I. (2023). Socioemotional wealth: A systematic literature review from a family business perspective. *European Research on Management and Business Economics*, *29*(2), 100218. https://doi.org/10.1016/j.iedeen.2023.100218

Hillman, A. J., Withers, M. C., & Collins, B. J. (2009). Resource dependence theory: A review. *Journal of Management*, *35*(6), 1404–1427. https://doi.org/10.1177/0149206309343469

Hirigoyen, G., & Poulain-Rehm, T. (2014). The corporate social responsibility of family businesses: An international approach. *International Journal of Financial Studies*, *2*(3), 240–265. https://doi.org/10.3390/ijfs2030240

Hsueh, J. W. J., De Massis, A., & Gomez-Mejia, L. (2023). Examining heterogeneous configurations of socioemotional wealth in family firms through the formalization of corporate social responsibility strategy. *Family Business Review*, *36*(2), 172–198. https://doi.org/10.1177/08944865221146350

Ibenrissoul, A., Yassine, A., & Kammoun, S. (2022). Corporate executives' perceptions of CSR in the listed Moroccan companies. *Oradea Journal of Business and Economics*, *7*(special), 19–35.

Jamali, D., Jain, T., Samara, G., & Zoghbi, E. (2020). How institutions affect CSR practices in the Middle East and North Africa: A critical review. *Journal of World Business*, *55*(5), 101127. https://doi.org/10.1016/j.jwb.2020.101127

Johnson, J. P., & Lenartowicz, T. (1998). Culture, freedom and economic growth: Do cultural values explain economic growth?. *Journal of World Business*, *33*(4), 332–334. https://doi.org/10.1016/S1090-9516(99)80079-0

Jost, J. T., Glaser, J., Kruglanski, A. W., & Sulloway, F. J. (2003). Political conservatism as motivated social cognition. *Psychological Bulletin*, *129*, 339–375.

Kammoun, S., Loukil, S., Romdhane, Y. B., & Ibenrissoul, A. (2020). The relationship between CSR, corporate governance, and firm performance: Evidence from Moroccan listed firms. In I. Paiva & L. Carvalho (Eds.),*Conceptual and theoretical approaches to corporate social responsibility, entrepreneurial orientation, and financial performance* (pp. 289–304). IGI Global. https://doi.org/10.4018/978-1-7998-2128-1.ch015

Kammoun, S., Romdhane, Y. B., Loukil, S., & Ibenrissoul, A. (2021). An examination of linkages between corporate social responsibility and firm performance: Evidence from Moroccan listed firms. *Estudios Gerenciales*, *37*(161), 636–646.

Kuttner, M., Feldbauer-Durstmüller, B., & Mitter, C. (2020). Corporate social responsibility in Austrian family firms: Socioemotional wealth and stewardship insights from a qualitative approach. *Journal of Family Business Management*, *11*(2), 238–253. https://doi.org/10.1108/JFBM-04-2019-0028

Kvale, S. (1996). The 1,000-page question. *Qualitative Inquiry*, *2*(3), 275–284. https://doi.org/10.1177/107780049900500105

Labelle, R., Hafsi, T., Francoeur, C., & Ben Amar, W. (2018). Family firms' corporate social performance: A calculated quest for socioemotional wealth. *Journal of Business Ethics*, *148*, 511–525. https://doi.org/10.1007/s10551-015-2982-9

Lamb, N. H., Butler, F., & Roundy, P. (2017). Family firms and corporate social responsibility: Exploring "concerns". *Journal of Strategy and Management*, *10*(4), 469–487. https://doi.org/10.1108/JSMA-02-2016-0010

Lamb, N. H., & Butler, F. C. (2018). The influence of family firms and institutional owners on corporate social responsibility performance. *Business & Society*, *57*(7), 1374–1406. https://doi.org/10.1177/0007650316648443

Le Breton-Miller, I., & Miller, D. (2009). Agency vs. stewardship in public family firms: A social embeddedness reconciliation. *Entrepreneurship Theory and Practice*, *33*(6), 1169–1191. https://doi.org/10.1111/j.1540-6520.2009.00339.x

López-González, E., Martínez-Ferrero, J., & García-Meca, E. (2019). Corporate social responsibility in family firms: A contingency approach. *Journal of Cleaner Production*, *211*, 1044–1064. https://doi.org/10.1016/j.jclepro.2018.11.251

Lumpkin, G. T., Martin, W., & Vaughn, M. (2008). Family orientation: Individual-level influences on family firm outcomes. *Family Business Review*, *21*(2), 127–138. https://doi.org/10.1111/j.1741-6248.2008.00120.x

Lv, P., Li, Y., & Mitra, D. (2020). CSR and performance of family businesses: A systematic review. *Australasian Accounting, Business and Finance Journal*, *14*(3), 75–85.

Ma, L. (2023). Corporate social responsibility reporting in family firms: Evidence from China. *Journal of Behavioral and Experimental Finance*, *37*, 100730. https://doi.org/10.1016/j.jbef.2022.100730

Mannheim, K. (1986). *Conservatism: A contribution to the sociology of knowledge*. (D. Kettler, V. Meja, & N. Stehr, Trans.). Routledge & Kegan Paul (Original work published 1927).

Mariani, M. M., Al-Sultan, K., & De Massis, A. (2023). Corporate social responsibility in family firms: A systematic literature review. *Journal of Small Business Management*, *61*(3), 1192–1246. https://doi.org/10.1080/00472778.2021.1955122

Marques, P., Presas, P., & Simon, A. (2014). The heterogeneity of family firms in CSR engagement: The role of values. *Family Business Review*, *27*(3), 206–227. https://doi.org/10.1177/0894486514539004

Michels, R. (1962). *Political parties*. Free Press.

Miller, D., Le Breton-Miller, I., & Scholnick, B. (2008). Stewardship vs. stagnation: An empirical comparison of small family and non-family businesses. *Journal of Management Studies*, *45*(1), 51–78. https://doi.org/10.1111/j.1467-6486.2007.00718.x

Minton, B. A., & Wruck, K. H. (2001). *Financial conservatism: Evidence on capital structure from low leverage firms*. SSRN 269608. https://dx.doi.org/10.2139/ssrn.269608

Nassiri, M. F., & Sabbari, A. (2020). The extrinsic and intrinsic complexity of the Moroccan family firms: A sociological contextualization. *European Journal of Business and Management*, *12*(23), 115–125. https://doi.org/10.7176/EJBM/12-23-13

Nekhili, M., Nagati, H., Chtioui, T., & Rebolledo, C. (2017). Corporate social responsibility disclosure and market value: Family versus nonfamily firms. *Journal of Business Research*, *77*, 41–52. https://doi.org/10.1016/j.jbusres.2017.04.001

Nisbet, R. A. (1952). Conservatism and sociology. *American Journal of Sociology*, *58*(2), 167–175. https://doi.org/10.1086/221116

Ourdi, A., Taghzouti, A., & Bourekkadi, S. (2021). *CSR practices in countries in transition: The case of Morocco* [E3S Web of Conferences]. 319, 01036. EDP Sciences. https://doi.org/10.1051/e3sconf/202131901036

Parada, M. J., Samara, G., Dawson, A., & Bonet, E. (2020). Prosperity over time and across generations: The role of values and virtues in family businesses. *Journal of Organizational Change Management*, *33*(4), 639–654. https://doi.org/10.1108/jocm-11-2018-0341

Pires, A. (1997). Échantillonnage et recherche qualitative: essai théorique et méthodologique. *La recherche qualitative. Enjeux épistémologiques et méthodologiques*, *169*, 113–169.

Radhakrishnan, A., David, D. J., Sridharan, S. V., & Davis, J. S. (2018). Re-examining supply chain integration: A resource dependency theory perspective. *International Journal of Logistics Systems and Management*, *30*(1), 1–30. https://doi.org/10.1504/IJLSM.2018.10012465

Songini, L., Seddio, P., & Faraudello, A. (2021). The why and how of corporate social responsibility in family business: A literature review. *International Journal of Transitions and Innovation Systems*, *6*(4), 341–365. https://doi.org/10.1504/ijtis.2020.10033282

Stock, C., Pütz, L., Schell, S., & Werner, A. (2023). Corporate social responsibility in family firms: Status and future directions of a research field. *Journal of Business Ethics, 190*(1), 1–61. https://doi.org/10.1007/s10551-023-05382-4

Tahri, W., & El Khamlichi, A. (2019). Disclosure and communication of the corporate social responsibility (CSR) in Morocco: The case of a bank. In Y. Baghdadi & A. Harfouche (Eds.), *ICT for a better life and a better world: The impact of information and communication technologies on organizations and society* (pp. 247–261). Springer. https://doi.org/10.1007/978-3-030-10737-6_16

Timur, K. (1988). The tenacious past: Theories of personal and collective conservatism. *Journal of Economic Behavior and Organization, 10*(2), 143–172. https://doi.org/10.1016/0167-2681(88)90043-1

Touate, S., & Bennouna, A. (2018). Practices of CSR in Moroccan SMEs: Status and issues. *International Journal of Management Excellence, 11*(2), 1574–1581. https://doi.org/10.17722/ijme.v11i2.1013

Uhlaner, L. M., van Goor-Balk, H. J. M., & Masurel, E. (2004). Family business and corporate social responsibility in a sample of Dutch firms. *Journal of Small Business and Enterprise Development, 11*(2), 186–194. https://doi.org/10.1108/14626000410537128

Vaismoradi, M., Jones, J., Turunen, H., & Snelgrove, S. (2016). Theme development in qualitative content analysis and thematic analysis. *Journal of Nursing Education and Practice, 6*(5), 100–110. https://doi.org/10.5430/JNEP.V6N5P100

Vlasic, G. (2022). Comparative analysis of the role of strategic orientation, strategic performance metric focus and strategic audacity in driving firm performance: Family businesses vs nonfamily businesses. *Journal of Family Business Management, 13*(1), 7–25. https://doi.org/10.1108/jfbm-03-2022-0048

Wickert, C. (2021). Corporate social responsibility research in the Journal of Management Studies: A shift from a business-centric to a society-centric focus. *Journal of Management Studies, 58*(8), E1–E17. https://doi.org/10.1111/joms.12775

Wu, J. (2018). The theoretical framework and application frontier of socioemotional wealth theory: A literature review from the perspective of family firm. *Modern Economy, 9*(01), 190. https://doi.org/10.4236/me.2018.91012

Yin, R. K. (1994). Discovering the future of the case study. Method in evaluation research. *Evaluation Practice, 15*(3), 283–290. https://doi.org/10.1177/109821409401500309

Zientara, P. (2017). Socioemotional wealth and corporate social responsibility: A critical analysis. *Journal of Business Ethics, 144*, 185–199. https://doi.org/10.1007/s10551-015-2848-1

Chapter 6

Corporate Entrepreneurship of Family Firms in the VUCA World

Tuncay Odabaş and Esra Gökçen Kaygısız

Giresun University, Giresun, Turkiye

Abstract

The "VUCA world" is an environment characterized by unprecedented levels of volatility, uncertainty, complexity, and ambiguity (VUCA). In such a turbulent environment, corporate entrepreneurship is key for all businesses, especially family firms. Corporate entrepreneurship is a concept that enables innovation, growth, and competitive advantage over competitors. It is a driving force for organizations to make changes in their structures and operations to respond to changes by using the limited resources they have in the environments in which they operate and to reduce the negative effects of shortening product life cycles. Family firms, which have an important place in the economies of countries, are indispensable players in economic activities, they need to think more strategically, and innovative and have an entrepreneurial perspective in ensuring their adaptation for competitive and growth purposes. In this study, the relationship between the place of family firms in the VUCA world and corporate entrepreneurship was tried to be established, and the corporate entrepreneurship of family firms was examined in line with their corporate logic. For this purpose, the news on the corporate websites of seven family companies operating in Türkiye and included in the 2023 Family Business Index was analyzed by content analysis method. Data were coded with thematic coding and findings were revealed. Common types of logic in family firms are market logic and efficiency and savings logic, with a hybrid characteristic consisting of a combination of market logic and efficiency and savings logic.

Keywords: Family firm; VUCA; entrepreneurship; corporate entrepreneurship; Türkiye

Entrepreneurial Behaviour of Family Firms:
Perspectives on Emerging Economies, 111–134

doi:10.1108/978-1-83753-934-520241006

1. Introduction

Today's world is very, unpredictable, complex, and contradictory. In a dynamic environment, it is important to be a part of change rather than resisting it for the continuity of both individual and institutional existence. Because of the effects of globalization, digitalization, and the fluctuating competitive environment, the world is in constant variation. This rapid change is creating a new environment called VUCA. Originating in the late 1990s, the military-derived acronym stands for volatility, uncertainty, complexity, and ambiguity, reflecting an unstable and changing business world. The new VUCA uncertainty that dominates the new world has become the new normal in both business and social life. Therefore, there is no option to go back to the old times in the VUCA world, but it offers great opportunities for companies when managed correctly.

In a world of rapid change, companies must embrace corporate entrepreneurship to navigate through events like pandemics, digital transformation, wars, and immigration, where uncertainty and complexity are on the rise. Today's competitive environment, powerful companies that engage in entrepreneurial behavior are successful and sustainable. Sustaining companies also bring along the welfare of the country's economy. Family-owned companies have an important share in the Turkish economy, as in the economies of most countries.

Whether family firms are entrepreneurial, or under what conditions they become entrepreneurial, is a topic of constant debate (Bettinelli et al., 2017; Minola et al., 2021). Research has sought to answer the question about the entrepreneurial attitudes and behaviors of family firms in various ways, both by elaborating different theoretical perspectives and by looking at the unique structures of such firms and the entrepreneurial families behind them (Campopiano et al., 2020; Kellermanns & Eddleston, 2006; Le Breton-Miller & Miller, 2018; Zellweger & Sieger, 2012). Researchers have also used metaphors to frame how entrepreneurial families pursue entrepreneurial opportunities, thus feeding into a legacy built through narratives of entrepreneurial practices across generations (Discua Cruz et al., 2021).

Therefore, the study aims to determine the corporate entrepreneurship of family firms operating in Türkiye and included in the 2023 Family Business Index (https://familybusinessindex.com/) within the framework of their corporate logic in the current VUCA environment. In addition, based on the differences in the management levels of the companies, it is aimed to analyze the effects of these differences on corporate logic. In the first section of the study, the general framework is presented and the concepts of VUCA and corporate entrepreneurship, which are the basic concepts of the research, are explained. The second section discusses the corporate entrepreneurship of family firms. In the third section, the purpose, sample, and method of the research are explained in detail. In the fourth section, where the research data are analyzed and the findings are presented, the corporate entrepreneurship of family firms in line with their corporate logic is evaluated. In the last section, the findings from the research data are interpreted and recommendations for future research are given.

2. Literature Review

2.1. VUCA World

The way we do business and the way we conduct business or think about business have transformed dramatically in the last decade. About 30 years ago, social scientists in the US Army coined the term "VUCA" to characterize the environment in which their students would have to operate in the future (Sarkar, 2016). VUCA is an acronym that refers to the variability, uncertainty, complexity, and ambiguity present in today's world. Although its origins are based on military origins, today it is becoming more and more popular every day to characterize the chaotic environment in which businesses operate (Yurdasever & Fidan, 2020). Indeed, both industry executives and authors from academia have produced an increasing number of books, articles, blog posts, and YouTube videos on VUCA and its effects on leaders and organizations (Baran & Woznyj, 2020).

Alkoç (2021) defines VUCA as the sum of efforts to produce, strategize, take action, manage people, and get results in an environment of uncertainty, volatility, and complexity. According to Abidi and Joshi (2018), VUCA is a concept that characterizes the volatile and chaotic business, economic, and physical environment that everyone faces, and how to manage it needs to be learned. VUCA provides a framework for businesses to shape both their current and future strategies (Johansen, 2007). It is also a dynamic term that encompasses the economic conditions created by the disappearance of borders as a result of globalization, a developing and changing technological environment, very different competitors and markets, highly volatile financial markets, and fickle consumers. These factors create uncertainty and complexity in their own right, but their effects are much more profound when they occur simultaneously (Turner & Margolis, 2012). In this context, in today's business world, many of these components come together at the same time and create a complex structure (Yurdasever & Fidan, 2020). Therefore, VUCA is now recognized as the "New World," and its permanent era and its effects will increase day by day (Alkoç, 2021).

Sarkar (2016) stated that to be successful in this world, some critical factors need to be implemented and listed these factors as follows: strong business fundamentals, innovation, fast-paced response, flexibility, managing change well, managing diversity both locally and globally, providing good market intelligence, strong collaboration with all relevant stakeholders such as customers, employees, and suppliers.

Experts and researchers have developed various approaches for businesses to survive in the VUCA world. The first of these is the "VUCA Prime" (vision, understanding, clarity, and agility) approach proposed by Bob Johansen, and the second is the "VUCA 2.0" (vision – vision, understanding – understanding, courage – courage, and adaptability – adaptability) approach proposed by Bill George (George, 2017; Lawrence, 2013). Another approach that has been developed and received widespread attention is McKinsey's "Three Horizons Model" shown in Fig. 6.1.

This model attempts to put the organizational thinking process into a certain perspective and offers a way out of the labyrinthine environment of the VUCA world.

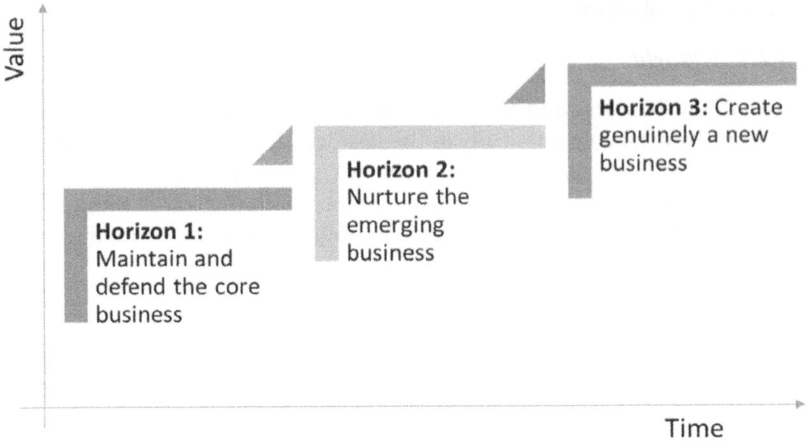

Fig. 6.1. McKinsey's Three Horizons: A Solution to Survive and Grow in a VUCA World. *Source*: Based on Sinha and Sinha (2020).

The first horizon is the time when businesses accept that the environment is no longer what it used to be and that existing businesses are obsolete. This period is the crossroads where businesses experiment with new ways of doing business. The second horizon is the point at which business decision-makers consider stepping out of their comfort zone it is the crossroads where business leaders abandon known and practised ways of working and try to replace them with new age modes and methods. The third horizon is the period when business leaders see reality. Therefore, it is the time when the current operations of businesses are reviewed, restructured, and implemented (Sinha & Sinha, 2020).

The different models that businesses rely on to strategize their businesses in the VUCA world have been mentioned above. These models aim to stay in balance in the VUCA world by developing positive solutions for each of the four sub-components that make up VUCA. However, it is important to understand the fundamental differences between the VUCA sub-components to create balance (Koç et al., 2021).

- Volatility refers to the speed, magnitude, nature, volume, and dynamics of change in a business, market, or industry.
- Uncertainty refers to the unpredictability of future events and problems.
- Complexity refers to the large number of diverse, layered, and interdependent factors that need to be considered.
- Ambiguity, on the other hand, refers to the fact that the reality of the events occurring cannot be seen (Bartolomeo, 2019).

Over the last decade, businesses have faced not only disruptive innovations stemming from accelerating technological advances because of digitalization and artificial intelligence (García-Villaverde et al., 2018) but also complex emerging market players that are growing, developing, and challenging Western dominance

(Li et al., 2019; Qaiyum & Wang, 2018). These increasing dynamics have been further intensified by the simultaneous unpredictability caused by the COVID-19 pandemic or significant economic downturns Pultz et al. (2021). The VUCA world has also questioned the way businesses operate in competitive markets. In this context, combining ethical practices with emerging technologies will lead organizations to success in the VUCA world.

2.2. Corporate Entrepreneurship

Because of globalization and sped-up change in recent years, organizations can only sustain their existence and gain competitive advantage by differentiating from their competitors through business, process, and product/service innovation (Kraus & Rigtering, 2017). The main reason for this situation is that in the dynamic and complex conditions of today's business world, the prerequisite for enterprises to achieve sustainable leading position is to see and evaluate opportunities, and their entrepreneurial capacity. Therefore, fostering an entrepreneurial atmosphere within a business and actively engaging in corporate entrepreneurship activities are valuable strategies for companies to outperform their competitors and achieve long-term economic and competitive advantages (Kaya et al., 2023; Kraus et al., 2012).

It is very difficult for businesses to gain and maintain industry leadership unless they can quickly adapt to changes under conditions surrounded by variable and turbulent environments with intense competition (Martín-Rojas et al., 2020). In changing market conditions, businesses need to become entrepreneurial and respond to new opportunities to sustain their profitability over time (Kuratko & Morris, 2018). For this reason, businesses that do not take entrepreneurial steps can be seen as setting themselves up for failure in today's business world. In this context, dynamic capabilities theory views entrepreneurial management as a key capability that can improve organizational flexibility and adaptability, enabling businesses to act strategically and embrace new opportunities (Teece, 2016). Corporate entrepreneurship, which is recognized as an effective method for achieving high levels of performance, has become a fundamental topic in management research (Kuratko & Audretsch, 2013).

The concept of corporate entrepreneurship has gained a strategic dimension and has become a concept that expresses the phenomenon of entrepreneurship in terms of all employees and the structure of the enterprise by including the internal and external environment (Arman, 2018).

Corporate entrepreneurship increases in importance day by day and enables organizations to innovate, grow, and gain competitive advantage over competitors (Erdem & Karadal, 2020). It is the set of activities within an organization to develop new products, services, processes, markets, ideas, strategies, technologies, and management approaches and to create different business areas (Zahra, 1991); a process that occurs within an existing business and leads to various innovative activities such as the development of new products, services, technologies, competitive strategies, and even business models (Antoncic & Hisrich, 2001; Kuratko & Audretsch, 2013); a strategic behavior or attitude in which individuals within the business undertake extra activities and will to break from routines to pursue new entrepreneurial opportunities (García-Morales et al., 2014); it is defined as a dynamic capability that enables businesses to address changing environments, quickly manage potential uncertainties, and remain competitive (Rehman et al., 2021).

The main point where corporate entrepreneurship differs from traditional entrepreneurship is that while traditional entrepreneurship adopts individual thinking and individual action, corporate entrepreneurship adopts the whole of the activities to be carried out by taking into account the innovative activities and changes in the organization in the process of creating a business for a new product or service. On the other hand, the main difference that distinguishes corporate entrepreneurship from entrepreneurship is that entrepreneurship is a phenomenon that creates new and small businesses, renewal existing businesses, ensuring their continuity and maintaining their competitive advantages in international markets, while corporate entrepreneurship is to create a new business with renewal and innovative activities within an existing organization (Van de Ven & Engleman, 2004). In this context, the main driving force underlying corporate entrepreneurship is to revitalize leadership, creativity, and innovation in businesses (Kuratko & Audretsch, 2013).

Entrepreneurship, recognizing or creating opportunities and then taking advantage of them, is a universal phenomenon. The entrepreneurial process occurs in different degrees and frequencies within organizations, such that some organizations are highly entrepreneurial while others are weak in terms of entrepreneurial orientation (Abazi-Alili et al., 2014; Dess & Lumpkin, 2005). The critical question for managers or decision-makers at this point is how entrepreneurial they want the business to be or the role that entrepreneurship should play within the business. When business managers do not know what they want to achieve, it becomes very difficult to encourage corporate entrepreneurship. Indeed, while employees are expected to think and act entrepreneurially, the starting point is to identify the desired outcomes of corporate entrepreneurship. Outcomes can take different forms, ranging from the creation of new ventures by the organization to innovative changes in the organization's strategy, business model, product portfolio, market boundaries, and operations. Fig. 6.2 shows these outcomes (Morris et al., 2009).

Corporate entrepreneurship activities flourish in enterprises where employees can easily express their ideas and thoughts and find the space to implement them. The success of corporate entrepreneurship activities depends on the strategy and integration of the enterprise (Goodale et al., 2011). While corporate entrepreneurship enables large enterprises to increase their profitability and continue their activities, it also contributes to the development and competitiveness of small enterprises (Zehir et al., 2012). Since it is used for different purposes in enterprises of different sizes, researchers with different variables have put the dimensions of corporate entrepreneurship, as well as its definition forward. In this context, corporate entrepreneurship is a multidimensional structure. While Saly (2001) emphasizes five different dimensions of corporate entrepreneurship (innovativeness, risk propensity, proactiveness, corporate entrepreneurship, and self-renewal), Zehir and Eren (2007) emphasizes four dimensions (new business

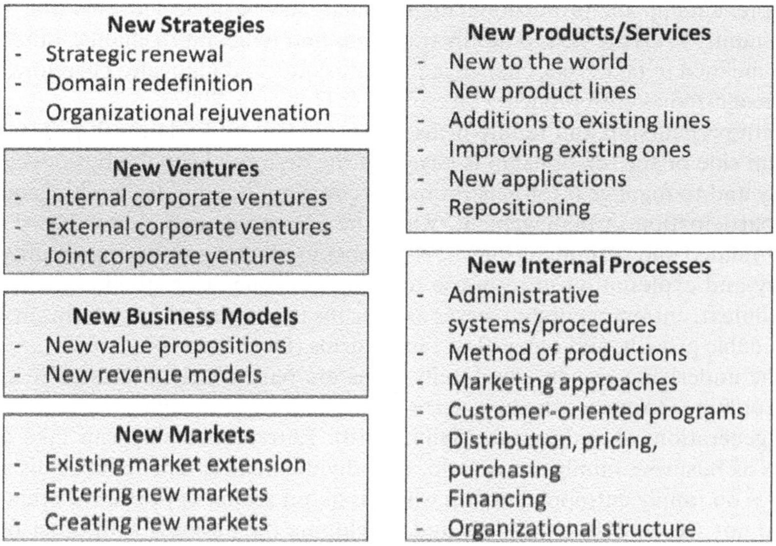

Fig. 6.2. Corporate Entrepreneurship Outcomes. *Source*: Based on Morris et al. (2009).

entrepreneurship, innovativeness, self-renewal, and pro-activeness). According to Zhang et al. (2008), corporate entrepreneurship includes three major components: innovation, entrepreneurship, and strategic renewal. In addition, based on previous research on the subject (Antoncic, 2007; Antoncic & Hisrich, 2001, 2003; Boukamcha, 2019; García-Morales et al., 2014; Jiménez-Barrionuevo et al., 2019; Martín-Rojas et al., 2020), corporate entrepreneurship is conceptualized in four dimensions. These dimensions are new business venturing, product/service/process innovation, self-renewal, and proactiveness. New business entrepreneurship refers to the creation of new businesses related to existing products or markets; innovation refers to product and service innovation; self-renewal refers to strategy reformulation and organizational change; and proactiveness refers to initiative risk-taking and competitive aggression (Antoncic, 2007).

2.3. Corporate Entrepreneurship of Family Firms

Family firms account for two-thirds or more of all businesses in developed and developing economies (Berrone et al., 2022). Therefore, family firms represent a worldwide phenomenon of great practical and theoretical importance (Davila et al., 2023).

Although family firms are present in every sector, each family firm has its unique characteristics. Therefore, researchers emphasize that family firms are not a homogeneous group (Discua Cruz & Howorth, 2008; Howorth et al., 2008). Family firms differ in terms of the diversity of goals and motives that drive them (Hall, 2001). In some family firms, business goals and objectives come before family goals and objectives, while in others, family goals and objectives come before business goals and objectives (Reid et al., 1999). As the business grows, sustainable entrepreneurship and professional management may be neglected. However, while some family firms are tied to family traditions and reluctant to change, others are more inclined to take risks, challenge the status quo, and innovate. Therefore, they are recognized as entrepreneurs (Westhead & Howorth, 2007).

Entrepreneurship and family firms share a means-end relationship. The family firm side of the relationship is based on the desire to keep the business in the family and to manage it for generations to come, reflected in leadership, control, and participation in management, while the entrepreneurial side is based on a well-founded and sustainable business proposition that develops opportunity discovery and exploitation in response to changes in the external environment. In this context, entrepreneurship serves as a means to the goal of long-term survival, sustainable growth, and renewal of family firms (Goel & Jones, 2016).

The underlying reason why family firms are particularly interested in entrepreneurship is to ensure the long-term survival and sustainability of the business over generations (Nordqvist & Melin, 2010). Entrepreneurship can take many forms as business, family, household, or individual entrepreneurship. This study focuses on family entrepreneurship which is about seeing opportunities that others do not see, as well as building and developing the business with other family members (Discua Cruz et al., 2013). The majority of entrepreneurs have established businesses as family firms. Therefore, families are an important source of resources, especially human capital, for start-ups (Aldrich & Cliff, 2003). Family firm researchers pay special attention to corporate entrepreneurship, which is a more specialized area of entrepreneurship Minola et al. (2021). There are several reasons underlying this special interest in corporate entrepreneurship. First, as an extension of organizational and strategic innovation, corporate entrepreneurship is necessary to overcome business challenges that affect the long-term competitiveness and survival of the business and enable the creation and use of socio-emotional wealth by the family (Gomez-Mejia et al., 2011). Second, strategic dimensions such as management processes, resources, and decision-making are influenced by family involvement, making family firms unique in terms of corporate entrepreneurship (Baltazar et al., 2023; Cruz & Nordqvist, 2012).

Corporate entrepreneurship is critical for family firms to survive, grow, and increase profitability (Rogoff & Heck, 2003; Salvato, 2004). Examples of corporate entrepreneurship include activities such as the search for new markets, product innovation, and process innovation (Covin & Slevin, 1991; 1991; Miller, 1983; Zahra et al., 2004). These entrepreneurial activities support the sustainability and success of family firms by contributing to both employment and wealth creation (Upton et al., 2001). Indeed, research has shown that corporate entrepreneurship increases revenue streams, empowers employees, and increases profitability (Barrett & Weinstein, 1998; Lumpkin & Dess, 1996; Zahra, 1996). The competitive environment in which businesses operate has become increasingly dynamic and uncertain since the 2000s. Therefore, it has become crucial for family firms to develop an entrepreneurial mindset that enables them to identify and capitalize on opportunities in their environment (Sirmon & Hitt, 2003).

Although corporate entrepreneurship is a crucial concept for both the survival and success of family firms across generations, few studies (Nordqvist, 2005;

Rogoff & Heck, 2003; Salvato, 2004) have examined how family firms view entrepreneurship. Moreover, little is known about why some family firms are more successful in corporate entrepreneurship than others (Nordqvist, 2005). Some studies have found that family firms are reluctant to undertake new ventures (Cabrera-Suárez et al., 2001), take risks (Morris, 1998), or support change (Levinson, 1989), while others have found that family firms that invest in and support entrepreneurship have higher performance potential (McCann et al., 2001). On the other hand, recent studies have developed a corporate entrepreneurship perspective specific to the family firm (Kellermanns & Eddleston, 2006). Beyond empirical contributions (Calabrò et al., 2016; Kotlar & Sieger, 2019; Lee et al., 2019), a balanced set of reviews (McKelvie et al., 2014; Minola et al., 2016) and conceptual studies (Randolph et al., 2019; Soleimanof et al., 2019) have been attracting attention on corporate entrepreneurship in family firms as a growing and maturing field.

The decision of family firms to invest in corporate entrepreneurship is not always an easy one. The family's control over the company may impose capital constraints that prevent the company from financing entrepreneurial activities (Carney, 2005). Indeed, family firms may be reluctant to invest in corporate entrepreneurship due to the risks, changes, and wealth preservation concerns associated with entrepreneurial activities (Carney, 2005; Chrisman et al., 2005). Moreover, the decision to invest in corporate entrepreneurship is binding on the family firm because family values and interests are integral to the company's goals and strategies (Sharma et al., 1996). While some family firms have a culture that fosters innovation and change (Vago, 2004; Zahra et al., 2004), in others, corporate entrepreneurship is not sufficiently supported due to a desire to maintain the family status quo or a lack of perception of opportunities in the environment (Gersick et al., 1997; Kepner, 1991; Salvato, 2004). Therefore, developing a family perspective that takes into account the attitudes and values of family members in family firms is of great importance in supporting corporate entrepreneurship.

López-Fernández et al. (2016) argue that family members are the oxygen that feeds the entrepreneurial fire in family firms; Randolph and Daspit (2017) argue that entrepreneurial activities to encourage innovation and growth in existing organizations are critical for an effective company and sustainable success. They also argued that for the success of the family firm, a forward-looking vision should be displayed, and company continuity should be given importance. Memili et al. (2010) argued that for family firms to achieve sustainable success and leave something to the next generations, they have to both take entrepreneurial risks and exhibit a competitive performance. They said that family firms become entrepreneurial to increase their performance and maintain their sustainability for generations. Salvato et al. (2010) argued that the family factor, which is dominant in family firms, can push the business to seize entrepreneurial opportunities for the future with strong emotional ties. Kotlar and Sieger (2019) investigated the willingness and ability of foreign managers in family firms to exhibit entrepreneurial behaviors as influenced by opportunistic tendencies, reversal of benevolent preferences, and identity-based incompatibilities. They concluded that family firms are less entrepreneurial than other firms across generations. Fang et al. (2021)

argued that managers or owners in decision-making positions in family firms should avoid narrow framing and have a holistic strategic perspective that enables them to engage in corporate entrepreneurship. Miller and Le Breton-Miller (2011) argue that family members shape entrepreneurial behavior in family firms and may engage in bold entrepreneurial activities to achieve financial success/growth. From a Turkish perspective, it can be said that Turkish companies, especially some conglomerates, can compete with other foreign companies in terms of their entrepreneurial characteristics and international financial success (Bloomberg, 2018) and that this success of companies is based on the fact that they are family-owned businesses (Hisarcıklıoğlu, 2019).

3. Methodology

3.1. Sample and Units of Analysis

The sample of the study consists of seven Turkish Family firms included in the 2023 Family Business Index. Units of analysis are the basic units in the document subjected to classification. These basic units are seven types: word, word group or expression, sentence, paragraph, person, theme, and content (Baş & Akturan, 2017). In this context, word, word group or expression, content, and theme were used as units of analysis in the study. While creating the coding form, the relevant literature was examined, and as a result of the examination, categories were created by making use of Thornton et al. (2005), Genç (2022), and Özkara and Kızıldağ (2015). The categories and subheadings in the coding form are as follows:

- *Market logic*: Growth, target, quality, competition, investment.
- *Productivity and savings logic*: Efficiency, performance, profit/profitability, ınnovation/ınnovative, wealthiness.
- *Cooperative logic*: Regional producer, cooperative enterprise/company/subsidiary, producer union/organization/organization, producer partner, producer, producer, being in favor of the producer/protecting the ınterest of the producer, ensuring that the producer is not victimized, ensuring that the producer does not suffer, not making the producer dependent on anyone/nobody, protecting/protecting/not leaving the producer alone.
- *Social responsibility logic*: Ethical responsibility, legal responsibility, economic responsibility.

3.2. Research Method

The research was conducted using content analysis, one of the qualitative research methods. Content analysis is a systematic, numerical, and unbiased analysis to measure the materials obtained both verbally and in writing (Wimmer & Dominick, 2000). Content analysis is the organization and interpretation of similar data by bringing them together within the framework of a specific concept or theme (Yildirim & Şimşek, 2013). The document analysis method was used as a data collection tool in the study. In the document analysis, the websites of the family

Table 6.1. Number of News on Family Firm Websites.

Family Firms	2016	2017	2018	2019	2020	2021	2022	2023	Total
Koç Holding A.S.	9	4	3	5	18	41	52	25	157
AG Anadolu Group Holding A.S.	7	5	5	5	5	4	3	–	34
Hacı Ömer Sabancı Holding A.S.	30	25	23	26	27	27	18	19	195
Zorlu Holding A.S.	–	–	–	–	22	21	18	2	63
Rönesans Holding A.S.	8	6	8	8	11	11	11	19	82
Borusan Holding A.S.	27	21	22	19	12	12	14	12	139
Doğuş Group	34	18	10	4	–	1	–	–	67

Source: Created by the authors.

companies included in the study were examined, and the news between 2016 and 2023 was used to determine the change in their corporate logic. The distribution of these news items is given in Table 6.1.

To determine the role of the news in changing the corporate logic of the corporate entrepreneur, 737 news articles between 2016 and 2023 on the websites of family firms were subjected to content analysis. In the analysis, predetermined corporate logic and the concepts that include this logic were identified from the news texts.

4. Data Analysis and Findings

In this section, the data collected for the research will be analyzed and the findings obtained will be presented. First, general information about the family firms included in the research will be given. Then, the data obtained to determine the corporate logic of family firms will be analyzed. Finally, the mechanisms behind the change in the corporate logic of family firms will be evaluated.

4.1. General Information on Family Firms

To determine the corporate logic of family firms and to reveal the events and actors that bring about changes in their corporate logic, their general situation should also be examined. In this study, seven family firms operating in Türkiye and included in the 2023 Family Business Index are analyzed, and their general outlook is given in Table 6.2.

According to Table 6.2, Koç Holding and Hacı Ömer Sabancı Holding have been in existence for almost a century. Koç Holding has more than 100 thousand employees and Sabancı Holding has more than 60 thousand employees. The ownership rate is above 50% in all of the companies. On the other hand, only the CEOs of Rönesans Holding and Doğuş Group are family members, while the CEOs of other companies are non-family members. When the family relations

Table 6.2. General Views of Family Firms.

Company	Founding Year	Revenues (Million TL)	Employees	Family	Shareholding (%)	No. of Directors		CEO
						Family Members	Other	
Koç Holding A.S.	1926	39.1	105.908	Koç	63.7	4	8	Not family
AG Anadolu Group Holding A.S.	1950	9.3	63.612	Özilhan ve Yazıcı	78	3	9	Not family
Hacı Ömer Sabancı Holding A.S.	1925	6.9	65.054	Sabancı	50.9	5	4	Not family
Zorlu Holding A.S.	1953	5.1	32.000	Zorlu	97	5	5	Not family
Rönesans Holding A.S.	1993	4.5	18.000	Ilıcak	90	1	6	From family
Borusan Holding A.S.	1944	3.7	11.757	Kocabıyık	76.19	2	4	Not family
Doğuş Group	1951	3.4	21.000	Şahenk	64.5	1	7	From family

Source: Created by the authors.

of the executives on the board of directors are analyzed, five executives at Hacı Ömer Sabancı and Zorlu Holding, four at Koç Holding, three at AG Anadolu Group Holding, and two at Borusan Holding are family members. It is noteworthy that Rönesans Holding has only one family member on its board of directors.

Out of the 500 companies featured in the 2023 Family Business Index, merely 29 are headed by female CEOs, and women occupy a mere 23% of board seats. Table 6.3 provides insight into the gender composition of board members in family firms operating within Türkiye, as included in the 2023 Family Business Index.

When Table 6.3 is analyzed, it is observed that the board structure of family firms is mostly composed of male directors (75%), while the ratio of female directors (25%) is lower than that of male directors. This result coincides with the result in the 2023 Family Business Index. It is noteworthy that Koç Holding and Hacı Ömer Sabancı Holding have four female directors each on their boards, while AG Anadolu Group Holding has one female director and Doğuş Group has no female directors.

While revealing the corporate logic of the family firms analyzed in the study, the diversification strategies of the companies within the framework of their corporate entrepreneurship should also be taken into consideration. In this context, Table 6.4 shows the subsidiaries owned by family firms in line with their diversification strategies.

As can be seen from Table 6.4, family firms have many subsidiaries in various sectors. Koç Holding focuses on the energy sector; AG Anadolu Group Holding on agriculture, energy, and industry; Hacı Ömer Sabancı Holding on industry; Zorlu Holding on textiles; Rönesans Holding on construction; Borusan Holding on distribution; and Doğuş Group on automotive. On the other hand, it is noteworthy that all companies operate in the energy sector. On the other hand, while Koç and AG Anadolu Group Holding started their businesses as a small grocery store, Sabancı Holding's cotton trade, Zorlu Holding's weaving loom, Rönesans Holding's construction sector, Borusan Holding's iron and steel trade and the export of agricultural products.

Table 6.3. Gender Distribution of the Board of Directors of Family Firms.

Company	**Number of Directors**	
	Male	**Female**
Koç Holding A.S.	8	4
AG Anadolu Group Holding A.S.	11	1
Hacı Ömer Sabancı Holding A.S.	5	4
Zorlu Holding A.S.	7	3
Rönesans Holding A.S.	5	2
Borusan Holding A.S.	4	2
Doğuş Group	8	0

Source: Created by the authors.

Table 6.4. Subsidiaries of Family Firms.

Koç Holding A.S.	Energy (11)	Finance (10)	Durable consumption (5)	Automotive (8)	Other sectors (18)		
AG Anadolu Group Holding A.S.	Beer group (1)	Soft drinks group (1)	Migros group (1)	Automotive group (3)	Agriculture, energy, and industry group (5)	Social institutions (3)	
Hacı Ömer Sabancı Holding A.S.	Bank (1)	Financial services (2)	Energy (2)	Industry (4)	Construction materials (3)	Retail (1)	Digital (1)
Zorlu Holding A.S.	Textile (4)	Energy (3)	Electronics, white goods telecommunications (2)	Real estate (3)	Mining and metallurgy	Other areas of activity (5)	
Rönesans Holding A.S.	Construction (9)	Real estate (4)	Health (1)	Energy (1)	Petrochemicals (1)		
Borusan Holding A.S.	Steel group (4)	Distributorship group (5)	Energy group (2)	Logistics group (1)			
Doğuş Group	Automotive (23)	Construction (2)	Publication group (1)	Food and beverage, tourism, and retail (5)	Real estate (5)	Technology (4)	Energy (4)

Source: Created by the authors.

In addition, Koç Holding operates in more than 150 countries, AG Anadolu Group Holding in 19 countries, Sabancı Holding in 14 countries, Zorlu Holding in 58 countries, Rönesans Holding in 30 countries, Borusan Holding in 12 countries, and Doğuş Group in 33 countries.

4.2. Findings on the Corporate Logic of Family Firms

The distribution of the types of corporate logic and the sub-codes of these logic types of the family firms included in the research are presented in Table 6.5. Each of the sub-codes of the types of corporate logic seen in family firms operating in Türkiye and included in the 2023 Family Business Index will be examined in detail in this section.

Four logic types were used to determine the corporate logic of family firms, but no findings were found regarding the cooperative logic among these logic types. The coding findings according to the types of corporate logic are given in Fig. 6.3.

As can be seen from the graph, the most coded corporate logic in family firms in Türkiye is the market logic with a rate of 77%. After this logic, the logic of efficiency and savings has a value of 18% and the logic of social responsibility has a value of 5%.

Market logic, the most common type of organizational logic in the study, was defined with five sub-codes. As seen in Fig. 6.4, "investment" is the most frequently used sub-code related to market logic. In other words, family firms in Türkiye act by market logic by emphasizing the importance of investment.

"Goal," the second most frequently coded sub-heading within market logic, was coded 383 times, which is an important finding. Another important indicator of market logic is the "growth" objective. Thus, other objectives of the market

Table 6.5. Types of Organizational Logic and Sub-codes.

Market Logic	Efficiency and Savings Logic	Cooperative Logic	Social Responsibility Logic
Growth (214)[a]	Efficiency (27)[a]	Producer (0)[a]	Ethical Responsibility (31)[a]
Goal (383)[a]	Performance (43)[a]	Regional Producer (0)[a]	Legal Responsibility (5)[a]
Quality (10)[a]	Profit/ Profitability (71)[a]	Cooperative Enterprise/ Company (0)[a]	Economic Responsibility (40)[a]
Competition (51)[a]	Innovation/ Innovative (105)[a]	Producer Association (0)[a]	
Investment (423)[a]	Wealthiness (9)[a]	Producer Partner (0)[a]	

[a]Indicates the number of repetitions of sub-codes.

Source: Created by the authors.

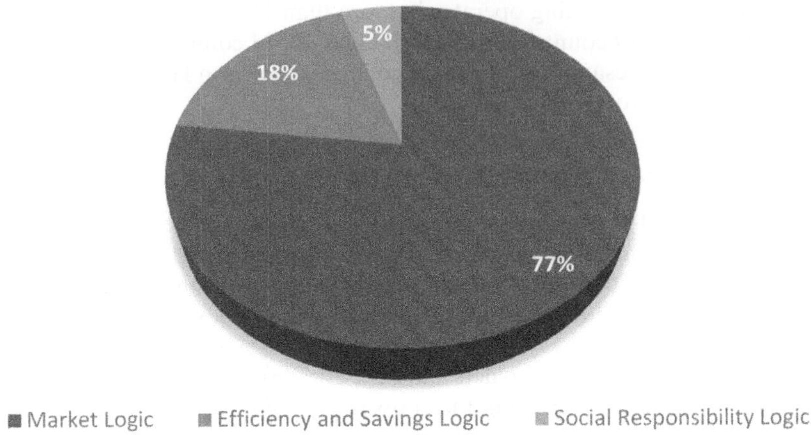

Fig. 6.3. Frequency of Corporate Logic of Family Firms. *Source*: Created by the authors.

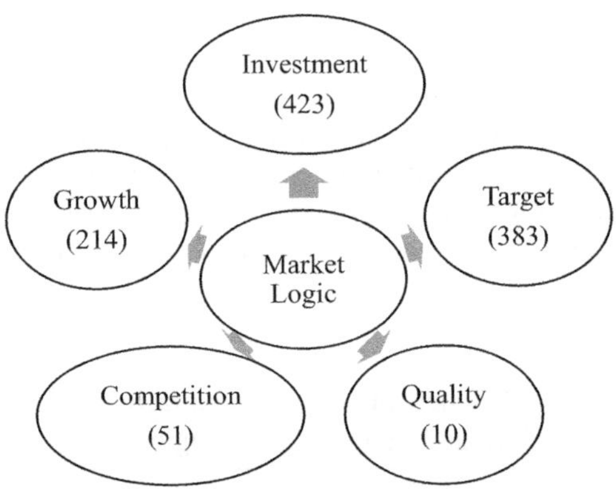

Fig. 6.4. Market Logic and Distribution of Sub-codes. *Source*: Created by the authors.

logic can be expected to be positively affected. "Competition" is the fourth important indicator of market logic with 51 coding. Competition is the basis of the focus in enterprises dominated by market logic.

The second most common type of logic in the family firms in the study is the efficiency and savings logic. The efficiency and savings logic are defined with five sub-codes and shown in Fig. 6.5. All of the sub-codes identified based on the literature were found in the news on the companies' websites. These are "innovation/innovative," "profit/profitability," "performance," "efficiency," and "wealth" in order of frequency.

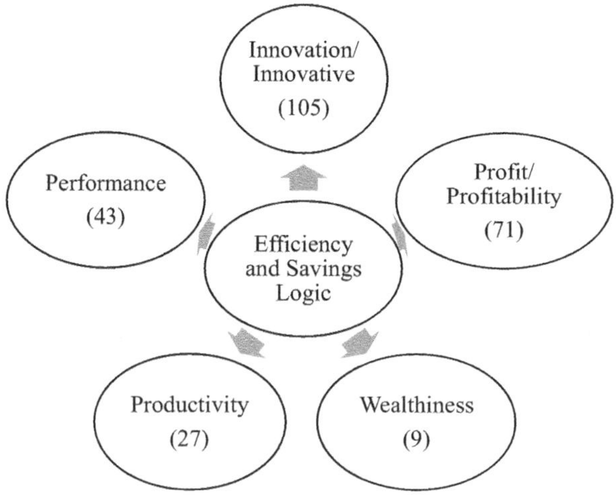

Fig. 6.5. Efficiency and Savings Logic and Distribution of Sub-codes. *Source*: Created by the authors.

According to Fig. 6.5, the most repeated sub-code under the logic of efficiency and savings is the concept of "innovation/innovator." The fact that family firms attach importance to innovation in a highly turbulent VUCA environment supports that they are not against change. The second most frequently used code within the logic of efficiency and savings is "profit/profitability." The primary purpose of the establishment of companies is to make a profit. Another important feature of the efficiency and savings logic is the "performance" objective. The performance sub-code comes to the forefront to increase the diversity of companies. Another important feature of the efficiency and savings logic is the emphasis on "efficiency." The efficiency sub-code stands out as the fourth key concept with 27 repetitions.

In the 2023 Family Business Index, another type of logic adopted by Turkish family firms other than the market logic and the logic of efficiency and savings is the logic of social responsibility. In the analyzed news articles, a total of 76 codings were made regarding the social responsibility logic, and most of these coding was realized under the sub-codes of "economic responsibility" and "ethical responsibility." Another code adopted by the social responsibility logic given in Fig. 6.6 is "legal responsibility."

Fig. 6.6 shows that the most frequently repeated code under the social responsibility logic is "economic responsibility." The logic of social responsibility, which plays an important role in the optimistic outlook of large companies, especially toward their environment, is also important for family firms. Family firms emphasize economic responsibility for the most under the logic of social responsibility. Another sub-code that family firms attach importance to is "ethical responsibility." At this point, the ethical responsibility perspective was coded 31 times and emerged as an important indicator of social responsibility logic.

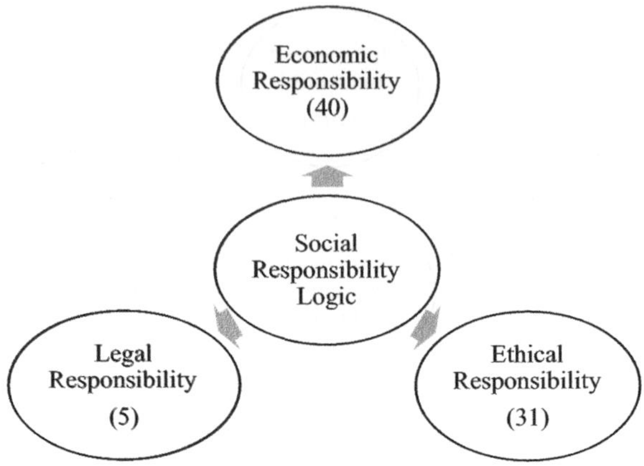

Fig. 6.6. Social Responsibility Logic and Sub-codes. *Source*: Created by the authors.

5. Conclusion and Discussion

In today's world, family firms, which are a dynamic element shaping the economies of countries, are in a key position both in terms of economic burden and social and political balance. It is very important for national economies that the activities of family firms continue to develop. This importance is even more significant and challenging, especially in the VUCA world, which is characterized by a high level of VUCA.

Within the framework of their corporate logic, this study examines the corporate entrepreneurship of family firms from Türkiye that are included in the 2023 Family Business Index in the VUCA world Four corporate logics were created with the adaptation of the corporate logic dimensions in the literature and the characteristics of these logic types were investigated.

Six of the family firms included in the study have a history of at least 70 years, while only Rönesans Holding has a history of 30 years. Koç Holding has 100,000 employees, AG Anadolu Group Holding has 63,000 employees, and Hacı Ömer Sabancı Holding has 65,000 employees. All the family firms were analyzed, and over 50% of the company is owned by family members. Only the CEOs of Rönesans Holding and Doğuş Group are family members, while the CEOs of the other companies are non-family members. The boards of directors of family firms are largely (75%) composed of men.

One of the results obtained in the study is the subsidiaries owned by family firms in line with their diversification strategies. As indicated in the findings of the study, the analyzed family firms have many subsidiaries in various sectors. In this framework, it can be said that the family firms under study attach importance to corporate entrepreneurship. It can be concluded that the family firms under study attach importance to corporate entrepreneurship based on the fact that they prioritize the "investment" logic, one of the types of corporate logic, more than others. However, it can be said that these businesses are growth and goal-oriented. In addition, generational differences in the perception of corporate entrepreneurship in family firms may strengthen or delay the growth of family wealth and, thus, affect the growth of the business. Indeed, Welsh et al. (2013) concluded in their study that subsequent generations in family firms also attach importance to corporate entrepreneurship and strengthen the growth of family wealth.

It can be said that the companies discussed in the study have been operating in various sectors and countries different from their main strengths since their establishment. In this context, it can be said that the companies have differentiated from their initial sectors and gained knowledge and experience in different sectors, thus giving importance to corporate entrepreneurship. The number of countries in which companies operate can also be shown as a criterion for evaluating how much they are corporate entrepreneurs. This result is like to the study of Erdirençelebi (2018). In the study, the entrepreneurial culture of family firms differed between generations, and it was determined that the second to third generation was more entrepreneurial.

The prevalent organizational logics within Turkish family firms are primarily market-oriented and focused on efficiency and cost savings. Family firms typically exhibit investment and target-oriented characteristics under the market logic, and they pursue innovation and profitability objectives under the efficiency and savings logic. This coexistence of market and efficiency-oriented logics within family firms signifies the presence of a hybrid corporate logic. Furthermore, it is evident that family firms prioritize expanding and diversifying their companies as a key objective. Although the companies examined in the study are sufficient to represent the sample population, the generalizability of the results is limited. This is because only Turkish family firms included in the 2023 Family Business Index were included in the study. In addition, another and the most important limitation of the research is that the data obtained from the companies' websites cover a specific period (2016–2023). These companies are also the leading companies in terms of profit rates and size in Türkiye. For this reason, it is thought that examining a larger sample group consisting of family firms that have survived as SMEs for two to three generations in future studies may contribute to the literature on the field. In addition, comparisons between family firms in different countries and Turkish family firms may provide different findings.

References

Abazi-Alili, H., Ramadani, V., & Gërguri-Rashiti, S. (2014). Determinants of innovation activities and their impact on the entrepreneurial businesses performance: Empirical evidence from Central and South Eastern Europe. *Proceedings of REDETE Conference*. Banja Luka, Bosnia and Herzegovina.

Abidi, S., & Joshi, M. (2018). *The VUCA learner*. Sage Publications.

Aldrich, H. E., & Cliff, J. E. (2003). The pervasive effects of family on entrepreneurship: Toward a family embeddedness perspective. *Journal of Business Venturing, 18*(5), 573–596.

Alkoç, Y. K. (2021). Yeni Dünya: Vuca Dünyası. *Sosyal, Beşeri ve İdari Bilimler Dergisi, 4*(10), 989–999.

Antoncic, B. (2007). Intrapreneurship: A comparative structural equation modeling study. *Industrial Management & Data Systems, 107*(3), 309–325.

Antoncic, B., & Hisrich, R. D. (2001). An integrative conceptual model. *Journal of Euromarketing*, *9*(2), 17–35.

Antoncic, B., & Hisrich, R. D. (2003). Clarifying the intrapreneurship concept. *Journal of Small Business and Enterprise Development*, *10*(1), 7–24.

Arman, M. (2018). Firmaların Kurumsal Girişimcilik Eğilimleri Üzerine Bir Araştırma. *Pamukkale Üniversitesi Sosyal Bilimler Enstitüsü Dergisi*, *33*, 277–291.

Baltazar, J. R., Fernandes, C. I., Ramadani, V., & Hughes, M. (2023). Family business succession and innovation: A systematic literature review. *Review of Managerial Science*, *17*(1), 2897–2920.

Baran, B. E., & Woznyj, H. M. (2020). Managing VUCA: The human dynamics of agility. *Organizational Dynamics*, *50*(2), 100787–101220.

Barrett, H., & Weinstein, A. (1998). The effect of market orientation and organizational flexibility on corporate entrepreneurship. *Entrepreneurship theory and practice*, *23*(1), 57–70.

Bartolomeo, M. (2019, November). VUCA prime–The answer to a VUCA dynamic. *The Axelos Blog*. Retrieved, August 11, 2023, from https://www.axelos.com/news/blogs/november-2019/vuca-prime-the-answer-to-a-vucadynamic.

Baş, T., & Akturan, U. (2017). *Nitel araştırma yöntemleri: NVivo 7.0 ile nitel veri analizi*. Seçkin Yayıncılık.

Berrone, P., Duran, P., G'omez-Mejía, L., Heugens, P. P., Kostova, T., & van Essen, M. (2022). Impact of informal institutions on the prevalence, strategy, and performance of family firms: A meta-analysis. *Journal of International Business Studies*, *53*, 1153–1177.

Bettinelli, C., Sciascia, S., Randerson, K., & Fayolle, A. (2017). Researching entrepreneurship in family firms. *Journal of Small Business Management*, *55*(4), 506–529.

Bloomberg. (2023, 12 10). *Türk aile şirketleri 2018'de cirolarını artırdı. 11 07, 2018.* Bloomberg: https://www.bloomberght.com/haberler/haber/2170699-turk-aile-sirketleri-2018-de-cirolarini-artirdi

Boukamcha, F. (2019). The effect of transformational leadership on corporate entrepreneurship in Tunisian SMEs. *Leadership & Organization Development Journal*, *40*(3), 286–304.

Cabrera-Suárez, K., De Saá-Pérez, P., & García-Almeida, D. (2001). The succession process from a resource-and knowledge-based view of the family firm. *Family Business Review*, *14*(1), 37–46.

Calabrò, A., Minola, T., Campopiano, G., & Pukall, T. (2016). Turning innovativeness into domestic and international corporate venturing: The moderating effect of high family ownership and influence. *European Journal of International Management*, *10*(5), 505–533.

Campopiano, G., Brumana, M., Minola, T., & Cassia, L. (2020). Does growth represent chimera or bellerophon for a family business? The role of entrepreneurial orientation and family influence nuances. *European Management Review*, *17*(3), 765–783.

Carney, M. (2005). Corporate governance and competitive advantage in family-controlled firms. *Entrepreneurship Theory and Practice*, *29*(3), 249–265.

Chrisman, J. J., Chua, J. H., & Sharma, P. (2005). Trends and directions in the development of a strategic management theory of the family firm. *Entrepreneurship Theory and Practice*, *29*(5), 555–575.

Covin, J. G., & Slevin, D. P. (1991). A conceptual model of entrepreneurship as firm behavior. *Entrepreneurship Theory and Practice*, *16*(1), 7–26.

Cruz, C., & Nordqvist, M. (2012). Entrepreneurial orientation in family firms: A generational perspective. *Small Business Economics*, *38*, 33–49.

Davila, J., Duran, P., Gómez-Mejía, L., & Sanchez-Bueno, M. J. (2023). Socioemotional wealth and family firm performance: A meta-analytic integration. *Journal of Family Business Strategy*, *14*(2), 100536.

Dess, G. G., & Lumpkin, G. T. (2005). The role of entrepreneurial orientation in stimulating effective corporate entrepreneurship. *Academy of Management Perspectives*, *19*(1), 147–156.

Discua Cruz, A., Hamilton, E., & Jack, S. L. (2021). Understanding entrepreneurial opportunities through metaphors: A narrative approach to theorizing family entrepreneurship. *Entrepreneurship & Regional Development*, *33*(5–6), 405–426.

Discua Cruz, A., & Howorth, C. (2008). Family business in Honduras: Applicability of agency and stewardship theories. In V. Gupta, N. Levenburg, L. Moore, J. Motwani, & T. Schwarz (Eds.), *Culturally-sensitive models of family business in Latin America* (pp. 222–243). ICFAI University Press.

Discua Cruz, A., Howorth, C., & Hamilton, E. (2013). Intrafamily entrepreneurship: The formation and membership of family entrepreneurial teams. *Entrepreneurship Theory and Practice*, *37*(1), 17–46.

Erdem, A. T., & Karadal, H. (2020). Kurumsallaşma, kurumsal girişimcilik ve örgütsel yenilikçilik ilişkilerinin xy kuşaklari açisindan analizi: Aile işletmelerinde bir araştirma. *Bolu Abant İzzet Baysal Üniversitesi Sosyal Bilimler Enstitüsü Dergisi*, *20*(2), 413–437.

Erdirençelebi, M. (2018). aile işletmelerinde nesiller arası girişimcilik kültürü. C.Ü. İktisadi ve İdari Bilimler Dergisi, Cilt 19, Sayı 2.

Fang, H. C., Memili, E., Chrisman, J. J., & Tang, L. (2021). Narrow-framing and risk preferences in family and non-family firms. *Journal of Management Studies*, *58*(1), 201–235.

García-Morales, V. J., Bolívar-Ramos, M. T., & Martín-Rojas, R. (2014). Technological variables and absorptive capacity's influence on performance through corporate entrepreneurship. *Journal of Business Research*, *67*(7), 1468–1477.

García-Villaverde, P. M., Rodrigo-Alarcón, J., Parra-Requena, G., & Ruiz-Ortega, M. J. (2018). Technological dynamism and entrepreneurial orientation: The heterogeneous effects of social capital. *Journal of Business Research*, *83*, 51–64.

Genç, Z. (2022). *Kurumsal Mantıklar ve Örgütlerdeki Kurumsal Mantık Değişimi: Türkiye'deki Zincir Oteller Üzerinde Bir Inceleme* [Doctoral dissertation]. Marmara Universitesi (Türkiye).

George, B. (2017). VUCA 2.0: *A strategy for steady leadership in an unsteady world*. Forbes. February 17th, 2017.

Gersick, K. E., Davıs, J. A., Hampton, M., & Lansberg, I. (1997). *Generation to generation: Life cycles of family business*. Harvard Business School Press.

Goel, S., & Jones, R. J. III (2016). Entrepreneurial exploration and exploitation in family business: A systematic review and future directions. *Family Business Review*, *29*(1), 94–120.

Gomez-Mejia, L. R., Cruz, C., Berrone, P., & De Castro, J. (2011). The bind that ties: Socioemotional wealth preservation in family firms. *The Academy of Management Annals*, *5*(1), 653–707.

Goodale, J. C., Kuratko, D. F., Hornsby, J. S., & Covin, J. G. (2011). Operations management and corporate entrepreneurship: The moderating effect of operations control on the antecedents of corporate entrepreneurial activity in relation to innovation performance. *Journal of Operations Management*, *29*(1–2), 116–127.

Hall, A. (2001). Towards an understanding of the strategy process in small family businesses: A multi-rational perspective. In D. Fletcher (Ed.), *Understanding the small family business* (pp. 32–45). Routledge.

Hisarcıklıoğlu, R. (2019). *TOBB Başkanı Hisarcıklıoğlu: Ekonomik Alanda İstiklal Mücadelesi Veriyoruz*. Retrieved July 21, 2023, from http://www.hurriyet.com.tr/gundem/tobb-baskani-hisarciklioglu-ekonomik-alanda-istiklal-mucadelesi-veriyoruz-41218648

Howorth, C., Rose, M., & Hamilton, E. (2008). Definitions, diversity and development: Key debates in family business research. In M. Casson, B. Yeung, A. Cassu, & N. Wadeson (Eds.), *Oxford handbook of entrepreneurship* (pp. 225–247). Oxford University Press.

Jiménez-Barrionuevo, M. M., Molina, L. M., & García-Morales, V. J. (2019). Combined influence of absorptive capacity and corporate entrepreneurship on performance. *Sustainability*, *11*(11), 3034.

Johansen, B. (2007). *Get there early: Sensing the future to compete in the present*. Berrett-Koehler Publishers.

Kaya, Z. Ö., Karaçay, G., Selim, Z., & Alpkan, L. (2023). Yetenek Yönetimi Uygulamalarının Örgüt Performansı İle İlişkisinde Kurumsal Girişimciliğin Aracılık Etkisi. *International Journal of Advances in Engineering and Pure Sciences*, *35*(2), 259–272.

Kellermanns, F. W., & Eddleston, K. A. (2006). Corporate entrepreneurship in family firms: A family perspective. *Entrepreneurship Theory and Practice*, *30*(6), 809–830.

Kepner, E. (1991). The family and the firm: A coevolutionary perspective. *Family Business Review*, *4*(4), 445–461.

Koç, M., Bir, Y., ve Özekenci, E. K. (2021). *VUCA Bileşenlerinin Ölçümlenmesi Üzerine Bir Ölçek Uyarlama Çalışması*. 20. Uluslararası İşletmecilik Kongresi, 102–119.

Kotlar, J., & Sieger, P. (2019). Bounded rationality and bounded reliability: A study of non-family managers' entrepreneurial behavior in family firms. *Entrepreneurship Theory and Practice*, *43*(2), 251–273.

Kraus, S., Pohjola, M., & Koponen, A. (2012). Innovation in family firms: An empirical analysis linking organizational and managerial innovation to corporate success. *Review of Managerial Science*, *6*(2), 265–286.

Kraus, S., & Rigtering, C. (2017). Strategic corporate entrepreneurship: A configuration approach-based case study. *International Journal of Entrepreneurial Venturing*, *9*(2), 101–121.

Kuratko, D. F., & Audretsch, D. B. (2013). Clarifying the domains of corporate entrepreneurship. *International Entrepreneurship and Management Journal*, *9*, 323–335.

Kuratko, D. F., & Morris, M. H. (2018). Corporate entrepreneurship: A critical challenge for educators and researchers. *Entrepreneurship Education and Pedagogy*, *1*(1), 42–60.

Lawrence, K. (2013). *Developing leaders in a VUCA environment* (pp. 1–15). UNC Executive Development.

Le Breton-Miller, I., & Miller, D. (2018). Beyond the firm: Business families as entrepreneurs. *Entrepreneurship Theory and Practice*, *42*(4), 527–536.

Lee, K., Makri, M., & Scandura, T. (2019). The effect of psychological ownership on corporate entrepreneurship: Comparisons between family and nonfamily top management team members. *Family Business Review*, *32*(1), 10–30.

Levinson, R. E. (1989). *Problems in managing a family-owned business* (Vol. 3). US Small Business Administration, Office of Business Development.

Li, X., Du, J., & Long, H. (2019). Dynamic analysis of international green behavior from the perspective of the mapping knowledge domain. *Environmental Science and Pollution Research*, *26*, 6087–6098.

López-Fernández, M. C., Serrano-Bedia, A. M., & Pérez-Pérez, M. (2016). Entrepreneurship and family firm research: A bibliometric analysis of an emerging field. *Journal of Small Business Management*, *54*(2), 622–639.

Lumpkin, G. T., & Dess, G. G. (1996). Clarifying the entrepreneurial orientation construct and linking it to performance. *Academy of management Review*, *21*(1), 135–172.

Martín-Rojas, R., Garrido-Moreno, A., & García-Morales, V. J. (2020). Fostering corporate entrepreneurship with the use of social media tools. *Journal of Business Research*, *112*, 396–412.

Mccann, J. E. III, Leon-Guerrero, A. Y., & Haley, J. D. Jr (2001). Strategic goals and practices of innovative family businesses. *Journal of Small Business Management*, *39*(1), 50–59.

McKelvie, A., McKenny, A., Lumpkin, G., & Short, J. C. (2014). Corporate entrepreneurship in family businesses: Past contributions and future opportunities. In L. Melin, M. Nordqvist, & P. Sharma (Eds.), *The Sage handbook of family business* (pp. 340–363). Sage Publications.

Memili, E., Eddleston, K. A., Kellermanns, F. W., Zellweger, T. M., & Barnett, T. (2010). The critical path to family firm success through entrepreneurial risk taking and image. *Journal of Family Business Strategy*, *1*(4), 200–209.

Miller, D., (1983) The correlates of entrepreneurship in three types of firms. *Management Science*, *29*(7), 770–791.

Miller, D., Le Breton-Miller, I., & Lester, R. H. (2011). Family and lone founder ownership and strategic behaviour: Social context, identity, and institutional logics. *Journal of management studies*, *48*(1), 1–25.

Minola, T., Campopiano, G., Brumana, M., Cassia, L., & Garrett, R. P. (2016). Corporate entrepreneurship in family business: The when and how. In F. W. Kellermanns & F. Hoy (Eds.), *The Routledge companion to family business* (pp. 311–340). Routledge.

Minola, T., Kammerlander, N., Kellermanns, F. W., & Hoy, F. (2021). Corporate entrepreneurship and family business: Learning across domains. *Journal of Management Studies*, *58*(1), 1–26.

Morris, M. H. (1998). From the editor: What is microenterprise development?. *Journal of Developmental Entrepreneurship*, *3*(2), V.

Morris, M. H., van Vuuren, J., Cornwall, J. R., & Scheepers, R. (2009). Properties of balance: A pendulum effect in corporate entrepreneurship. *Business Horizons*, *52*(5), 429–440.

Nordqvist, M. (2005). Familiness in top management teams: Commentary on Ensley and Pearson's "an exploratory comparison of the behavioral dynamics of top management teams in family and nonfamily new ventures: Cohesion, conflict, potency, and consensus". *Entrepreneurship Theory and Practice*, *29*(3), 285–291.

Nordqvist, M., & Melin, L. (2010). Entrepreneurial families and family firms. *Entrepreneurship & Regional Development*, *22*(3–4), 211–239.

Özkara, B., & Kızıldağ, D. (2015). *Holding formu değişiyor mu?* Bir kurumsal girişimcilik örneği.

Pultz, S., Hansen, M. P., & Jepsen, H. (2021). Planning for a job: The trying experience of unemployment during the COVID-19 crisis in Denmark. *International Perspectives in Psychology: Research, Practice, Consultation*, *10*(4), 228.

Qaiyum, S., & Wang, C. L. (2018). Understanding internal conditions driving ordinary and dynamic capabilities in Indian high-tech firms. *Journal of Business Research*, 90, 206–214.

Randolph, R. V., Li, Z., & Daspit, J. J. (2017). Toward a typology of family firm corporate entrepreneurship. *Journal of Small Business Management*, 57(3), 1102–1118.

Randolph, R. V., Li, Z., & Daspit, J. J. (2019). Toward a typology of family firm corporate entrepreneurship. *Journal of Small Business Management*, *57*(3), 1102–1118.

Rehman, N., Mahmood, A., Ikram, A., & Ahmad, A. (2021). Firing on all cylinders: Configuring information technology around the constituents of corporate entrepreneurship to outperform in SME sector. *Plos One*, *16*(9), e0256539.

Reid, R., Dunn, B., Cromie, S., & Adams, J. (1999). Family orientation in family firms: A model and some empirical evidence. *Journal of Small Business and Enterprise Development*, *6*(1), 55–67.

Rogoff, E. G., & Heck, R. K. Z. (2003). Evolving research in entrepreneurship and family business: Recognizing family as the oxygen that feeds the fire of entrepreneurship. *Journal of Business Venturing*, *18*(5), 559–566.

Salvato, C. (2004). Predictors of entrepreneurship in family firms. *The Journal of Private Equity*, *7*(3), 68–76.

Salvato, C., Chirico, F., & Sharma, P. (2010). A farewell to the business: Championing exit and continuity in entrepreneurial family firms. *Entrepreneurship & Regional Development*, *22*(3–4), 321–348.

Saly, A. W. (2001). Corporate entrepreneurship: Antecedents and consequences of entrepreneurship in large firms Amsterdam. *Management*, *39*, 615–641.

Sarkar, A. (2016). We live in a VUCA World: The importance of responsible leadership. *Development and Learning in Organizations: An International Journal*, *30*(3), 9–12.

Sharma, P., Chrisman, J. J., & Chua, J. (Eds.). (1996). *A review and annotated bibliography of family business studies*. Kluwer Academic Publishing.

Sinha, D., & Sinha, S. (2020). Managing in a VUCA world: Possibilities and pitfalls. *Journal of Technology Management for Growing Economies*, *11*(1), 17–21.

Sirmon, D. G., & Hitt, M. A. (2003). Managing resources: Linking unique resources, management, and wealth creation in family firms. *Entrepreneurship theory and practice*, *27*(4), 339–358.

Soleimanof, S., Singh, K., & Holt, D. T. (2019). Micro-foundations of corporate entrepreneurship in family firms: An institution-based perspective. *Entrepreneurship Theory and Practice*, *43*(2), 274–281.

Teece, D. J. (2016). Dynamic capabilities and entrepreneurial management in large organizations: Toward a theory of the (entrepreneurial) firm. *European Economic Review*, *86*, 202–216.

Thornton, P. H., Jones, C. & Kury, K. (2005). Institutional Logics and Institutional change in organizations: Transformation in accounting, architecture, and publishing. In C. Jones & P. H. Thornton (Eds.), *Transformation in Cultural Industries (Research in the Sociology of Organizations, Vol. 23)*, (pp. 125–170). Emerald Group Publishing Limited, Leeds. https://doi.org/10.1016/S0733-558X(05)23004-5

Turner, C., & Margolis, G. (2012). *Volatility: Threat or opportunity?* Retrieved August 01, 2023, from http://info.steelwedge.com/rs/steelwedge/images/sw_industryweek_oct_2012.pdf

Upton, N., Teal, E. J., & Felan, J. T. (2001). Strategic and business planning practices of fast growth family firms. *Journal of Small Business Management*, *39*(1), 60–72.

Vago, M. (2004). Integrated Change Management©: Challenges for family business clients and consultants. *Family Business Review*, *17*(1), 71–80.

Van de Ven, A. H., & Engleman, R. M. (2004). Central problems in managing corporate innovation and entrepreneurship. In K. Jerome & C. C. Andrew (Eds.), *Advances in Entrepreneurship, Firm Emergence and Growth (Advances in Entrepreneurship, Firm Emergence and Growth, Vol. 7)*, (pp. 47–72). Emerald Group Publishing Limited, Leeds. https://doi.org/10.1016/S1074-7540(04)07003-5

Welsh, D. H., Memili, E., Rosplock, K., Roure, J., & Segurado, J. L. (2013). Perceptions of entrepreneurship across generations in family offices: A stewardship theory perspective. *Journal of Family Business Strategy*, *4*(3), 213–226.

Westhead, P., & Howorth, C. (2007). 'Types' of private family firms: An exploratory conceptual and empirical analysis. *Entrepreneurship and Regional Development*, *19*(5), 405–431.

Wimmer, R. D., & Dominick, J. R. (2000). *Mass media research*. Cengage Learning.

Yildirim, A., & Şimşek, H. (2013). *Sosyal bilimlerde nitel araştırma yöntemleri*. Seçkin Yayıncılık.

Yurdasever, E., & Fidan, Y. (2020). KOMB (VUCA) dünyası ve yeni liderlik becerileri. *İnsan ve Toplum Bilimleri Araştırmaları Dergisi*, *9*(2), 1638–1664.

Zahra, S. A. (1996). Goverance, ownership, and corporate entrepreneurship: The moderating impact of industry technological opportunities. *Academy of management journal*, *39*(6), 1713–1735.

Zahra, S. A. (1991). Predictors and financial outcomes of corporate entrepreneurship: An exploratory study. *Journal of Business Venturing*, *6*(4), 259–285.

Zahra, S. A., Hayton, J. C., & Salvato, C. (2004). Entrepreneurship in family vs. non-family firms: A resource-based analysis of the effect of organizational culture. *Entrepreneurship Theory and Practice*, *28*(4), 363–381.

Zehir, C., & Eren, M. S. (2007). Field research on impacts of some organizational factors on corporate entrepreneurship and business performance in the Turkish automotive industry. *Journal of American Academy of Business*, *10*(2), 170–176.

Zehir, C., Müceldili, B., & Zehir, S. (2012). The impact of corporate entrepreneurship on organizational citizenship behavior and organizational commitment: Evidence from Turkey SMEs. *Procedia-Social and Behavioral Sciences*, *58*, 924–933.

Zellweger, T., & Sieger, P. (2012). Entrepreneurial orientation in long-lived family firms. *Small Business Economics*, *38*, 67–84.

Zhang, Z., Wan, D., & Jia, M., (2008) Do high performance human resource practices help corporate entrepreneurship? The mediating role of organizational citizenship behaviour. *Journal of High Technology Management Research*, *19*, 128–138.

Chapter 7

Gender Bias and Family Firms Leadership in Africa: Evidence from Nigeria

Joy E. Akahome[a] *and Ida Skubis*[b]

[a]*Federal University, Nigeria*
[b]*Silesian University of Technology, Poland*

Abstract

This study investigates the motivations and challenges of Nigerian women in leadership roles in male-dominated family firms. It addresses the literature gap in gender dynamics within these businesses, particularly in Nigeria, where such enterprises are economically significant yet often display gender biases due to cultural and societal norms. Using qualitative methods and a multiple case study approach, the research analyzes the experiences of eight women leading family firms. It identifies three key motivations for these women: acquiring necessary skills and capabilities, career development, and enhancing quality of life, influenced by personal growth, job satisfaction, and balancing work and family. The study also highlights three main challenges: the glass ceiling effect, traditional gender roles, and primogeniture, leading to stereotypes, societal pressures, and often relegating women to subordinate roles or presenting significant leadership hurdles.

Keywords: Leadership; management; business; entrepreneurship; women entrepreneurs

Entrepreneurial Behaviour of Family Firms:
Perspectives on Emerging Economies, 135–159

doi:10.1108/978-1-83753-934-520241007

1. Introduction

Despite monumental technological advancements, the family, and by extension, the family firm, remains a crucial influencer of global development. According to Payne (2020), the family constitutes a crucial element of the worldwide business economy and deserves scholarly attention. Many factors combine to define family firms as major purveyors of socio-economic development in the economy (Post & Byron, 2015).

According to the Family Firm Institute (2017), family firms account for about two-thirds of all businesses around the globe. They generate approximately 70–90% of the yearly gross domestic product and create 50–80% of jobs for a large number of people worldwide. There is a plethora of evidence in the extant literature supporting this assertion. For instance, Ramadani and Hoy (2015) in a review allude that family firms represent the majority of companies and are an important source for job generation in most countries (Hacker & Dowling, 2012; Hoy & Sharma, 2010; Ramadani et al., 2013).

Family Business Review defines a family firm as one that is solely managed by family members. The criteria for a family firm to succeed involve a combination of goals that are not necessarily financial. These goals include perseverance, commitment, pride in accomplishments, and satisfaction (Samara et al., 2019). A family firm is successful when there is coexistence among the family in achieving their values to grow their firm (Payne, 2020). In Nigeria, 53% of family firms export their products, which are less than the global average for family firms (PWC, 2020).

Limited empirical evidence suggests gender as an antecedent of performance in managing Nigerian family firms. Yet, the observed level of bias against the female gender in Nigeria's family firms is mind-boggling and potentially antithetical to family firm development. Such bias originates from the patriarchal and male chauvinistic culture prevalent in Nigeria, as in most other African cultures. Accordingly, there has been a low representation of female business leaders, which inadvertently denies family firms the demonstrated resilience of most Nigerian women, arguably invaluable for family firm success.

In the World Economic Forum Gender Gap Report (2018), Nigeria was ranked 133 out of 149 countries, where only 20% of women have a business enterprise and 12% of these women are members of board directors in companies. Therefore, gender bias pervades every organizational decision, even in the national assembly, where only 6% of women are given the opportunity for a position. The PWC survey (2018) found less representation of women in the global arena, where 80% of business owners are men, and women occupy just 30% of the leadership positions in Nigerian family firms. Cultural and religious beliefs (Owoyemi & Olusanya, 2014), socio-historical trajectories (Alex-Hart, 2016), and socio-cultural expectations of traditional society (Wang, 2010) are some sources of gender bias.

The spillover of gender bias as a socio-cultural construction into society's values and perceptions in business decisions is well-argued. For instance, Ryan et al. (2016) and Keating and Little (1997) trace gender bias with regard to the selection of a business successor, which leads to the consideration of men as more valuable in business than women. This bias usually leads to wives, daughters, or even sisters being excluded as potential successors (Griffeth et al., 2006), even with demonstrable acumen to manage the business better.

Most women who join family firms in male-dominated fields find it difficult to progress through the ranks. Even when they are allowed to serve in the business, they face more obstacles than their male counterparts (Xie et al., 2020). The primary incentives for Nigerian female social entrepreneurs to start and continue their enterprises include money/income, passion for societal change, independence, and societal acceptance. Notably, the motives of independence and societal change are expressed from a distinctly female perspective, emphasizing desires for more time for family, children, and self, and to empower other women (Skubis et al., 2023).

Most women have to learn to work harder for respect and recognition (Labaki, 2020). Factors such as education, networking, and experience help women succeed (Labaki, 2020). Curimbaba (2002) discovered that a female child who succeeds in the family firm often does so because of the absence of a male child in the family. Even when the female child assumes the role of the leader of the business, it is usually only temporary (Martin, 2001), due primarily to marriage and inheritance practices. The female responsibility in the home is often seen as domestic in nature, even when it comes to accepting the potential of females in the workplace (Jimenez, 2009).

Previous studies have examined female successors of family firms in other countries (Campopiano et al., 2019; Eddleston & Sabil, 2019; Glover, 2014; Humphreys, 2013; Labaki, 2020; Otten-Pappas, 2013; Sharma & Kaur, 2019). However, there is a gap in investigating women who engage in male-dominated family firms in Nigeria. There is a scarcity of empirical studies examining gender bias and the role of women in family firm leadership in the African context, with a specific focus on Nigeria. While there is a growing body of research on gender and family firms globally, there is a notable gap in understanding the unique challenges and opportunities faced by women in Nigerian family firms.

This study seeks to answer two research questions: What are the lived experiences of Nigerian women regarding their unique opportunities and challenges in managing or leading a male-dominated family firm? Therefore, the objective of the study is to formulate a description by recounting the lived experiences of Nigerian women regarding their motivation and challenges in assuming leadership positions in a male-dominated family firm.

This chapter's analysis adds to the current limited body of literature that deals with female leadership in Nigerian family firms, with obvious theory development and practice implications for family firms in predominantly patriarchal cultural settings. After this brief introduction, the rest of the chapter follows this structure: a brief review of literature, materials and methodology, analysis and findings, discussion, theoretical and practical implications, and concluding remarks.

2. Literature Review

2.1. Nigerian Culture Regarding Working Women

Nigerian cultural practices have negatively affected women's rights, leading to gender discrimination and inequality (Durojaye et al., 2014). There are several differences between Nigerian men and women in the areas of politics, education, social, and economic aspects (Okoyeuzu et al., 2012). Traditionally, Nigerian women's jobs have centered on engaging in domestic activities (Bankole & Adeyeri, 2014). However, their involvement in career development has changed the structure of the Nigerian family (Kahkha et al., 2014).

The Nigerian government has made laws and policies to address the issue of gender inequalities, yet these women still experience inequality and discrimination (Durojaye et al., 2014). To eradicate this issue, Durojaye et al. (2014) suggested the creation of education awareness campaigns, legal reforms, and the adoption of a quota system.

Nigerian women find it difficult to strike a balance between work and family. This problem prevents women from participating in top management jobs (Okonkwo, 2013). This gender inequality and discrimination extend to families, as a child grows up to be a parent; boys are given freedom and respect, while girls are restricted and treated as dependents, only to be given out in marriage (Okonkwo, 2013).

The Nigerian culture provides men with the position of occupying prestigious offices and control of basic resources, while women often occupy low-skill jobs and receive lower pay (Okonkwo, 2013). Ntoimo and Isiugo-Abanihe (2014) examined how the patriarchal structure limits the desire of Nigerian women to marry. Patriarchy is a system based on gender differentiation where the father, as the head of the home, is given authority and control over the women and children.

Moreover, the lack of opportunities for Nigerian women reduces their opportunities and interferes with their family and personal well-being. The glass ceiling effect in Nigeria prevents women from progressing to top-level positions. This phenomenon perpetuates the cycle of poverty in the country (Kolade & Kehinde, 2013). However, progress has been made in including Nigerian women in public offices (Ebohon, 2012). 33 Nigerian women formed 7.6% of the 470 legislators, and ministerial positions are increasingly occupied by women (Ebohon, 2012). Nigerian women have realized that the deterioration of political and social values is caused by male-dominated rule (Ebohon, 2012).

There is a lack of women in management and in professions traditionally suited for men (Kolade & Kehinde, 2013) although women have taken an interest in occupations like nursing, teaching, and male-dominated businesses like driving, mechanics, banking, and telecommunications (Kolade & Kehinde, 2013). Despite this, few Nigerian women occupy top managerial positions in oil and gas, manufacturing, construction, and banking (Kolade & Kehinde, 2013). Nigerian women are faced with the dual role of mother and worker; therefore, the tension increases as they manage to progress in their careers while family demands more of their time (Bankole & Adeyeri, 2014). It is important to understand how women cope with these roles.

2.2. Female Successor in Family Firm

There has been an increase in the number of women managers in family firms in several countries (Smith, 2007). It is noted that women own over 30% of American family firms (Astrachan, 2002), while most conceptual research conducted focuses on women in family firms (Hisrich & Fulop, 1997). These studies have investigated the roles women play in family firms, gender bias, and, most importantly, succession planning (Sabharwal, 2015). In observing the role of women in family firms, it has been discovered that women often show more dependence and concern for others compared to their male counterparts, who are mostly independent in nature (Sabharwal, 2015). Women are seen to exhibit softer emotions and be more receptive in their roles as leaders in family firms (Sabharwal, 2015). Several variables have been studied in family firms when comparing females to males, including skills and capabilities attributed to females in leadership positions.

- *Leadership style*: Various studies on differences in leadership style between males and females found no significant difference in their management and leadership styles (Powell, 1990), while Eagly et al. (1995) found that both sexes are equally effective in their leadership styles. Some studies have shown that women managers exhibit leadership that is collaborative and promotes teamwork (Moore & Buttner, 1997). Other researchers suggest women exhibit a democratic leadership style (Eagly & Johnson, 1990), while others believe women have developed interpersonal skills, which are the best determinant for examining female entrepreneurs (Buttner, 2001).
- *Family membership conflict*: Regarding family conflict in the business, most researchers have indicated that women's involvement in the family firm leads to lesser conflict compared to when a male family member is the manager (Bjornberg & Nicholson, 2007).
- *Succession plans*: This involves the founder of the business letting go and passing control and authority to the next person (Cadieux, 2007). A study by Haberman and Danes (2007) investigated father-to-son and father-to-daughter succession plans and discovered significant differences in communication patterns and information sharing. Vera and Dean (2005) noted that women face more challenges than men in the succession process. Choosing a successor in a family firm is influenced by the culture present in every country (Schenkel et al., 2016), and parents create perceptions for their children concerning the family firm.
- *The use of outside advisors*: Schenkel et al. (2016) suggest that using outside advisors has been a focus of research on women in family firms. Research has indicated that women are more likely to seek outside advisors, such as consultants, to make informed decisions rather than relying on individual systematic practices, as women have shown less confidence in decision-making and prefer to solicit the opinions of others to build a supportive network.
- *Long-term planning*: Strategic planning or long-term planning has been emphasized in the literature (Filbeck & Lee, 2000). Including a female member in the family firm allows for better decision-making regarding the firm's affairs (Daspite et al., 2016). Females can process and react to information more effectively while making decisions under risk.
- *The influence of the business owner and their intention of going public*: When the founder of the business has the right to choose their successor regardless of the person's knowledge of the business (Daspite et al., 2016), some family members may not contribute successfully to the company's growth if choosing the first son is the criterion for running the firm (Choi & Park, 2014). Some research

has analyzed selection criteria and gender as it relates to succession (Dumas, 2003). Schlepphorst and Moog (2014) have revealed that personal traits are important factors in choosing a successor rather than using gender or birth order although gender is still an important factor in succession in family firms.

2.3. Positive Contributions of Female Leadership or Successor in Family Firm

Efficient leadership involves implementing inclusive policies, using resources realistically, and concentrating on attaining systemic objectives (Skubis et al., 2023a). Research has revealed the positive effect of women in business as they assume leadership positions. It shows that female involvement in family firms has led to the success of the firm due to several motivational factors. The study carried out by Samara et al. (2019) shows that women's intrinsic traits, such as understanding, creativity, and intuition, make them better leaders in handling conflict and crises. For example, females holding political offices have been praised for managing the COVID-19 crisis (Forbes, April 13, 2020).

Family firms have a large percentage of women in roles of governance rather than occupying managerial roles (Orozo-Collazos et al., 2019). While the glass ceiling effect has prevented women from gaining top management positions in non-family firms, family firms can provide better opportunities for women to exert their influence in the decision-making process. Family firms may be able to eradicate glass ceiling issues and create a conducive environment for women to achieve superior performance in their jobs (Amore et al., 2014; Samara et al., 2019).

Another factor reveals that female successors or leadership in family firms will lead to an increased level of profit for the business (Orozo-Collazos et al., 2019). Numerous studies have shown that women have a positive influence on the performance of the firm (Bøhren & Staubo, 2014; Campopiano et al., 2019; Eddleston & Sabil, 2019; Jeong & Harrison, 2017). This is why organizations are gradually disregarding the glass ceiling and establishing support for and promotion of their female employees (Bøhren & Staubo, 2014; Jeong & Harrison, 2017). By increasing female leadership in family firms, a good example can be set for communities to reach out to policymakers in a bid to instill gender equality.

Women's influence in family firms is important because a woman is seen as the glue that keeps the family together. However, men are often influenced by power and the need to control others. Women are more emotional beings than men and are more concerned with building relationships (Eddleston & Sabil, 2019). Women can improve the reputation of the family firm by providing and supporting philanthropic efforts (Campopiano et al., 2019). As women become more visible in family firms, their role as emotional beings can strengthen the longevity of the business, build harmony, and create a reputation that leads to the success of the firm (Eddleston & Sabil, 2019). Recognizing women's role in family firms will serve as a role model for other female generations.

The exclusion of women from top management positions leads to many missed opportunities and creates risks because women tend to make less risky decisions than men, partly due to the lack of women in business. A sure way of improving risk management would be to have a gender-balanced management team in the business to realize the positive effect of women (Gallucci et al., 2015; Lyngsie & Foss, 2017). Family firms with females at the top management level outperform others that lack female representation in the management team. Research has shown that females in management positions create more value than those that lack women (Campopiano et al., 2019; Eddleston & Sabil, 2019). Therefore, family firms are successful in promoting female leadership. The contribution of women ensures the success of the business and creates business continuity over several generations (Labaki, 2020).

2.4. Opportunities for Women Successors in a Male-dominated Family Firm

2.4.1. Having the Gift of Skill and Capacity

Research has shown that women are more skillful and have the capacity to outperform their male counterparts in terms of demonstrating social skills, improving the quality of their work life, satisfying customers, and focusing on personal growth (Humphreys, 2013). The feminine style of management is indicative of the ways women communicate analyze and solve problems.

Women often emphasize their personal experiences on the job. They tend to communicate more easily and exhibit a tendency to care for and respect their fathers, rather than taking responsibility on their own in solving business problems. Vera and Dean (2005) acknowledged that women are more trustworthy, attentive, caring, collaborative, supportive, and deliberate in making decisions. Pyromalis et al. (2004) observed that women perform better in the areas of job satisfaction and succession opportunities, as well as in improving the performance of the firm. Women handle conflict better than men when pursuing socio-economic benefits and securing financial commitments.

Training is an important component in producing able entrepreneurs who can contribute to the economy (Aneke, 2017). Skill-based training and the delivery of managerial skills are essential in strengthening entrepreneurs and improving their businesses (Aneke, 2017). Female owners of family firms must have the right resources, skill set, and knowledge to perform excellently (Yildiz et al., 2019). If these women have acquired the necessary education and experience for the business, then managing it should not be a problem (Bettinelli et al., 2019). By exhibiting this competence, women could gain advantages in monetary returns and other aspects (Mcguinness et al., 2017; Xie et al., 2020).

2.4.2. To Develop a Professional Career

Securing a female successor in the business should be encouraged by the family because it can provide women with the opportunity to have a flexible schedule and increase their job satisfaction. Females often see their involvement in the business as a source of pride, especially when assisting the family in filling the position as the head of the company (Schröder et al., 2011).

Vera and Dean (2005) recognized several advantages for women working in family firms, including the hope and dream of devoting time to grow the family firm, the pride of carrying on the family tradition, sharing family values, and the flexibility of dealing with children and husbands while devoting time to the business. Family firms are often sought as an option by women in their quest to develop their own careers.

Moreover, female successors should not be undervalued. Instead, families should protect and train their daughters as competent successors from the outset, rather than bringing them in only when a critical incident will force them to do so. A fraction of daughters join the company because it fits naturally into their passion or career interest, or because they are willing to work for and with the family (Akhmedova et al., 2019). They are motivated to become professionals rather than just income earners. Gaining intrinsic motivation would lead women to enjoy their jobs and increase their satisfaction with their work (Akhmedova et al., 2019).

2.4.3. Improving Work Life

Research has shown that 90% of women who work in family firms do so on a full-time basis and are also responsible for domestic chores and raising the children (Bianco et al., 2015; Bøhren & Staubo, 2014). These women often feel it is normal to perform the roles of a wife, mother, and manager. In summary, daughters expect their fathers to approve of their leadership and give them responsibilities similar to their brothers in managing the business (Otten-Pappas, 2013). Therefore, family firms can provide daughters with work-life balance and job security, allowing them to raise children and devote time to their personal needs. Women pay a higher cost than men when it comes to balancing work with family life. However, in family firms, there is often a creation of human resources practices that provide resources and support for women to balance their work and family lives (Ely & Padavic, 2020).

2.5. Challenges of Women Leaders or Successor in Family Firm

2.5.1. Glass Ceiling Effect

The glass ceiling is a roadblock that generally prevents women from progressing to higher positions in the corporate hierarchy (Kiaye & Singh, 2013). This glass ceiling includes barriers such as gender stereotypes, discrimination against women, and gender segregation in the workplace. It identifies barriers at the individual, organizational, and societal levels that hinder ambitious women from climbing the corporate ladder.

According to a Business Standard Report (2018), in India, only 25% of women are in the labor force. Even among these, 25% of professional women are not allowed promotion to top management positions. A study by Sampson and Moore (2008) identified glass ceiling issues in England, where women are paid less and progress less to higher positions despite having the same level of education and experience as their male counterparts. Kiaye and Singh (2013) identified some organizational and societal barriers within a Durban firm in South Africa. The organization was less supportive of women's growth, and these women faced sexual abuse by men. Sever (2016) conducted a study in Istanbul and considered the attitudes of women toward their work. These women were found to be more exhausted, less ambitious, and more family-oriented.

A study by Oge et al. (2014) discovered that women working at Turkiye University were reluctant to take authority from their bosses due to distractions from home despite possessing the required qualities to become successful leaders. In Nigeria, Ganiyu et al. (2018) noted that women progressed to a certain level in their careers before facing glass ceiling issues such as family-related issues, lack of supportive network mechanisms, cultural stereotypes, and religious convictions. The glass ceiling may cause a brain drain crisis in Nigeria, reflecting the broader challenges of gender inequality and lack of support that female entrepreneurs face in the country (Skubis et al., 2023b).

In view of the extant literature, it is evident that gender roles and stereotypes that have existed in different countries have made massive contributions to the discrimination women face. In the past, women have been responsible for taking care of the home, and men have understood that this would affect their ability to manage a business.

2.5.2. Traditional Roles

A study by Martin (2001) suggests that the exclusion of women from managing the family firm is attributed to the traditional roles played by women – as wives, mothers, or sisters. These roles are often more closely related to family roles rather than business roles, leading to the belief that women are not suitable for handling family firms and are more domestic in nature (Bianco et al., 2015; Jimenez, 2009).

Marshack (1994) discovered that traditional gender stereotypes were evident in the tasks assigned to each partner. If women were given the opportunity to be included in the business, they would often assume a less important or prominent role, such as a secretary, while men would be responsible for more prestigious positions, like an executive in the company. Gender may influence factors such as attitudes men have toward the family firm, which could affect the growth of the business.

However, Williams et al. (2013) have inspired parents to teach and groom their children, whether male or female, to manage the family firm. Given that women are often the caretakers of their wards, they can instill the values of the family and firm in the children (Dugan et al., 2011).

2.5.3. Primogeniture

Primogeniture is an ideology that expresses the underrepresentation of women in family firms, suggesting that men are preferable to women in leading or managing certain jobs or taking up executive positions (Ahrens et al., 2015). This system continues to dominate the value system of family firms. A situation often arises where a son is expected to head the family firm, with daughters excluded from joining the business despite their educational qualifications.

A seven-year study carried out in Denmark indicated that being a male first-born is a major factor in appointing him as the executive of the company. The male child has a higher chance of being appointed than the female (Bennedsen et al., 2007). Some research has provided insight into why daughters are not successors in family firms. It is often believed that it is the father's responsibility to protect his daughter from problems that may arise in managing the company, and because of this, daughters are given menial jobs or low-level tasks (Dumas, 1992; Glass & Cook, 2016).

Another perspective on women's exclusion from the business is that fathers may not believe their daughters have the strength, capacity, or experience to run the business. In family succession, sons are groomed with the expectation of heading the family firm, while daughters often miss the opportunity for such roles. In Germany, only 23% of females are allowed to succeed in a family firm regardless of their higher level of education and experience. Men are still considered the more preferable choice.

3. Methodology

The research design conducted a qualitative study using a case study approach to understand the motivation and challenges women face in managing a male-dominated family firm. There is limited data on women who have managed family firms in Nigeria. However, these women have shown a positive trend based on a survey of women's leadership in Nigerian family firms. A qualitative study is appropriate to provide an understanding of phenomena such as their motivation and challenges (Moleong, 2013).

This study uses a multiple case study approach to gain an in-depth understanding of the subject. A qualitative study was employed to understand the lived experiences of respondents without having predetermined assumptions. A qualitative multiple case study allows the researcher to capture full and meaningful characteristics of real-life situations and can provide an awareness of events while answering the questions of what, how, and why (Yin, 2017).

Additionally, this method supports the objective of the study and provides data to answer the research question. Yin (2017) recommends a case study approach when the research addresses explanatory questions such as how or why something happened, or a descriptive question asking what happened.

The goal of a multiple case study is to provide a rich and powerful picture of human interaction, which is preferred over a single case study. When a study involves more than one person, it is considered a multiple-case study. A multiple case study was used by sampling women leaders in an attempt to replicate the same findings across multiple cases, such as interviewing several women and discovering consistent results or responses.

3.1. Sampling Technique

The study participants were chosen using a purposive sampling technique (Oliver, 2006) because it focuses more on obtaining precise and rich data to gain better and clearer information about the subject, rather than on the number of respondents in the study. The criteria for choosing the respondents included individuals such as female directors, managers, and owners of the business. The study focused on understanding women's motivation and challenges in assuming a leadership role in a male-dominated family firm.

Based on these criteria, the study used eight cases of family firms in Nigeria. The intention of the study was not to generalize but rather to generate meaningful information for the study.

3.2. Data Collection

The data collection was gathered through a series of interviews with the participants who represent different Nigerian ethnic groups and engage in male-dominated family firm. The main method of data collection used in the study was an in-depth semi-structured interview. This approach allows researchers to explore deeply when more information is needed. The study involved the collection of both primary and secondary data. Meanwhile, the use of secondary data, which consists of academic journals, government agency data, and news articles, supports the study.

The interview process was conducted at the location of the family firm, with each interview lasting approximately 30–44 minutes. The researcher is often referred to as the instrument because their knowledge and skills are important for producing quality, accurate research (Rowley, 2012). The researcher collected data using open-ended, semi-structured interview questions. The semi-structured interview is a process of pairing questions that is guided by identifying themes in a consistent and organized manner to elicit responses from respondents (Qu & Dumay, 2011). Member checking was completely done in the study because it enhances the reliability of the study (Stake, 2011). For example, to validate the research and ensure reliability, respondents were asked to review the transcribed document to find any errors or relevant information that was not included during the interview. Member checking is when the respondents validate the interview, improving the accuracy and credibility of the study (Mero-Daffe, 2011).

Data cleansing was done after member checking to detect or remove irrelevant data. After data cleansing, the researcher entered the transcribed interview data into the computer-assisted qualitative data analysis software called NVivo. NVivo assisted in providing codes, themes, and interpretation of data.

3.3. Data Analysis Procedure

To ensure the validity and reliability of the data used in the study, respondents' interviews were transcribed and read by the interviewees to ensure the accuracy of responses. Eight women who have been successors of the family firm for over five years were interviewed for the study. They possessed deep knowledge and experience in responding to the questions. To facilitate the conversation, the researchers used appropriate prompts regarding the questions for the interview.

The data collected were categorized into further information beyond the interview questions and responses of the respondents. There was recognition of patterns that provided a thematic analysis. During content analysis, the themes were differentiated after the discovery of repeated responses in the multiple case study (Vaismoradi et al., 2015).

In identifying common relationships across multiple case studies during the coding of the interview, the researchers could justify the cataloging of various themes (Saldana, 2015). In developing a case study database, the words were identified, and documented, and themes were revealed, ensuring adequacy and reliability of the data (Yin, 2017). Content analysis was used in organizing and analyzing the interviews, which assisted in the development of themes (Yin, 2017).

4. Findings

4.1. Demographic Information (Profile of the Participant)

The method of gathering information from each respondent was through an interview. The personal profiles of the respondents were gathered for the study to provide a deep understanding of the subjects for the research (Table 7.1).

The family firms analyzed in this article are male-dominated. These include businesses in the hotel, transportation, construction, filling stations, welding and fabrication, furniture, and electrical appliances sectors.

Most Nigerian women enjoy the possibility of leading the staff in a company. While the ages of the successors vary, it is confirmed that they are all over 30 years of age. Based on the results, family firms have implemented gender equality in choosing the next person to succeed as the owner of the business, while some are passed onto the next generation that is capable of leading the business in terms of their experience, skills, traits, and behavior.

In Case 1, the respondent hails from the western part of Nigeria and has a master's degree. She inherited the business from her late husband and has been in charge for 20 years. Case 2, from the eastern part of Nigeria, has earned a bachelor's degree and has been involved in the welding and fabrication business for 5 years. She learned the skill from her late father and decided to set up the business with her husband. Case 3 is a single woman from the western part of Nigeria with a bachelor's degree, who inherited a 10-year-old hotel business from her father because she is an only child.

Cases 4–7 have secondary school leaving certificates. Case 4 inherited the transportation business from her husband. She is a widow with three children and has been operating the business for five years. Case 5, a divorced woman from the southern part of Nigeria, inherited her father's furniture business, which has been in existence for 18 years. Her brothers allowed her to assume the leadership role because of her devotion, expertise, and traits toward the business. Case 6, also from the southern part of Nigeria, decided to further her education to use the academic knowledge to improve her business. She inherited the business from her deceased elder brother, with whom she established the business 10 years ago. Case 7, who finished secondary school and gained experience from her father before he died, comes from the western part of Nigeria. She is single with a child and has been in the business for 10 years. Case 8 is a married woman who inherited the hotel business from her father. She has a bachelor's degree and has been running the business for 10 years.

Table 7.1. Profile of the Respondents.

Case Study	Description	Sample Details
Case 1	Currently operates a fuel filling station business in three branches across three Nigerian states: Delta, Bayelsa, and Port Hardcourt	60 years old 2nd generation Educational background: master's degree Founder: male Year founded: 2000 Number of employees: 15 Number of family member employees: 7
Case 2	Operates welding and fabrication business in Bayelsa state	45 years old 2nd generation Educational background: bachelor's degree Founder: male Year founded: 2015 Number of employees: 16 Number of family member employees: 10
Case 3	Operates a three-star hotel in Bayelsa state	45 years old 2nd generation Educational background: bachelor's degree Founder: male Year founded: 2010 Number of employees: 20 Number of family member employees: 15
Case 4	Operates a transportation business	40 years old 2nd generation Educational background: secondary school education Founder: male Year founded: 2015 Number of employees: 6 Number of family member employees: 6

(*Continued*)

Table 7.1. (*Continued*)

Case Study	Description	Sample Details
Case 5	Operates a furniture business	39 years old 2nd generation Educational background: secondary school education Founder: male Year founded: 2002 Number of employees: 30 Number of family member employees
Case 6	Sells electronics and electrical appliances	37 years old 2nd generation Educational background: secondary school education Founder: male Year founded: 2010 Number of employees: 4 Number of family member employees: 4
Case 7	Operates a gas, fuel, and kerosene filling station	47 years old 2nd generation Educational background: secondary school education Founder: male Year founded: 2010 Number of employees: 12 Number of family member employees: 10
Case 8	Operates a two-star hotel	48 years old 2nd generation Educational background: bachelor's degree Founder: male Year founded: 2010 Number of employees: 8 Number of family member employees: 8

The research data have revealed that Nigerian family firms led by women have considerable longevity, meaning they can exist for over 10 years. Family firms in Nigeria that have existed for more than five years are seen as large enterprises and can also be assessed from internal and external environmental factors. On average, these family firms have 4–20 employees, which include some family members as staff.

The research objective is to explore the motivation and challenges of female leaders in a male-dominated family firm. Therefore, the data were collected to answer the two research questions: (1) What motivates a female leader in a male-dominated family firm? (2) What challenges do female leaders face in a male-dominated family firm? The data reached saturation when the interview responses became repetitive.

In this study, several themes emerged. The dominant ones under the motivation for female leaders' involvement in a male-dominated family firm are possessing the required skills and capability, to develop a professional career and to provide quality of life. Their answers revealed the motives that provided them with the advantages and benefits that drove them to be involved in the family firm.

4.2. Experiences

4.2.1. Possessing the Required Skills and Capability for the Business

The women acknowledged the possession of experience attitude and behavior to engage in a leadership role. The women were taught by the business owner before passing on the business to them. Excerpts from different respondents stated:

> This job is very tedious and requires a lot of learning and mastering of skills. I wouldn't be running the headship of the business, if I didn't possess the experience for the business (Case 2).
>
> My father chose me because he trusts that I can manage the business profitably rather than my brothers who would rather waste the profit for his own personal gain (Case 3).
>
> Another response from Case 5 stated that "I was chosen to manage the business because of my good decision making and ability to take risks" (Case 5).

4.2.2. Developing a Professional Career

Another fundamental theme that is crucial in this study is the aspect of self or personal improvement in the business. Case 3 stated that she wasn't focused on the business for the sole of making a profit. She also saw herself as one who could provide professional solutions to other companies.

> I also wanted to leverage my corporate experience to help small business owners to build their sales, gain profit that could stand the test of time.
>
> I wanted to build a career for myself.

This is also expressed by being a consultant in the business:

> I want a career where people can come to me for advice on this business.

4.2.3. Quality of Life

Quality of life is the feeling of satisfaction that is associated with a job and life. Quality of life refers to the time and ability to engage in activities you love doing, expressed in the areas of being an innovator, trendsetter, flexibility, and better income.

Case 3 narrated how close she was to her grandfather. She didn't want to work for several hours when she wouldn't get the time to enjoy her earnings. She experienced a poor quality of life.

> When I lost my grandpa to stroke, it led me to redefine my life and think about the impact I want to create for myself. I didn't want to work for almost 14 hours in a day for someone else. I didn't want to sacrifice my quality of life so I decided to focus on the business.

4.2.4. Being an Innovator and a Trendsetter

Case 4 is realistic about setting an inspiration for other women. She believes she can change the traditional belief system that women are only wired for domestic purposes.

> She shared that; "I was a miserable housewife who wanted to show people that I wanted more out of life. I can just sit and think about some wonderful creative ideas and when I implement them, it manifests into something beautiful."

4.2.5. Work at My Own Time (Work Flexibility)

Case 1 exuded a relief of freedom from going to work every day and flexibility to focus on her own family firm and taking care of the kids. She stated almost the same scenario:

> I had a job that I would wake up around 5 am in the morning, prepare my kids for school before heading to work.

4.2.6. Higher-income and Independence

Case 2 narrated a scenario where she expressed her passion for independence and wanting to earn a better income.

> I had this deep sense of passion to make more money for myself and my children. I knew that If I continued with the salary-paid job I had, I would not have been able to send my kids to good schools and live comfortably.

4.3. Challenges that These Women Face in Managing the Family Firm

Three themes were formulated in viewing the challenges that women face in family firms. These are Glass ceiling effects which are expressed in the form of pervasive stereotypes of caregiving abilities. The second theme is the traditional role which was expressed in the area of societal expectations and belief about women's leadership abilities and lack of acceptance. The third theme is primogeniture which is expressed as incompetence and exhibiting an un-lady-like behavior.

4.3.1. Glass Ceiling Effect

This is expressed in the form of a pervasive stereotype of being a caregiver.

4.3.2. Pervasive Stereotype

There is a generalization about women being only caregivers and even if she decides to get a paid job outside being a mother, it shouldn't be something as big as taking the position of an executive in the company. This pervasive stereotype has occurred in the situation of Case 1 where her family members don't treat her with respect when she delegates. They would rather listen to her husband. This pervasive stereotype is observed when she is seen as domestic in nature meaning that women are only caregivers and should be treated as such.

Case 1 shared a story of how the challenge from the business shaped her life.

> It is so appalling to see that most men still think women should be domestic in nature. we shouldn't work, just sit at home and cater to the children. It sounds absurd in this day and age.

4.4. Traditional Roles

4.4.1. Societal Expectations and Beliefs About Women's Leadership Abilities

This societal expectation is expressed in terms of lack of acceptance, lack of financial and emotional support, incompetence, and unladylike behavior from the family of the participant. Ada's husband and his family have shown a lack of acceptance for my accomplishment.

4.4.2. Lack of Acceptance

Case 3 also said that she struggles with finding acceptance in owning the business.

> My father's brothers have tried to disinherit me from my father's property, and they don't take kindly to me managing this business as the head.

4.4.3. Lack of Financial and Emotional Support

Even Cases 5–8 shared that her husband's family are not in support of her running the business.

> I expect my husband's brothers to have sympathy on me to provide for my children. They went as far as taking me to court because of this business (Case 5).

4.4.4. Primogeniture

Primogeniture is the ideology or perspective that expresses women's underrepresentation in family firm and that men are preferable to women in leading or managing certain jobs or positions (Ahrens et al., 2015).

4.4.5. Incompetence

Case 1 experienced some comments from her staff in the company.

> I heard one of the men who works with me saying why should I be giving instructions on the job he knows better than I do. They think I am not cut out for this business because it is male-dominated.

4.4.6. Unlady-like Behavior

Expecting me to handle a smaller position in the office because he believes I am a woman, and I should tend to my children instead of the business. Case 8 expressed shock when her brother told her that she shouldn't be too involved in the business. She needed to take the back seat while he headed the company.

> Just focus on the children, you don't need to stress yourself for this business. You are a woman. This is a man's job; I can handle it better.

5. Discussion

This study has provided an understanding of the gender bias issues that Nigerian women face in assuming leadership roles in family firms. The objective of the study was to investigate the motivation and challenges of female involvement in male-dominated family firms. In response to this objective, research questions were posed to explore the experiences of these women. The research questions are: What motivates your involvement in the male-dominated family firm? What are the challenges you experience in running the business?

This study investigated eight women who come from different cultural backgrounds and work in various male-dominated industries. Their companies have been in existence for over 10 years, where they assume leadership roles. Four out of the eight participants have a bachelor's degree, and the other four have a secondary school certificate.

The first research question asked about their motive for involvement in the family firm. The responses describe the benefits or advantages derived from being a leader in the family firm. The participant responses are categorized into three themes: possessing the required skills and capability, developing a professional career, and improving the quality of life. The first theme involves possessing the skills, capabilities, and attitude for the business. This aligns with Daspite et al. (2016), who stated that when a female member of the family is included in the family firm, it allows them to make better decisions on the affairs of the firm because females can easily process and react to information while making decisions under risk. Possessing the right skills, like having an educational experience, is expressed in areas of formally or informally acquired skills and abilities over the years of learning the job.

According to Humphreys (2013), females usually emphasize their personal experiences on the job. The responses also reflect an attitude of confidence, intelligence, competence, and a "determination to prove myself." This is in accordance with Otten-Pappas (2013), who suggests that daughters expect their fathers to approve of their leadership and give them responsibilities similar to their brothers in managing the business. Aneke (2017) approved of the fact that skill-based training and delivery of managerial skills are essential in strengthening the entrepreneur and improving their business, which would bring out the attitude to outperform above the expectations of others. The second theme, developing a professional career, is in agreement with Akhmedova et al. (2019), who state that women are motivated to become more professional rather than just income earners. Gaining intrinsic motivation would lead women to enjoy their jobs or increase their satisfaction with the job.

The third theme, improving quality of life, expresses the participant's role in being an innovator, and trendsetter, and having flexibility in balancing work and family life, along with better income. This is in agreement with Vera and Dean (2005), who recognized some advantages for women working in the family firm, such as the hope and dream of devoting time to growing the family firm, the pride of carrying the family tradition, sharing family values, and the flexibility of dealing with children and husbands while devoting time to the business. Also, Ely and Padavic (2020) state that in family firms, there is a creation of human resources practices that provide resources and support for women to balance their work life with family life.

The second research question asks about the challenges experienced in running the business. Three themes were formulated in viewing the challenges that women face in family firms. These are the glass ceiling effect, traditional roles, and primogeniture. The first is the glass ceiling effect, expressed as pervasive stereotypes that assume the feminine role to be caregivers and hold insignificant/small positions in a company so that they don't get obstructed from their traditional roles given by society.

The second theme, traditional roles, is expressed as societal expectations about women's leadership abilities, which include the male's lack of acceptance, financial and emotional support, and their view that these women are incompetent and unladylike (aggressive behavior). These obstacles relate to a study by Martin (2001), who posits that the exclusion of women from managing the family firm is attributed to the traditional roles played by women as wives, mothers, and sisters. These roles are often more closely related to family roles rather than business roles.

The third theme, primogeniture, aligns with the research of Ganiyu et al. (2018), which states that women progressed to a certain level in their career before they were faced with glass ceiling issues like family-related issues, lack of supportive network mechanisms, cultural stereotypes, and religious convictions. Thus, the present study reveals the presence of gender bias in women's leadership in family firms.

6. Conclusion

This research has revealed a new study about women's leadership in Nigerian family firms. The primary purpose is to provide the researcher with the experiences of Nigerian women who are involved in the ownership, management, or leadership of male-dominated family firms. These women narrated their motivations and the challenges they experienced in the family firm.

The case presented in this research shows that the motivations for these women's involvement were possessing the required skills and capability, developing a professional career, and providing a quality of life. Their challenges faced included the glass ceiling effect, which is expressed in the form of pervasive stereotypes of caregiving abilities. The second theme is the traditional role, expressed in terms of societal expectations and beliefs about women's leadership abilities and lack of acceptance. The third theme is primogeniture, expressed as perceived incompetence and exhibiting unladylike behavior.

However, this study has some limitations that cannot be ignored. There is limited literature in Nigeria that promotes women's leadership in family firms, and only a handful of women are given the right of ownership in these businesses. Only eight cases in Nigeria were examined in the study, which brings another limitation. Therefore, the study cannot be generalized; it can only be used to deduce meaningful information about women's leadership in male-dominated family firms. Another limitation is that the study only focuses on women involved in male-dominated family firms and excludes other business areas.

The research contributes to Nigerian family firms where women are allowed to become owners or leaders. Therefore, this study has made several contributions; the main contribution of this chapter is that, to the best of the researcher's knowledge, this is the first study that has investigated female leaders in male-dominated Nigerian family firms. The managerial contribution of the chapter focuses on how family firms can improve women's career interests, create job satisfaction, and enhance the skills and experiences of Nigerian women. The practical contribution has several aspects. First, family firms should design programs to develop executive positions for women, such as creating mentorship programs. Second, given that female participation in family firms can lead to success, these businesses should increase women's involvement or encourage women to take on executive positions to move the business forward. There should be implementation of training programs, especially in the area of improving quality of life or work-life balance for women. Finally, the Nigerian government should adhere to the gender equality act that includes women in various careers and eliminates discrimination against women in certain jobs.

The government should also pay more attention to programs that assist in widening women's participation and increasing their knowledge, skills, and experience in male-dominated businesses, which can benefit the family and create the ability to cope with the challenges of the business. The whole family should be involved in the program so that they can be taught how to model positive behavior to assist women in business.

Further research can be conducted to expand the scope of the region and the business area. The issue of female involvement in other parts of Africa, or Africa as a whole, could be another area for further study.

References

Ahrens, J. P., Landmann, A., & Woywode, M. (2015). Gender preferences in the CEO successions of family firms: Family characteristics and human capital of the successor. *Journal of Family Business Strategy*, *6*(2), 86–103.

Akhmedova, A., Cavallotti, R., Marimon, F., & Campopiano, G. (2019). Daughters' careers in family business: Motivation types and family-specific barriers. *Journal of Family Business Strategy*, *11*(3), 100307.

Alex-Hart, B. (2016). *What's ethnicity got to do with it? The workplace lived experience of ethnic minority (Ijaw) women in the Nigerian civil service* [PhD thesis]. University of East London.

Amore, M. D., Garofalo, O., & Minichilli, A. (2014). Gender interactions within the family firm. *Management Science*, *60*(5), 1083–1097.

Aneke, E. O., Derera, E., & Bomani, M. (2017). An exploratory study of challenges faced by women entrepreneurs in the construction industry in South Africa. *International Journal of Business and Management Studies*, *9*(2), 35–51.

Astrachan, J. (2002). Editor's notes. *Family Business Review*, *15*(1), 23–47.

Bankole, A. O., & Adeyeri, D. A. (2014). Work schedule and family life of married women in the Nigerian banking industry: A study of selected banks in Lagos. *IFE Centre of Psychological Studies*, *12*, 6002–6015. http://www.ifepsychologia.org/

Bennedsen, M., Nielsen, K. M., Pérez-González, F., & Wolfenzon, D. (2007). Inside the family firm: The role of families in succession decisions and performance. *The Quarterly Journal of Economics*, *122*(2), 647–691.

Bettinelli, C., Del Bosco, B., & Giachino, C. (2019). Women on boards in family firms: What we know and what we need to know. In *The Palgrave handbook of heterogeneity among family firms* (pp. 201–228). Palgrave Macmillan. https://doi.org/10.1007/978-3-319-77676-7_9

Bianco, M., Ciavarella, A., & Signoretti, R. (2015). Women on corporate boards in Italy: The role of family connections. *Corporate Governance: An International Review*, *23*(2), 129–144.

Bjornberg, A., & Nicholson, N. (2007). The family climate scales – Development of a new measure for use in family business research. *Family Business Review*, *20*(3), 229–246.

Bøhren, Ø., & Staubo, S. (2014). Does mandatory gender balance work? Changing organizational form to avoid board upheaval. *Journal of Corporate Finance*, *28*, 152–168.

Business Standard Report. (2018). *Just around 25% of India's workforce is female, says McKinsey report*. https://wap.business-standard.com/article-amp/economy-policy/justaround-25-of-india-s-workforce-is-female-says-mckinseyreport-118062000034_1.html

Buttner, E. H. (2001). Examining female entrepreneurs' management style: An application of a relational frame. *Journal of Business Ethics*, *29*(3), 253–269.

Cadieux, L. (2007). Succession in small and medium-sized family businesses: Toward a typology of predecessor roles during and after instatement of the successor. *Family Business Review*, *20*(2), 95–109.

Campopiano, G., Rinaldi, F. R., Sciascia, S., & De Massis, A. (2019). Family and non-family women on the board of directors: Effects on corporate citizenship behavior in family-controlled fashion firms. *Journal of Cleaner Production*, *214*, 41–51.

Choi, S., & Park, C. (2014). Glass ceiling in Korean civil service: Analyzing barriers to omen's career advancement in the Korean government. *Public Personnel Management*, *43*(1), 118–139.

Curimbaba, F. (2002). The dynamics of women's roles as family business managers. *Family Business Review*, *15*(3), 239–252.

Daspite, J. J., Holt, D. T., Chrisman, J. J., & Long, R. G. (2016). Examining family firm succession from a social exchange perspective: A multiphase, multistakeholder review. *Family Business Review*, *29*(1), 44–64.

Dugan, A. M., Krone, S. P., LeCouvie, K., Pendergast, J. M., KenyonRouvinez, D. H., & Schuman, A. M. (2011). *A woman's place: The crucial roles of women in family business*. Macmillan.

Dumas, C. (1992). Integrating the daughter into family business management. *Entrepreneurship Theory and Practice*, *16*(4), 41–56.

Dumas, C. (2003). Understanding the father-daughter and the father-son dyads in family-owned businesses. *Family Business Review*, *2*(1), 23–33.

Durojaye, E., Okeke, B., & Adebanjo, A. (2014). Harmful cultural practices and gender equality in Nigeria. *Gender and Behaviour*, *12*, 6169–6181. http://www.ajol.info/index.php/gab

Eagly, A., & Johnson, B. (1990). Gender and leadership style: A meta-analysis. *Psychological Bulletin*, *108*, 233–256.

Eagly, A., Karau, S., & Makhajani, M. (1995). The science and politics of comparing women and men. *American Psychologist*, *50*(3), 145–158.

Ebohon, S. I. (2012). Feminizing development: The political sociology of female tokenism in the Nigerian project. *African and Asian Studies*, *11*, 410–443. https://doi.org/10.1163/15692108-12341242

Eddleston, K. A., & Sabil, G. (2019). Women in family firms: Unsung heroes of business-owning families. In V. L. Crittenden (Ed.), *Go-to-market strategies for women entrepreneurs* (pp. 185–194). Emerald Publishing. https://doi.org/10.1108/978-1-78973-289-420191023

Ely, R., & Padavic, I. (2020). What's really holding women back? It's not what most people think. *Harvard Business Review*, *98*(2), 58–67.

Family Firm Institute. (2017). *Global data points*. Family Firm Institute.

Filbeck, G., & Lee, S. (2000). Financial management techniques in family businesses. *Family Business Review*, *13*(3), 201–216.

Forbes. (2020). *Top 100 companies for diversity*. Forbes.

Gallucci, C., D'amato, A., & Santulli, R. (2015). Women on board of directors and firm performance: The moderating role of female ownership. Empirical evidence from the Italian wine industry. *Journal of Financial Management, Markets and Institutions*, *3*(2), 225–244.

Ganiyu, R. A., Oluwafemi, A., Ademola, A. A., & Olatunji, O. I. (2018). The glass ceiling conundrum: Illusory belief or barriers that impede women's career advancement in the workplace. *Journal of Evolutionary Studies in Business*, *3*(1), 137–166.

Glass, C., & Cook, A. (2016). Leading at the top: Understanding women's challenges above the glass ceiling. *The Leadership Quarterly*, *27*(1), 51–63.

Glover, J. L. (2014). Gender, power and succession in family farm business. *International Journal of Gender and Entrepreneurship*, *6*(3), 276–295.

Griffeth, R., Allen, D., & Barrett, R. (2006). Integration of family owned business succession with turnover and life cycle models: Development of a successor retention process model. *Human Resource Management Review*, *16*(4), 490–507.

Haberman, H., & Danes, S. (2007). Father-daughter and father-son family business management transfer comparison: Family FIRO model application. *Family Business Review*, *20*(2), 163–184.

Hacker, J., & Dowling, M. (2012). Succession in family firms: How to improve family satisfaction and family harmony. *International Journal of Entrepreneurship and Small Business*, *15*(1), 76–99.

Hisrich, R., & Fulop, G. (1997). Women entrepreneurs in family business: The Hungarian case. *Family Business Review*, *10*(3), 281–302.

Hoy, F., & Sharma, P. (2010). *Entrepreneurial family firms*. Pearson Prentice Hall.

Humphreys, M. M. (2013). Daughter succession: A predominance of human issues. *Journal of Family Business Management*, *3*(1), 24–44.

Jeong, S.-H., & Harrison, D. A. (2017). Glass breaking, strategy making, and value creating: Meta-analytic outcomes of women as CEOs and TMT members. *Academy of Management Journal*, *60*(4), 1219–1252.

Jimenez, R. M. (2009). Research on women in family firms' current status and future directions. *Family Business Review*, *22*(1), 53–64.

Kahkha, A. O., Kahrazeh, A., & Armesh, H. (2014). Corporate entrepreneurship and firm performance important role of small and medium enterprise. *International Journal of Academic Research in Business and Social Sciences*, *4*(6), 8–25. https://doi.org//10.6007/ijarbss/v4-i6/916

Keating, N., & Little, H. (1997). Choosing the successor in New Zealand family farms. *Family Business Review*, *10*(2), 157–171.

Kiaye, R. E., & Singh, A. M. (2013). The glass ceiling: A perspective of women working in Durban. *Gender in Management: An International Journal*, *28*(1), 28–42.

Kolade, O. J., & Kehinde, O. (2013). Glass ceiling and women career advancement: Evidence from Nigerian construction industry. *Iranian Journal of Management Studies*, *6*(1), 79–99.

Labaki, R. (2020). Research methods on emotions in family business. In *Handbook of qualitative research methods for family business* (pp. 351–388). Edward Elgar Publishing.

Lyngsie, J., & Foss, N. J. (2017). The more, the merrier? Women in top-management teams and entrepreneurship in established firms. *Strategic Management Journal*, *38*(3), 487–505.

Marshack, K. J. (1994). Copreneurs and dual-career couples: Are they different? *Entrepreneurship: Theory & Practice*, *19*(1), 49–69.

Martin, J. (2001). *Organizational culture: Mapping the terrain*. SAGE Publications.

Martin, L. (2001). More jobs for the boys? Succession planning in SMEs. *Women in Management Review*, *16*(5), 222–231.

Mcguinness, P. B., Vieito, J. P., & Wang, M. (2017). The role of board gender and foreign ownership in the CSR performance of Chinese listed firms. *Journal of Corporate Finance*, *42*, 75–99.

Mero-Daffe, A. (2011). *Survey of organizational development techniques*.

Moleong, L. J. (2013). *Metodologi Penelitian Kualitatif (Edisi Revisi)*. PT Remaja Rosdakarya.

Moore, D., & Buttner, E. (1997). *Women entrepreneurs: Moving beyond the glass ceiling*. Sage.

Nigeria, A. B., Olusanya, M., & Ajayi, O. (2018). *Entrepreneurship in Nigeria: Challenges and opportunities*.

Ntoimo, L. F. C., & Isiugo-Abanihe, U. (2014). Patriarchy and singlehood among women in Lagos, Nigeria. *Journal of Family Issues*, *35*, 1980–2008.

Oge, S., Karasoy, A., & Kara, O. (2014). A research on glass ceiling syndrome career barriers of women academics. *International Journal of Social, Behavioral, Educational, Economic, Business and Industrial Engineering*, *8*(9), 3011–3020.
Okonkwo, E. A. (2013). Attitude towards gender equality in South-Eastern Nigerian culture: Impact of gender and level of education. *IFE Center for Psychological Studies*, *11*, 5579–5585. http://www.ifepsychologia.org/content/gender-and-behaviour
Okoyeuzu, C. R., Obiamaka, P. E., & Onwumere, J. U. J. (2012). Shaping the Nigerian economy: The role of women. *Acta Universitatis Danubiuse, Œconomica [Danubiuse University, Economics]*, *8*(4), 15–24. http://journals.univ-danubius.ro/index.php/oeconomica/article/view/1093
Oliver, P. (2006). *Purposive sampling. The sage dictionary of social research methods* (pp. 244–245). Sage Publications.
Orozo-Collazos, C., Ratten, V., Dana, L.-P., & Ramadani, V. (2019). Entrepreneurial dynamics in family businesses. In V. Ratten, L.-P. Dana, & V. Ramadani (Eds.), *Entrepreneurship and Family Business* (pp. 123–145). Springer. https://doi.org/10.1007/978-3-030-12345-6_9
Otten-Pappas, D. (2013). The female perspective on family business successor commitment. *Journal of Family Business Management*, *3*(1), 8–23.
Qu, S. Q., & Dumay, J. (2011). The qualitative research interview. *Qualitative Research in Accounting & Management*, *8*(3), 238–264. https://doi.org/10.1108/11766091111162070
Owoyemi, O., & Olusanya, O. (2014). Org gender: A precursor for discriminating against women in paid employment in Nigeria. *American Journal of Business and Management*, *3*(1), 10–14.
Payne, G. T. (2020). Family business review in 2020: Focus on the family. *Family Business Review*, *33*(1), 6–9. https://doi.org/10.1177/0894486520904460.
Post, C., & Byron, K. (2015). Women on boards and firm financial performance: A meta-analysis. *Academy of Management Journal*, *58*(5), 1546–1571.
Powell, G. (1990). One more time: Do male and female managers differ? *Academy of Management Executive*, *4*(3), 68–75.
PwC. (2020). *PwC family business survey 2020*. PricewaterhouseCoopers.
Pyromalis, V., Kalkanteras, T., Rogdaki, M., & Sigalas, G. (2004). An integrated framework for testing the success of the family business succession process according to gender specificity. *Proceeding of the Academy of Family Business*, *2*(2), 1–6.
Ramadani, V., Fayolle, A., Gerguri, S., & Aliu, E. (2013). The succession issues in family firms: Evidence from Macedonia. *5th E-LAB international symposium of entrepreneurship on family entrepreneurship: A new field of research*. EM Lyon Business School.
Ramadani, V., & Hoy, F. (2015). Context and uniqueness of family businesses. In L. P. Dana & V. Ramadani (Eds.), *Family businesses in transition economies: Management, succession and internationalization* (pp. 5–37). Springer. https://doi.org/10.1007/978-3-319-14209-8_2
Rowley, J. (2012). Conducting research interviews. *Management Research Review*, *35*(3/4), 260–271.
Ryan, M. K., Haslam, S. A., Morgenroth, T., Rink, F., Stoker, J., & Peters, K. (2016). Getting on top of the glass cliff: Reviewing a decade of evidence, explanations, and impact. *The Leadership Quarterly*, *27*(3), 446–455.
Sabharwal, M. (2015). From glass ceiling to glass cliff: Women in senior executive service. *Journal of Public Administration Research and Theory*, *25*(2), 399–426.
Saldana, J. (2015). *The coding manual for qualitative researchers* (3rd ed.). SAGE Publications.
Samara, G., Jamali, D., & Lapeira, M. (2019). Why and how should SHE make her way into the family business boardroom? *Business Horizons*, *62*(1), 105–115.
Sampson, S. D., & Moore, L. L. (2008). Is there a glass ceiling for women in development? *Nonprofit Management and Leadership*, *18*(3), 321–339. https://doi.org/10.1002/nml.185

Schenkel, M. T., Yoo, S. S., & Kim, J. (2016). Not all created equal. Examining the impact of birth order and role identity among descendant CEO sons on family firm performance. *Family Business Review*, *29*(4), 380–400.

Schlepphorst, S., & Moog, P. (2014). Left in the dark: Family successors' requirement profiles in the family business succession process. *Journal of Family Business Strategy*, *5*(4), 358–371.

Schröder, E., Schmitt-Rodermund, E., & Arnaud, N. (2011). Career choice intentions of adolescents with a family business background. *Family Business Review*, *24*(4), 205–321.

Sever, H. (2016). The comparison of glass ceiling perception of employees working in public and private enterprises. *American Journal of Industrial and Business Management*, *6*, 577–588.

Sharma, S., & Kaur, R. (2019). Glass ceiling for women and its impact on women's career progression in the Indian service sector: The moderating role of family structure. *International Journal of Indian Culture and Business Management*, *18*(2), 235–250.

Skubis, I., Akahome, J., & Bijańska, J. (2023a). Green innovations in healthcare sector in Nigeria. *Scientific papers of Silesian University of Technology – Organization and management series* (No. 176). http://dx.doi.org/10.29119/1641-3466.2023.176.33

Skubis, I. Akahome, J., & Bijańska, J. (2023b). The brain drain syndrome and the role of responsible leadership in health care service organisation in Nigeria. *Scientific papers of Silesian University of Technology – Organization and management series* (No. 176). http://dx.doi.org/10.29119/1641-3466.2023.176.34

Skubis, I., Akahome, J., & Wodarski, K. (2023). Exploring the characteristics, motivation, challenges, and support system of female social entrepreneurs in Nigeria. *Scientific papers of Silesian University of Technology – Organization and management series* (No. 180, pp. 603–628).

Smith, M. (2007). *Women take charge of more family companies but face added hurdles* (pp. 1–2). Family Business, Caledonian Family Business Centre.

Stake, R. E. (2011). *Qualitative research: Studying how things work*. Guilford Press.

Vaismoradi, M., Turunen, H., & Bondas, T. (2015). Content analysis and thematic analysis: Implications for conducting a qualitative descriptive study. *Nursing & Health Sciences*, *15*(3), 398–405.

Vera, C., & Dean, M. (2005). An examination of the challenges daughters faces in family business succession. *Family Business Review*, *18*(4), 321–345.

Wang, C. (2010). Daughter exclusion in family business succession: A review of the literature. *Journal of Family and Economic Issues*, *31*(4), 475–484.

Williams, D. W., Zorn, M. L., Russell Crook, T., & Combs, J. G. (2013). Passing the torch: Factors influencing transgenerational intent in family firms. *Family Relations*, *62*(3), 415–428.

World Economic Forum. (2018). *The global gender gap report 2018*. World Economic Forum.

Xie, J., Nozawa, W., & Managi, S. (2020). The role of women on boards in corporate environmental strategy and financial performance: A global outlook. *Corporate Social Responsibility and Environmental Management*, *27*(5), 2044–2059.

Yildiz, S., Meydan, C., Taştan Boz, İ., & Sakal, Ö. (2019). Do the quota applications for women on boards improve financial performance? *Sustainability*, *11*(21), 5901.

Yin, R. K. (2017). *Case study research and applications: Design and methods* (6th ed.). SAGE Publications.

Chapter 8

Entrepreneurial Behaviour of Family Firms in the United Arab Emirates (UAE): Navigating Cultural Dynamics and Emerging Market Realities

Anushka Lydia Issac

Westford University College, United Arab Emirates

Abstract

This chapter thoroughly explores the intersection of family entrepreneurship, cultural dynamics, and emerging markets, with a specific focus on the United Arab Emirates (UAE). Examining the entrepreneurial behaviour of family firms, it delves into how these enterprises navigate cultural intricacies, seize emerging market opportunities, and contribute to local and global entrepreneurship ecosystems. The dynamic interplay between family dynamics and entrepreneurial pursuits is scrutinized, unravelling influences on resource allocation, succession planning, risk-taking, and innovation within UAE family firms. This exploration contributes valuable insights into the evolving landscape of family entrepreneurship, serving as a resource for researchers, policymakers, and practitioners. The research employs a comprehensive methodology involving case studies, shedding light on how these enterprises adapt, pivot, and exhibit resilience in response to the challenges and opportunities presented by emerging markets. Case studies provide valuable insights into the strategies employed by UAE family firms, contributing to a nuanced understanding of the evolving landscape of family entrepreneurship. This chapter serves as a valuable resource for researchers, policymakers, and practitioners seeking insights

Entrepreneurial Behaviour of Family Firms:
Perspectives on Emerging Economies, 161–181

Published under exclusive licence by Emerald Publishing Limited
doi:10.1108/978-1-83753-934-520241008

into the intricate interplay of family entrepreneurship, cultural dynamics, and emerging markets.

Keywords: Entrepreneurial behaviour; family firms; emerging markets; cross-cultural management and family firm resilience

1. Introduction

In the heart of the UAE, where business, culture, and markets converge, family-owned enterprises grapple with the intersection of tradition and innovation. This region, renowned for its forward-thinking approach, has positioned itself as a global hub for commerce and ingenuity, with family firms playing a pivotal role in the economic landscape (Government of Dubai, 2023; United Arab Emirates Government, 2023). This critical introduction sets the stage for a comprehensive exploration of the intricate relationship between family entrepreneurship, cultural influences, and the realities of a rapidly evolving market in the UAE. The UAE, a nation characterized by its forward-looking vision, has emerged as a global hub of commerce and innovation (Government of Dubai, 2023; Jabeen & Faisal, 2018; Kellermanns et al., 2008). A substantial segment of the economic fabric of the UAE is composed of family firms. These enterprises are profoundly rooted in cultural values while concurrently exhibiting a robust alignment with the intricacies of the contemporary business milieu (Krasus et al., 2011; Roveli et al., 2022). Situated at the juncture of tradition and innovation, these entities adeptly utilize their cultural underpinnings to navigate the intricacies inherent in emerging markets, showcasing a notable degree of adaptability (Kardos, 2012; Levinsohn, 2013).

This chapter centres on the question: 'How do cultural dynamics and emerging market realities influence the entrepreneurial behaviour of family firms in the UAE, and what strategies do these businesses employ to navigate and capitalize on these factors?' The inquiry aims to dissect the intricate relationship between cultural influences, the evolving market context, and the adaptive strategies deployed by family firms. In adopting a critical lens, the chapter endeavours to illuminate the symbiotic relationship between cultural dynamics and market realities, unravelling the strategies, challenges, and successes that define the entrepreneurial landscape (Denison et al., 2004; Krauss et al., 2023; Vracheva et al., 2019). The objective extends beyond mere documentation, seeking to elucidate how family firms harness cultural heritage for innovative purposes. It delves into the reconciliation of tradition with modernity, embracing change while safeguarding legacy, and leveraging cultural values to create economic and societal impact (Jasir et al., 2023; Krueger et al., 2021; Vracheva et al., 2019).

The UAE qualifies as an 'emerging economy' due to its rapid economic development, diversification efforts, and significant progress across various sectors.

The term 'emerging economy' is typically applied to nations undergoing rapid industrialization and experiencing substantial economic growth. In the UAE's case, strategic investments, ambitious infrastructure projects, and proactive economic policies contribute to its recognition as an emerging economy on the global stage. This status implies ongoing development, innovation, and adaptability, aligning with the themes explored in the entrepreneurial behaviour of family firms within the UAE.

1.1. Cultural Resonance as a Catalyst for Entrepreneurial Behaviour and Emerging Market Realities: The Nexus of Opportunity and Challenge

Culture, as an omnipresent force, exerts a profound influence on every facet of business operations within family enterprises. From decision-making processes to strategies for growth, the roots of these businesses intertwine closely with the cultural fabric of the UAE (Günzel-Jensen & Robinson, 2017; Romero-Galisteo et al., 2022). This interplay between culture and entrepreneurship is both intricate and intriguing, as family firms harmonize traditional values with the demands of a globalized economy. The notion of 'Filial Piety', where reverence for elders and familial harmony is paramount, shapes governance structures, succession planning, and risk-taking strategies within these enterprises (Jabeen & Faisal, 2018; Kellermanns et al., 2008).

The rapid ascension of the UAE as an emerging market has presented entrepreneurs with enticing opportunities on a global scale. However, this trajectory, particularly for family firms, is not without its challenges, as articulated by Arif Amiri, the CEO of DIFC Authority: 'Family firms are uniquely complex and require different services and handling than other types of businesses'. This insight, shared in an op-ed for Dubai-based Arabian Business magazine, emphasizes the distinctive nature of family enterprises (DIFC, 2023; Jasir et al., 2023; Samara, 2021). Navigating the uncharted terrain of a perpetually evolving market, these enterprises are compelled to deftly negotiate the complexities arising from regulatory frameworks, competitive landscapes, and technological disruptions. Confronted with the imperative of preserving cultural authenticity amid the pursuit of innovative strategies, family firms grapple with the dual challenge of remaining both relevant and competitive (Denison et al., 2004; Krueger et al., 2021).

Throughout this chapter, a diverse array of case studies is drawn upon to paint a comprehensive picture of family entrepreneurship in the UAE. The experiences of renowned family firms, the trajectories of emerging enterprises, and the perspectives of scholars converge to provide a holistic understanding of how these enterprises navigate the cultural and market currents that shape their journey (Denison et al., 2004; Krueger et al., 2021). The chapter seeks to contribute not only to academic discourse but also to the practical knowledge that informs the decisions of entrepreneurs, policymakers, and stakeholders invested in the evolving entrepreneurial landscape of the UAE (Bodolica et al., 2015; Jasir et al., 2023; Samara, 2021).

2. Cultural Foundations of Family Entrepreneurship in the UAE: Nurturing Innovation, Shaping Strategies, and Fostering Sustainable Growth

The domain of family entrepreneurship in the UAE manifests as a complex fabric intricately interwoven with cultural elements, fundamentally influencing the essence of these enterprises (Ang, 2018). In this critical analysis, we explore the profound impact exerted by cultural values, traditions, and societal norms on the entrepreneurial conduct of family firms in the UAE. It becomes evident that these enterprises transcend mere existence within the confines of the business sphere; rather, they are deeply entrenched in the cultural heritage of the region, drawing upon it as a source for driving innovation, shaping business strategies, and fostering sustainable growth (Ang, 2018; Chan, 2018). This contrasts with the often-short-term focus prevalent in Western business cultures. The concept of '*Barakah*', deeply ingrained in Emirati culture, encapsulates the belief in spiritual blessings that accompany the ethical accumulation of wealth. Family firms adopt strategies that reflect this belief, emphasizing responsible business practices and community involvement (Ang, 2018; Chan, 2018; Vracheva et al., 2019; Xie, 2022).

In the UAE, the symbiotic relationship between cultural values and economic pursuits is strikingly apparent in the realm of family entrepreneurship. While economic success is valued, it is often measured against the backdrop of cultural preservation and societal cohesion. Family firms understand the importance of contributing positively to their communities and adhering to cultural norms of benevolence and generosity. One of the most significant manifestations of this approach is the concept of 'Takaful', which translates to solidarity and mutual support. Family firms, such as the Al Nowais Group, channel their resources to support community initiatives, education, and healthcare projects (Abu Dhabi Media Office, 2024; Saadiya Ahmad, 2023; Shireena Al Nowais, 2022). This confluence of economic prosperity and cultural responsibility fosters an ecosystem where sustainable growth benefits both the enterprise and society at large.

Nevertheless, traversing the juncture of culture and entrepreneurship is not devoid of challenges. The swift modernization and cosmopolitan influences characterizing the UAE have introduced dynamics that occasionally pose challenges to traditional values. Family firms are confronted with the imperative of delicately balancing cultural authenticity with the imperatives of a globalized business environment (Dzenopoljac et al., 2022). Particularly in scenarios where cultural values intersect with gender dynamics, the adaptive response becomes paramount. While strides have been made in the UAE towards gender equality, certain enduring traditional expectations persist. Family firms are increasingly reassessing their structures and practices to ensure inclusivity while upholding cultural norms. The cultural underpinnings of family entrepreneurship in the UAE reveal a compelling narrative of innovation, strategic acumen, and sustainable growth. These enterprises are not passive recipients of cultural heritage; rather, they actively engage, utilizing their roots to imbue their ventures with authenticity, ethical considerations, and a forward-looking ethos (Ramadani et al., 2023). Negotiating the delicate path between tradition and progress, family firms in the UAE shed light on the potential of harmonizing cultural values with entrepreneurial aspirations. Their journey underscores the significance of culture as a facilitator, a catalyst, and a reservoir of resilience in shaping the trajectory of family entrepreneurship in the UAE and beyond.

3. Innovative Practices and Emerging Market Realities: Navigating UAE's Entrepreneurial Landscape

Within the dynamic economic landscape of the UAE, family firms play a dual role as custodians of cultural heritage and trailblazers of innovation. Operating in the context of an emerging market, these enterprises establish their distinctive position by spearheading innovative methodologies with implications extending beyond familial boundaries (Kargwell, 2015). This analytical discourse delves into the compelling narrative elucidating how family firms in the UAE strategically leverage their intrinsic familial networks, flexible organizational structures, and entrepreneurial mindset to adeptly navigate the intricate interplay of challenges and opportunities inherent in a dynamically evolving economic milieu (Ahmad et al., 2021; Kargwell, 2015).

The entrepreneurial stage in the UAE is distinguished by its unique cultural ethos – a multifaceted tapestry interweaving tradition, ambition, and cosmopolitan influences. Amidst this amalgamation, family firms assume the dual role of custodians preserving cultural continuity while simultaneously redefining the landscape of innovation (Ahmad et al., 2021). These enterprises discern that familial networks transcend mere social constructs; they are intricate matrices of interconnected relationships fostering resilience and innovation. Grounded in the Emirati concept of 'Al-Majlis', a traditional communal gathering space, family firms are adeptly incorporating ancient customs into contemporary business methodologies. These gatherings serve as platforms for knowledge exchange, deliberation on challenges, and collaborative problem-solving. The interchange of ideas within these familial networks frequently catalyses innovative approaches to address the exigencies of the market (Datta et al., 2020; De Man, 2022; Madichie & Gallant, 2012).

The Emirati concept of 'Al-Majlis' plays a pivotal role in shaping the entrepreneurial landscape of family firms in the UAE. This traditional gathering space holds cultural significance and is adapted by family firms into contemporary practices to foster resilience, innovation, and a sense of community. The 'Al-Majlis' gatherings are typically facilitated or moderated by a respected family member or an external facilitator with expertise in family firm dynamics. This ensures that discussions remain focussed, constructive, and aligned with the goals of the family and the business. 'Al-Majlis' gatherings are often organized regularly, providing a structured platform for family members involved in the business to come together. The frequency can vary based on the specific family traditions and business needs. These gatherings may take the form of formal meetings or informal discussions, creating an environment conducive to open dialogue. The gatherings are inclusive, encompassing family members across different generations and roles within the business. This inclusivity is essential for building a sense of unity, shared purpose, and collective responsibility. It allows for the involvement of both experienced elders and younger family members, fostering intergenerational learning.

The 'Al-Majlis' gatherings offer a range of benefits that contribute to the strength and resilience of family firms in the UAE. In the informal setting of 'Al-Majlis', experienced family members share valuable knowledge, wisdom, and practical insights gained over the years. This serves as a platform for the transfer of expertise to newer members entering the business, fostering a continuous learning environment. Family firms often rely on consensus-based decision-making. 'Al-Majlis' provides a dedicated space for open discussions where family members express their opinions, raise concerns, and collectively arrive at decisions aligned with the family's values and long-term vision for the business. During challenging times or crises, the familial networks established through 'Al-Majlis' become instrumental. The supportive environment and shared problem-solving approach cultivated in these gatherings enhance the family's ability to navigate difficult situations and make informed decisions. The exchange of ideas within the 'Al-Majlis' setting sparks innovation by combining traditional values with contemporary business practices. This adaptability allows family firms to respond effectively to changing market demands, technological advancements, and other dynamic factors that impact the business landscape. 'Al-Majlis' plays a significant role in reinforcing the cultural continuity of both the family and the business. It serves as a space where cultural values, customs, and rituals are not only celebrated but also integrated into the day-to-day operations of the business. This alignment with cultural ethos contributes to the distinctive identity of family firms in the UAE.

The inherent adaptability characteristic of family firms often situates them as vanguards in acclimating to emerging market dynamics. The UAE witnesses a landscape marked by swift transformations propelled by technological advancements, evolving consumer preferences, and global economic fluctuations (Datta et al., 2020; Madichie & Gallant, 2012). Unencumbered by intricate hierarchies, family firms demonstrate a proclivity for prompt responses to these shifts, employing agile strategies to capitalize on opportunities and mitigate risks. The illustrative case of the Jashanmal Group underscores this agility, particularly within the context of the retail sector disrupted by e-commerce. Leveraging an intimate understanding of the local market, the group recalibrated its business model by incorporating online platforms and optimizing its supply chain. This strategic manoeuvre not only preserved its competitive edge but also aligned with the familial values of adaptability and perseverance (Madichie & Gallant, 2012; Yasin & Khansari, 2022).

The entrepreneurial mindset is deeply ingrained in the fabric of family firms in the UAE, reflecting an inherent drive to explore unexplored territories, tap into untapped markets, and consistently innovate. This ethos transcends the confines of the business domain, resonating throughout the society they impact (Dutot & Van Horne, 2015; Tipu & Ryan, 2016). Evident in the pioneering spirit of these enterprises, their influence extends beyond immediate commercial interests. The evolution of the Thumbay Group, originating as a small clinic and expanding into a diverse conglomerate spanning healthcare, education, and research, exemplifies this trajectory (Bakhouche et al., 2020; Dutot & Van Horne, 2015). This expansion serves as a testament to their entrepreneurial resilience and dedication to addressing unmet societal needs. As family firms venture into opportunities beyond their primary competencies, they underscore their profound impact on diversifying the UAE's economy (Bakhouche et al., 2020; Xie, 2022).

In the realm of family-owned businesses, Gulf Marketing Group (GMG) exemplifies the imperative of innovation for competitiveness. With a diverse portfolio of international brands and homegrown concepts, GMG's documented vision, 'Innovate, Differentiate and Elevate to Be the Marketplace Leader', underscores their commitment to innovation. Mohammad A. Baker, highlighting the changing business landscape, emphasizes the need for retailers to adapt to new ways of doing business. In a context where costs are rising, physical boundaries are disappearing due to ubiquitous internet access, and retailers aim to align with global standards, GMG advocates a proactive approach to change the traditional retail model. This perspective aligns with their vision and positions innovation as a driving force in maintaining leadership in the marketplace (PwC, 2019).

3.1. Innovating Through Technology Adoption and Digital Transformation

Family firms in the UAE are actively leveraging technology adoption and digital transformation as integral components of their entrepreneurial strategies, aligning with the rapidly evolving business landscape. Abdullah Al Majdouie, Group President, and Vice Chairman, underscores the significance of industry expertise and staying at the forefront of developments to maintain competitiveness. He emphasizes,

> Businesses need to be more aware of the direction of their industries as it influences both bottom-down profit and top-line growth. We need to know where the sector is going in the next five to ten years, or we will fall behind. At Al Majdouie, we keep on top of developments and make plans of action. We are looking into the future, re-evaluate business models, and move ahead. (PwC, 2019)

This commitment to foresight and adaptability is reflected in the seamless integration of innovative technologies by family firms in the UAE. The adoption of e-commerce platforms has emerged as a strategic move, enabling these enterprises to extend their reach, adapt to evolving consumer preferences, and bolster their market presence (Dressler & Paunovic, 2021). Leveraging digital marketing tools and strategies, family firms are expanding their brand visibility. Social media, search engine optimization, and online advertising play pivotal roles in reaching and engaging with diverse audiences, both locally and globally. The adoption of data analytics tools allows family firms to gather and analyse relevant market information. This data-driven approach facilitates informed decision-making, helping them identify trends, understand customer behaviour, and optimize operational processes (Nambisan et al., 2019).

In the rapidly evolving landscape of family firms in the UAE, the imperative to navigate the digital future is unmistakable. It calls for the meticulous development of a digital strategy that not only embraces technological advancements but also aligns seamlessly with the unique ethos of family enterprises. Imad Abuizz, Partner and Middle East Technology Leader at PwC, emphasizes the essence of this journey, stating, 'Family firms need to develop a digital strategy that will carry them into the future' (PwC, 2019).

Family firms are incorporating automation and smart technologies into their operations. From smart manufacturing processes to automated inventory management systems, these innovations enhance efficiency, reduce costs, and contribute to overall business sustainability. As family firms digitize their operations, cybersecurity becomes a top priority. Implementing robust cybersecurity measures safeguards sensitive business information, customer data, and financial transactions, ensuring the trust and confidence of stakeholders. Some family firms actively engage with technology startups, fostering a culture of innovation. Collaborations and partnerships with startups bring fresh ideas and novel solutions, injecting entrepreneurial spirit into established family enterprises (Dressler & Paunovic, 2021; Nambisan et al., 2019). Recognizing the importance of continuous innovation, family firms allocate resources to research and development. This investment allows them to stay at the forefront of technological advancements, explore new markets, and diversify their product or service offerings. Embracing the principles of Industry 4.0, family firms are integrating smart technologies, the internet of things, and artificial intelligence into their manufacturing processes. This not only enhances production efficiency but also positions them as leaders in the era of digital industrialization.

4. Sustainability and Social Entrepreneurship: Weaving Impact into UAE's Family Firms

In the UAE, family firms find themselves at the juncture of tradition and progress, integrating cultural values with endeavours towards sustainable development and societal welfare. This scholarly exploration probes the intricate interplay between sustainability, social entrepreneurship, and the entrepreneurial pursuits of family firms in the UAE (Denison et al., 2004; Vracheva et al., 2019). Aligned with the UAE's steadfast commitment to sustainable practices and holistic societal progress, this examination elucidates how these enterprises intertwine their operations with lasting impact, concurrently contributing to the broader development goals of the UAE while pursuing entrepreneurial objectives (Denison et al., 2004; Krueger et al., 2021).

Integral to the ethos of family firms in the UAE is the acknowledgement that economic prosperity is intricately intertwined with environmental stewardship and social welfare. Serving as custodians of cultural values, these enterprises perceive their entrepreneurial endeavours as conduits for effecting meaningful change (Denison et al., 2004; Jasir et al., 2023). This perspective seamlessly aligns with the UAE's dedication to sustainability, exemplified by initiatives such as 'UAE Vision 2021' and the '2030 Agenda for Sustainable Development'. Family firms recognize their role transcends profit generation; they are pivotal in steering societal progress. The Al Ghurair Group provides a tangible example, having established the 'Awqaf & Minors Affairs Foundation'. By allocating a portion of profits to support education, healthcare, and community development, the Al Ghurair family exemplifies that the pursuit of profit and societal well-being need not be mutually exclusive (Ang, 2018; Chan, 2018; Vracheva et al., 2019; Xie, 2022).

The arid landscape of the UAE has prompted innovative sustainability practices with global resonance. Family firms, deeply rooted in the Emirati context, leverage their inherent ingenuity to contribute to this blueprint for progress (Ang, 2018). From renewable energy initiatives to water conservation strategies, these enterprises integrate sustainability into their operations, driven by a sense of responsibility to preserve the environment for future generations. The case of Masdar City serves as a paradigmatic illustration (Denison et al., 2004; Vracheva et al., 2019). Developed by the Mubadala Investment Company, this sustainable urban development project epitomizes innovation by amalgamating cutting-edge technologies with sustainable design principles. Through initiatives like Masdar City, family firms seamlessly intertwine their economic pursuits with environmental consciousness, setting a precedent for sustainable urban development in the region (Denison et al., 2004).

Social entrepreneurship is an inherent facet of family firms in the UAE, demonstrating an intrinsic capacity to identify societal gaps and address them with innovative solutions. These enterprises leverage their entrepreneurial acumen to forge connections between market opportunities and social impact, effectively contributing to the UAE's commitment to creating a better future for its citizens (Majumdar & Varadarajan, 2013). The establishment of the Al Ansari Exchange Charity Foundation by the Al Ansari family is illustrative of this entrepreneurial philanthropy. Leveraging the success of their financial services business, the family has created a platform to channel resources into impactful community projects spanning education, healthcare, and social empowerment (Jabeen et al., 2017). This integration of entrepreneurship and social impact echoes the UAE's call for sustainable and inclusive development.

UAE's family firms, propelled by cultural values and entrepreneurial spirit, profoundly enrich the nation's development agenda. These enterprises function not solely as economic engines but as critical contributors to the nation's social fabric (Al Matroushi et al., 2020). Their symbiotic relationship with the UAE's development goals propels them beyond traditional business boundaries, fostering collaborations and partnerships that catalyse societal progress. The Khalifa Fund for Enterprise Development stands as an exemplar of this collaborative spirit (Facchini et al., 2021). Founded by the Khalifa family, this initiative supports Emirati entrepreneurs, nurturing innovation and diversifying the economy. By doing so, family firms intertwine their resources and expertise with the UAE's strategic goals, fostering a vibrant ecosystem of innovation and economic growth (Khalifa & Dhiaf, 2016). Sustainability and social entrepreneurship have become integral components of the UAE's entrepreneurial narrative, intricately woven into the fabric of family firms. These enterprises serve as agents of positive change, not only generating economic value but also advancing societal well-being and environmental stewardship (Ahmed et al., 2018). As they navigate the dynamic landscape of the UAE, family firms resonate with the nation's aspirations, manifesting a harmonious integration of tradition, entrepreneurship, and sustainable progress. Their contributions echo the UAE's commitment to a future where prosperity transcends economic growth and embraces the holistic well-being of its people and planet (Kargwell, 2012; Saji, 2018).

5. Multigenerational Dynamics and Succession Planning: Navigating the Continuity of UAE's Family Firms

In the UAE, family firms occupy a distinctive realm where legacy and innovation intersect. This scholarly exploration delves into the intricate fabric of multigenerational dynamics and succession planning within UAE's family firms (Goby & Erogul, 2011; Kargwell, 2012; Saji, 2018). Functioning as custodians of cultural heritage and catalysts for economic growth, these enterprises grapple with the intricacies of transitioning leadership from one generation to the next while preserving their values and entrepreneurial ethos.

Family firms in the UAE transcend mere economic entities, embodying carriers of cultural legacies with values transcending generations. The transfer of leadership from one generation to the next entails a nuanced dance between conserving cultural heritage and accommodating the imperatives of contemporary entrepreneurship (Ahmed et al., 2018; Saji, 2018). This transition is guided by deeply ingrained values, such as 'Hemayah', representing the protection and safeguarding of family interests. The dynamic interplay of cultural continuity and generational change finds exemplification in the Al-Futtaim Group (Ahmed et al., 2018; Khalifa & Dhiaf, 2016). The transition of this conglomerate from a modest trading business to a diversified multinational corporation underscores the meticulous art of succession planning (Facchini et al., 2021; Khalifa & Dhiaf, 2016). By cultivating a culture of adaptability and continuous learning, the Al-Futtaim family ensures a seamless transformation that respects tradition while championing innovation (Al Matroushi et al., 2020; Facchini et al., 2021).

5.1. Cultural Intelligence in Global Markets: The Vital Asset for UAE's Family Firms

In the global landscape, cultural intelligence (CQ) emerges as a crucial asset that distinguishes successful family firms in the UAE. Going beyond basic cultural awareness, CQ entails the ability to adapt and navigate effectively within diverse cultural settings. Successful family enterprises recognize the importance of aligning strategies, products, and services with local norms and preferences (Randrianasolo et al., 2020). For instance, the Al Habtoor Group has showcased high CQ by tailoring its offerings in hospitality, real estate, and automotive sectors to meet the unique expectations of various international markets.

Effective cross-cultural communication is paramount for family firms operating globally. Entities like the Al Tayer Group, engaged in luxury retail and other sectors, prioritize open dialogue and value diverse perspectives to foster a workplace culture that transcends cultural barriers. Leveraging diversity for innovation is another hallmark of family firms with high CQ. The Al Jaber Group, spanning construction, energy, and infrastructure, benefits from a culturally diverse workforce, tapping into a rich pool of insights and approaches to drive innovation (Dangmei, 2016). Cultural sensitivity is crucial to avoid unintentional cultural faux pas in global operations. The Majid Al Futtaim Group, with a significant presence in various countries, maintains high CQ by tailoring its retail practices to respect local customs, religious observations, and social norms. Strategic talent management, reflecting a culturally diverse workforce, is a strategic aspect of CQ, as exemplified by the Easa Saleh Al Gurg Group (Dangmei, 2016; Randrianasolo et al., 2020). Intentional initiatives such as diversity and inclusion programmes, cross-cultural training, and the formation of multicultural teams contribute to embedding CQ in operational practices for family firms in the UAE. The outcomes of high CQ extend beyond individual business success. Family enterprises with elevated CQ not only thrive in global markets but also contribute to enhancing the UAE's reputation as a culturally adaptive and inclusive business hub. Their success stories underscore the symbiotic relationship between CQ, global competitiveness, and the preservation of the Emirati cultural identity.

5.2. Collaborative Endeavours: Family Firms and Societal Progress

Family firms in the UAE play a pivotal role in societal progress through strategic collaborations with governmental and non-governmental organizations. Beyond their economic contributions, these enterprises actively engage in partnerships that extend into the realms of education, healthcare, sustainability, and social empowerment. Such collaborations underscore the family firms' commitment to holistic development, aligning their efforts with the broader vision of the UAE. By forging meaningful alliances, these businesses become catalysts for positive change, leveraging their resources and influence to address pressing societal challenges and contribute to the advancement of the nation.

Al Ghurair Group and educational foundations. The Al Ghurair family, operating through the Al Ghurair Group, has established noteworthy collaborations with educational foundations, emphasizing their commitment to enhancing access to quality education. These collaborations extend to partnerships with governmental bodies and non-governmental organizations (NGOs) to establish scholarships, educational programmes, and infrastructure development (Eshtrefi, 2023; Zain & Kassim, 2012). The Al Ghurair Group's initiatives contribute significantly to the nation's human capital development, reflecting a strategic alignment with the broader educational goals of the UAE. By actively participating in educational initiatives, the family firm not only supports individual students but also plays a pivotal role in shaping the educational landscape of the country (Gamal & Hassan, 2021; Zain & Kassim, 2012).

Thumbay Group and healthcare initiatives. The Thumbay Group, originating as a small clinic, has demonstrated a strong commitment to addressing healthcare challenges through collaborations with governmental health authorities and non-profit organizations. Their initiatives span a wide spectrum, encompassing community health camps, partnerships for medical research, and infrastructure development (Crescent Enterprises, 2019; Jain, 2005). These efforts closely align with the UAE's vision for a healthy society, showcasing the Thumbay Group's dedication to contributing to public health outcomes. By actively engaging with healthcare initiatives, the family firm emerges as a key player in the advancement of the UAE's healthcare sector and the well-being of its citizens (Crescent Enterprises, 2019).

Majid Al Futtaim Group and sustainability organizations. The Majid Al Futtaim Group has strategically collaborated with governmental and non-governmental sustainability organizations to promote environmental consciousness. Through initiatives such as eco-friendly mall designs, waste reduction programmes, and the adoption of renewable energy, the group actively contributes to the UAE's sustainability goals (Gamal & Hassan, 2021; Sadiq & Gebba, 2022). By integrating sustainability practices into its business operations, the Majid Al Futtaim Group not only aligns with global environmental priorities but also positions itself as a responsible corporate entity that considers long-term environmental impacts in its decision-making processes (Sadiq & Gebba, 2022).

Al Habtoor Group and social empowerment. The Al Habtoor Group engages in impactful collaborations with governmental bodies and NGOs to spearhead community development programmes. These programmes, addressing initiatives for skill development, employment generation, and social empowerment, are intricately aligned with the UAE's vision for inclusive growth. Through these collaborations, the Al Habtoor Group demonstrates a commitment to social responsibility, actively participating in initiatives that contribute to the holistic development of communities and individuals within the UAE (Gamal & Hassan, 2021; Namaki, 2008).

Al Tayer Group and technology incubators. The Al Tayer Group has forged strategic collaborations with governmental innovation agencies and technology incubators to foster entrepreneurship and innovation. These partnerships encompass mentorship programmes, startup incubation initiatives, and joint ventures that contribute to the UAE's aspirations of becoming a global innovation hub. By actively supporting technology incubators and fostering innovation, the Al Tayer Group positions itself at the forefront of technological advancements, contributing to the country's economic diversification and knowledge-based economy (Dani, 2014; Schuette, 2013).

Jashanmal Group and disaster relief organizations. The Jashanmal Group exemplifies a commitment to social responsibility through active collaborations with governmental and non-governmental disaster relief organizations. In times of crises, such as natural disasters or pandemics, these collaborations enable swift and effective responses, showcasing the Jashanmal Group as a reliable pillar of support during challenging times. The family firm, through its involvement in disaster relief, underscores the importance of corporate social responsibility and community support in times of need (Gasparski Wojciech et al., 2011).

Al Ansari exchange and charitable foundations. The Al Ansari family, operating through the Al Ansari Exchange, forms impactful alliances with charitable foundations and governmental bodies to address pressing social issues. These collaborations span initiatives in education, healthcare, and community welfare, reflecting the family's commitment to philanthropy (Afghan, 2011). Through active participation in charitable initiatives, the Al Ansari Exchange contributes to the well-being of communities, emphasizing the role of family firms as agents of positive social change (Ansari, 2014; Dana et al., 2019).

Economic development partnerships. The Khalifa Fund for Enterprise Development plays a pivotal role in economic development by strategically collaborating with entrepreneurial families. Through avenues such as funding, mentorship, and collaborative projects, these partnerships contribute significantly to diversifying the economy and nurturing innovation (Sisodia et al., 2020). By actively supporting entrepreneurial families, the Khalifa Fund fosters a vibrant ecosystem that fuels economic growth and contributes to the realization of the UAE's economic diversification goals (Al Maainah, 2021).

The partnerships between family firms and governmental or non-governmental organizations in the UAE exemplify a commitment to societal progress that goes beyond profit-driven endeavours. Through collaborative initiatives, these businesses contribute to the nation's human capital development, promote a healthy society, advance environmental sustainability, and empower local communities. The impact of these collaborations extends far beyond immediate economic considerations, painting family firms as key players in fostering a socially responsible and inclusive society in the UAE. As they continue to forge alliances and engage in initiatives that transcend traditional business boundaries, family enterprises in the UAE solidify their role as active contributors to the broader well-being of the nation.

5.3. Balancing Tradition and Innovation

The intergenerational transition within family firms in the UAE inherently introduces a dynamic interplay between tradition and innovation, necessitating adept navigation to reconcile historical roots with forward-thinking strategies. Striking a delicate balance, these enterprises, exemplified by the Al Naboodah Group, a venerable entity with a 150-year history, adeptly integrate traditional craftsmanship and values into innovative pursuits within sectors such as construction and real estate. This seamless harmonization underscores their proficiency in managing the complexities inherent in multigenerational dynamics (Ahmad et al., 2021; Jabeen et al., 2017; Majumdar & Varadarajan, 2013).

Succession planning, beyond its logistical facets, emerges as a nuanced orchestration focussed on preserving the familial identity and vision. Recognizing the pivotal role of preparation for the next generation, exemplified by the Easa Saleh Al Gurg Group, family firms in the UAE prioritize equipping successors with requisite skills, values, and a forward-looking perspective. This commitment, manifested through education, professional development, and leadership nurturing, ensures a seamless intergenerational transition, where emerging leaders are poised to guide the enterprise into the future while upholding its historical legacy (Dutot & Van Horne, 2015; Tipu & Ryan, 2016).

Multigenerational dynamics are characterized by the transfer of wisdom and knowledge, extending beyond formal education to a lived experience. In the context of UAE's family firms, this exchange, exemplified by the entrepreneurial journey of the Al Tayer Group, becomes a catalyst for innovation and adaptability. Acknowledging the significance of learning across generations, the Al Tayer family, engaged in luxury fashion, automobiles, and real estate, leverages the synergy between digital fluency introduced by the younger generation and seasoned insights from the older generation. This collaborative approach results in an agile business model capable of thriving amid dynamic market shifts (Ang, 2018; Bakhouche et al., 2020; Chan, 2018; Dutot & Van Horne, 2015; Xie, 2022).

6. Globalization and Internationalization: Navigating the Expansive Horizons of UAE's Family Firms

In the dynamic economic milieu of the UAE, family firms concurrently function as custodians of cultural heritage and protagonists in the sphere of globalization. This analytical discourse delves into the intricate interplay between globalization and internationalization within the framework of family firms in the UAE. As these enterprises transcend geographical confines, they navigate the intricate dynamics of global markets while steadfastly upholding their local values, thereby contributing substantively to the nation's economic growth and global positioning (McCabe, 2001).

While often used interchangeably, globalization and internationalization encapsulate distinct dimensions that exert profound influences on family firms in the UAE. Globalization signifies the interconnectivity of economies and cultures, transcending geographical limitations, while internationalization pertains to the strategic expansion of business operations across borders (Anand, 2015). Together, these dynamics reshape family firms, propelling them into the global arena while scrutinizing their capacity to bridge cultural nuances.

Family firms in the UAE, deeply entrenched in cultural heritage, concurrently exhibit acute global vision. This distinctive synthesis positions them as global entities without compromising their cultural authenticity. Acknowledging that international market entry necessitates more than mere adaptation to new business practices, these enterprises emphasize strategic alignment between global aspirations and local values (Anand, 2015; McCabe, 2001; Tight, 2021). The Majid Al Futtaim Group, a multinational conglomerate rooted in the UAE, exemplifies this harmonious coexistence of global vision and local values. Through meticulous curation of shopping malls and entertainment complexes across various countries, the group strikes a balance between universal retail practices and culturally sensitive offerings. This exemplifies how globalization and internationalization converge to amplify the cultural essence of their brand while catering to diverse markets (McCabe, 2001; Tight, 2021).

Operating on a global scale necessitates heightened cultural competence extending beyond conventional market research. Family firms in the UAE recognize that global success hinges on an in-depth understanding of the cultural nuances shaping consumer behaviours, preferences, and business interactions. This awareness enables them to tailor their offerings to resonate with diverse clientele, irrespective of geographical distances (Anand, 2015; Tight, 2021). The Jumeirah Group's foray into international hospitality markets serves as an epitome of this cultural competence. Their luxury hotels seamlessly embody the ethos of Emirati hospitality while adeptly adapting to the distinct cultural expectations of each location. This harmonious integration of cultural sensitivity with international ambitions positions family firms to flourish in the global arena (Anand, 2015; Tight, 2021).

6.1. Challenges of Globalization: Homogenization Versus Differentiation

While globalization offers access to diverse markets, it concurrently presents the challenge of homogenization, requiring family firms to navigate a careful path to avoid dilution of their distinctive identity in the pursuit of global recognition. The nuanced task entails balancing alignment with global trends while preserving unique cultural attributes (Anand, 2015; McCabe, 2001). The narrative of the Al Shaya Group's venture into global retail serves as a case study illustrating this challenge. Through the introduction of renowned international brands to Middle Eastern markets, the group ensured that each outlet maintained its cultural authenticity, mitigating the risk of homogenization and fostering a loyal customer base appreciative of both global offerings and local sensibilities (Anand, 2015; McCabe, 2001).

The internationalization journey for family firms in the UAE transcends mere geographic expansion, evolving into a transformative journey that often catalyses innovation. Navigating unfamiliar markets compels these enterprises to embrace novel perspectives, engage in cross-cultural collaborations, and adapt their products and services to meet global standards. The global footprint of the Al Jaber Group, spanning construction, energy, and infrastructure, serves as an illustration of this innovation catalyst (McCabe, 2001; Tight, 2021). Undertaking large-scale projects worldwide exposed the group to diverse technological landscapes and industry practices, resulting in the cross-pollination of ideas, methodologies, and technologies that spurred innovation, benefiting both local and international ventures (Anand, 2015).

The expansion of family firms across borders extends beyond financial gains, fostering global networks that can be leveraged for local impact. These networks serve as conduits for knowledge exchange, partnership formation, and the infusion of best practices from around the world, amplifying the family firms' capacity to drive change beyond their immediate markets (Anand, 2015; McCabe, 2001). The international ventures of the Al Habtoor Group exemplify this multiplier effect, with global networks facilitating knowledge transfer that enriches local initiatives. This reciprocal exchange underscores how internationalization enhances not only economic growth but also the overall development of the UAE. In the narrative of UAE's family firms, globalization and internationalization emerge as intertwined narratives of expansion and cultural preservation (McCabe, 2001; Tight, 2021). These enterprises adeptly navigate the intricate global market landscape while upholding the essence of their cultural heritage. As they transcend borders, they serve as ambassadors of Emirati values, transcending cultural differences to leave a lasting impact on diverse global communities. UAE's family firms stand as a testament to the nation's prowess in bridging tradition and progress, enriching the global economy while safeguarding its unique cultural identity (Anand, 2015).

7. Challenges in Balancing Globalization and Cultural Authenticity: A Closer Look

Family firms in the UAE confront distinctive challenges at the crossroads of globalization and cultural authenticity, where the imperative for global expansion intersects with the need to safeguard their unique identity (Alkaabi & Ramadani, 2023). The pervasive risk of cultural dilution emerges as a common hurdle, with the potential pressure to conform to global norms threatening the Emirati cultural essence. For example, the Al Shaya Group encountered this challenge during its global retail expansion, necessitating meticulous brand management to strike a delicate balance between international appeal and local cultural sensitivity (Ramadani et al., 2023).

Adapting products or services to meet global standards while preserving cultural nuances poses another delicate task. Family firms entering the hospitality sector, such as the Jumeirah Group, grapple with the challenge of aligning their luxury offerings with international standards while ensuring the preservation of Emirati hospitality values. Furthermore, the struggle to balance alignment with global trends and the maintenance of local identity is particularly evident in family firms within the fashion industry, exemplified by luxury retail entities like the Al Tayer Group (Jokhio, 2023). They navigate the challenge of staying globally relevant in fashion trends while retaining the traditional elements that define their brands. Effective communication of a consistent global brand image while respecting cultural sensitivities demands nuanced strategies to avoid misconceptions about the brand's identity. This is especially pertinent for family firms engaged in media and entertainment, such as Majid Al Futtaim, which must carefully navigate content production to ensure global appeal without undermining local values (James et al., 2010).

While these challenges are complex, successful family firms have navigated them by employing strategic approaches. Examples include the Al Shaya Group's meticulous brand management strategies, emphasizing cultural sensitivity in marketing and in-store experiences. Similarly, the Jumeirah Group has prioritized hiring local staff and incorporating Emirati design elements in its international hotels to preserve the authenticity of its brand (James et al., 2010; Jokhio, 2023). Family firms overcoming these challenges often leverage thorough market research, and local talent in global operations, and engage in cross-cultural collaborations, not only preserving their cultural authenticity but also enhancing their global competitiveness.

8. Conclusion

The investigation into the entrepreneurial behaviour of family firms in the UAE has unveiled a complex tapestry interwoven with cultural resonance, innovative practices, multigenerational dynamics, sustainability, and global engagement. This chapter provides a comprehensive understanding of how family firms in the UAE navigate the intricacies of an emerging market while preserving their heritage and contributing to both national and global objectives (Kargwell, 2012; Saji, 2018). These family firms stand as noteworthy embodiments of cultural continuity and entrepreneurial innovation, serving as guiding beacons for businesses globally. The dynamic interplay between preserving ancestral values and pioneering new frontiers has elevated these enterprises to prominence, establishing them as essential pillars of the UAE's economic and cultural evolution (Al Matroushi et al., 2020; Facchini et al., 2021; Jabeen et al., 2017; Khalifa & Dhiaf, 2016).

From the microcosm of multigenerational dynamics to the macrocosm of globalization, family firms in the UAE epitomize a spectrum of traits redefining entrepreneurship. The chapter has elucidated how these enterprises leverage familial networks, agility, and entrepreneurial mindsets to pioneer innovative practices, enhancing their market positions. Their profound commitment to sustainability and societal well-being underscores their role as drivers of holistic development. The common thread weaving through these narratives is the symbiotic relationship between tradition and innovation (Ahmad et al., 2021; Kargwell, 2015; Majumdar & Varadarajan, 2013). UAE's family firms perceive tradition not as an impediment but as a catalyst for transformative growth. Their strategies resonate not only locally but also globally, showing that a robust foundation of cultural values is not a hindrance to internationalization but a catalyst for global impact. The entrepreneurial journey of UAE's family firms is intertwined with the nation's broader development agenda. These enterprises act as agents of change, aligning their operations with the UAE's strategic objectives to foster economic diversification, inclusivity, and sustainability (Datta et al., 2020; Madichie & Gallant, 2012; Yasin & Khansari, 2022). By navigating the delicate balance of cultural preservation and the demands of an interconnected world, they contribute significantly to the nation's global standing.

As the UAE progresses towards an increasingly interconnected future, this chapter's exploration of family entrepreneurship serves as a guiding compass. The insights gleaned from the intersection of culture, innovation, multigenerational dynamics, sustainability, and globalization offer a roadmap applicable to businesses worldwide. The family firms in the UAE encapsulate the nation's adeptness at harmonizing its rich cultural heritage with the dynamic palette of modern entrepreneurship (Ang, 2018; Bakhouche et al., 2020; Chan, 2018; Xie, 2022). The entrepreneurial behaviour of these family firms in the UAE stands as a testament to the nation's resilience, adaptability, and visionary approach. Beyond being economic entities, these enterprises serve as narrators of a cultural legacy, innovators, and promoters of progress (Denison et al., 2004; Krueger et al., 2021). As they continue navigating the evolving landscape of the UAE's entrepreneurial ecosystem, they illuminate a trajectory that seamlessly blends the past with the future, transcending boundaries, and inspiring future generations.

References

Abu Dhabi Media Office. (2024, March 8). *M42 launches dedicated women's preventive health clinic Laha Wellness Hub*.https://www.mediaoffice.abudhabi/en/health/m42-lau

Afghan, N. (2011). Succession in family businesses: Kinship culture and Islamic law of inheritance. *Business Review*, *6*(2), 104–118. https://doi.org/10.54784/1990-6587.1197

Ahmad, S. F., Hermayen, A., & Bhavani, G. (2021). Knowledge discovery in surveys using machine learning: A case study of women in entrepreneurship in UAE (pp. 514–518).

2021 International conference on computational intelligence and knowledge economy (ICCIKE). https://doi.org/10.1109/ICCIKE51210.2021.9410798

Ahmed, G., Amponsah, C. T., & Deasi, S. S. (2018). Exploring the dynamics of women entrepreneurship: A case study of UAE. *International Journal of Business & Applied Sciences*, *7*(3), 2471–8858.

Al Maainah, K. (2021). *Multiple perspectives of a knowledge-based innovation ecosystem: The case of Khalifa Fund for enterprise development in the UAE*. Salford Business School.

Al Matroushi, H., Jabeen, F., Matloub, A., & Tehsin, M. (2020). Push and pull model of women entrepreneurship: Empirical evidence from the UAE. *Journal of Islamic Accounting and Business Research*, *11*(3), 588–609. https://doi.org/10.1108/JIABR-02-2017-0020

Anand, B. (2015). Reverse globalization by internationalization of SME's: Opportunities and challenges ahead. *Procedia – Social and Behavioral Sciences*, *195*, 1003–1011. https://doi.org/10.1016/j.sbspro.2015.06.359

Ang, J. (2018). Cultural heritage and innovation. *Buletin Ekonomi Moneter Dan Perbankan*, *21*(2), 142–148. https://doi.org/10.21098/bemp.v21i1.961

Ansari, I. F. (2014). The CEO succession decision in listed family firms [Degree of Doctor of Philosophy]. In *School Accounting & Finance Section*. Cardiff Business School.

Bakhouche, A., Elchaar, R., & Emam, M. (2020). *Survey of financing options and key challenges faced by SMEs in the UAE* (pp. 115–145). IGI Global. https://doi.org/10.4018/978-1-5225-9377-5.ch006

Bodolica, V., Spraggon, M., & Zaidi, S. (2015). Boundary management strategies for governing family firms: A UAE-based case study. *Journal of Business Research*, *68*(3), 684–693. https://doi.org/10.1016/j.jbusres.2014.08.003

Chan, C. S. C. (2018). Sustainability of indigenous folk tales, music and cultural heritage through innovation. *Journal of Cultural Heritage Management and Sustainable Development*, *8*(3), 342–361. https://doi.org/10.1108/JCHMSD-06-2017-0044

Crescent Enterprises. (2019). *Resilience in diversity*. https://www.crescententerprises.com/media/annual-and-sustainability-report-2019-2020.pdf

Dangmei, J. (2016). *Cultural intelligence: Bridging the cultural differences in the emerging markets*. http://ssrn.com/abstract=2847336

Dani, S. (2014). Middle East retail: Fostering growth despite challenges. *International Journal of Management and Social Sciences Research (IJMSSR)*, *3*(4), 41–47. https://www.researchgate.net/publication/324676612

Datta, K. S., Adkins, O., & Fitzsimmons, J. R. (2020). *Entrepreneurship and social media influencers in an Islamic context* (pp. 121–139). Springer. https://doi.org/10.1007/978-3-030-43453-3_7

De Man, A. (2022). Two pre-Islamic places of worship in the tourism landscape of the UAE. *Religions*, *13*(8), 715. https://doi.org/10.3390/rel13080715

Denison, D., Lief, C., & Ward, J. L. (2004). Culture in family-owned enterprises: Recognizing and leveraging unique strengths. *Family Business Review*, *17*(1), 61–70. https://doi.org/10.1111/j.1741-6248.2004.00004.x

DIFC. (2023, July 17). *Family businesses are on the rise in Dubai: here's why*. https://www.difc.ae/whats-on/blogs/family-businesses-are-rise-dubai-heres-why

Dressler, M., & Paunovic, I. (2021). Sensing technologies, roles and technology adoption strategies for digital transformation of grape harvesting in SME wineries. *Journal of Open Innovation: Technology, Market, and Complexity*, *7*(2), 123. https://doi.org/10.3390/joitmc7020123

Dutot, V., & Van Horne, C. (2015). Digital entrepreneurship intention in a developed vs. emerging country: An exploratory study in France and the UAE. *Transnational Corporations Review*, *7*(1), 79–96. https://doi.org/10.5148/tncr.2015.7105

Dzenopoljac, V., Gërguri-Rashiti, S., Ramadani, V., & Dana, L.-P. (2022). *The context for business in Kuwait* (pp. 259–275). World Scientific. https://doi.org/10.1142/9789811229695_0012

Eshtrefi, L. (2023). *Family business in the United Arab Emirates* (pp. 121–141). Springer. https://doi.org/10.1007/978-3-031-17262-5_7

Facchini, F., Jaeck, L., & Bouhaddioui, C. (2021). Culture and entrepreneurship in the United Arab Emirates. *Journal of the Knowledge Economy*, *12*(3), 1245–1269. https://doi.org/10.1007/s13132-020-00663-z

Gamal, S., & Hassan, S. (2021). *Family business in Egypt-planning, advantages and disadvantages, problems solving for expanding and challenges.*

Gasparski Wojciech, W., Kwiatkowski, S., & Ryan Leo, V. (2011). Towards an understanding of Islam and Muslim entrepreneurship in the Middle East. In *Entrepreneurship: Values and Responsibility* (Vol. 1). Routledge.

Goby, V. P., & Erogul, M. S. (2011). Female entrepreneurship in the United Arab Emirates: Legislative encouragements and cultural constraints. *Women's Studies International Forum*, *34*(4), 329–334. https://doi.org/10.1016/j.wsif.2011.04.006

Government of Dubai. (2023, April 3). *Mohammed Bin Rashid launches strategy to transform Dubai into World's creative economic capital*. https://mediaoffice.ae/en/news/2021/April/03-04/Mohammed-Bin-Rashid-Launches-Strategy-to-Transform-Dubai-into-Worlds-Creative-Economic-Capital

Günzel-Jensen, F., & Robinson, S. (2017). Effectuation in the undergraduate classroom: Three barriers to entrepreneurial learning. *Education + Training*, *59*(7/8), 780–796. https://doi.org/10.1108/ET-03-2016-0049

Jabeen, F., & Faisal, M. N. (2018). Imperatives for improving entrepreneurial behavior among females in the UAE. *Gender in Management: An International Journal*, *33*(3), 234–252. https://doi.org/10.1108/GM-03-2016-0042

Jabeen, F., Faisal, M. N., & Katsioloudes, M. (2017). Entrepreneurial mindset and the role of universities as strategic drivers of entrepreneurship. *Journal of Small Business and Enterprise Development*, *24*(1), 136–157. https://doi.org/10.1108/JSBED-07-2016-0117

Jain, P. C. (2005). Indian entrepreneurs in the Gulf countries: Some case studies. *India Quarterly: A Journal of International Affairs*, *61*(4), 123–142. https://doi.org/10.1177/097492840506100405

James, U., Nhan, T. V., & Phung, N. (2010). *"Real Culture" preservation, authenticity, and change in Hoi An's heritage tourism industry "Real Culture" preservation, authenticity, and change in Hoi An's heritage tourism industry*. https://digitalcollections.sit.edu/isp_collection

Jasir, M., Khan, N. U., & Barghathi, Y. (2023). Stewardship theory of corporate governance and succession planning in family businesses of UAE: Views of the owners. *Qualitative Research in Financial Markets*, *15*(2), 278–295. https://doi.org/10.1108/QRFM-08-2021-0135

Jokhio, E. Z. (2023). *Cultural diversity in a globalized world: Navigating interconnected realities*. https://ssrn.com/abstract=4589308

Kardos, M. (2012). The relationship between entrepreneurship, innovation and sustainable development. Research on European Union countries. *Procedia Economics and Finance*, *3*, 1030–1035. https://doi.org/10.1016/S2212-5671(12)00269-9

Kargwell, S. A. (2012). A comparative study on gender and entrepreneurship development: Still a male's world within UAE cultural context. *International Journal of Business and Social Science*, *3*(6), 44–55.

Kargwell, S. A. (2015). Landscaping of emerging women entrepreneurs in the MENA countries: Activities, obstacles, and empowerment. *International Journal of Business and Social Science*, *6*(2), 222–232. www.ijbssnet.com

Kellermanns, F. W., Eddleston, K. A., Barnett, T., & Pearson, A. (2008). An exploratory study of family member characteristics and involvement: Effects on entrepreneurial behavior in the family firm. *Family Business Review*, *21*(1), 1–14. https://doi.org/10.1111/j.1741-6248.2007.00107.x

Khalifa, A. H., & Dhiaf, M. M. (2016). The impact of entrepreneurship education on entrepreneurial intention: The UAE context. *Polish Journal of Management Studies, 14*(1), 119–128. https://doi.org/10.17512/pjms.2016.14.1.11

Krueger, N., Bogers, M. L. A. M., Labaki, R., & Basco, R. (2021). Advancing family business science through context theorizing: The case of the Arab world. *Journal of Family Business Strategy, 12*(1), 100377. https://doi.org/10.1016/j.jfbs.2020.100377

Levinsohn, D. (2013). Disembedded and beheaded? – A critical review of the emerging field of sustainability entrepreneurship. *International Journal of Entrepreneurship and Small Business, 19*(2), 190. https://doi.org/10.1504/IJESB.2013.054963

Madichie, N. O., & Gallant, M. (2012). Broken silence: A commentary on women's entrepreneurship in the United Arab Emirates. *The International Journal of Entrepreneurship and Innovation, 13*(2), 81–92. https://doi.org/10.5367/ijei.2012.0071

Majumdar, S., & Varadarajan, D. (2013). Students' attitude towards entrepreneurship: Does gender matter in the UAE? *Foresight, 15*(4), 278–293. https://doi.org/10.1108/FS-03-2012-0011

McCabe, L. T. (2001). Globalization and internationalization: The impact on education abroad programs. *Journal of Studies in International Education, 5*(2), 138–145. https://doi.org/10.1177/102831530152004

Namaki, M. S. S. El. (2008). Strategic behavior. In *Strategy and entrepreneurship in Arab countries* (pp. 155–170). Palgrave Macmillan UK. https://doi.org/10.1057/9780230288652_8

Nambisan, S., Wright, M., & Feldman, M. (2019). The digital transformation of innovation and entrepreneurship: Progress, challenges and key themes. *Research Policy, 48*(8), 103773. https://doi.org/10.1016/j.respol.2019.03.018

PwC. (2019). *Future-proofing Middle East family businesses*. https://www.pwc.com/m1/en/publications/documents/family-business-survey-2019.pdf

Ramadani, V., Dzenopoljac, V., Zainal, M., & Dzenopoljac, A. (2023). *Family business in Kuwait* (pp. 33–51). Springer International Publishing. https://doi.org/10.1007/978-3-031-17262-5_3

Randrianasolo, A., Semenov, A., Arnold, M., & Reynolds, K. (2020). A model of cultural intelligence and global identity. *Journal of Consumer Marketing, 37*(7), 821–832. https://doi.org/10.1108/JCM-05-2019-3244

Romero-Galisteo, R. P., González-Sánchez, M., Gálvez-Ruiz, P., Palomo-Carrión, R., Casuso-Holgado, M. J., & Pinero-Pinto, E. (2022). Entrepreneurial intention, expectations of success and self-efficacy in undergraduate students of health sciences. *BMC Medical Education, 22*(1), 1–7. https://doi.org/10.1186/s12909-022-03731-x

Saadiya Ahmad. (2023, August 10). *The healthcare industry in the Middle East: Challenges and opportunities*. Arabian News.

Sadiq, M., & Gebba, T. R. A. (2022). Financial performance, firm value, transparency and corporate governance. Evidences from family-owned business in UAE. *Transnational Corporations Review, 14*(3), 286–296. https://doi.org/10.1080/19186444.2021.1938496

Saji, B. S. (2018). Effectiveness of innovation and entrepreneurship education in UAE higher education. *Academy of Strategic Management Journal, 17*(4), 1–10.

Samara, G. (2021). Family businesses in the Arab Middle East: What do we know and where should we go? *Journal of Family Business Strategy, 12*(3), 100359. https://doi.org/10.1016/j.jfbs.2020.100359

Schuette, L. (2013). *Process optimization with the Six Sigma DMAIC approach using the example Danzas AEI Emirates LLC (Deutsche Post DHL Group) (Project)*. https://repositorio.iscte-iul.pt/handle/10071/5960

Shireena Al Nowais. (2022, September 21). *Abu Dhabi's Ma'an receives Dh480 million in donations to support social initiatives*. National News.

Sisodia, G. S., Awad, E., Alkhoja, H., & Sergi, B. S. (2020). Strategic business risk evaluation for sustainable energy investment and stakeholder engagement: A proposal for energy policy development in the Middle East through Khalifa funding and land subsidies. *Business Strategy and the Environment*, *29*(6), 2789–2802. https://doi.org/10.1002/bse.2543

Tight, M. (2021). Globalization and internationalization as frameworks for higher education research. *Research Papers in Education*, *36*(1), 52–74. https://doi.org/10.1080/02671522.2019.1633560

Tipu, S. A. A., & Ryan, J. C. (2016). Predicting entrepreneurial intentions from work values. *Management Decision*, *54*(3), 610–629. https://doi.org/10.1108/MD-09-2015-0387

United Arab Emirates Government. (2023). *Dubai creative economy strategy*. https://u.ae/en/about-the-uae/strategies-initiatives-and-awards/strategies-plans-and-visions/finance-and-economy/Dubai-Creative-Economy-Strategy

Vracheva, V. P., Abu-Rahma, A., & Jacques, P. (2019). Effects of context on the entrepreneurial intent of female students from the United Arab Emirates. *Education + Training*, *61*(6), 700–717. https://doi.org/10.1108/ET-01-2018-0014

Xie, J. (2022). Innovative design of artificial intelligence in intangible cultural heritage. *Scientific Programming*, *2022*, 1–8. https://doi.org/10.1155/2022/6913046

Yasin, N., & Khansari, Z. (2022). Exploring the enterprise landscape for business incubators in the UAE. In D. Hyams-Ssekasi & F. Agboma (Eds.), *Entrepreneurship and change* (pp. 191–208). Springer International Publishing. https://doi.org/10.1007/978-3-031-07139-3_8

Zain, M., & Kassim, N. M. (2012). Strategies of family businesses in a newly globalized developing economy. *Journal of Family Business Management*, *2*(2), 147–165. https://doi.org/10.1108/20436231211261880

Chapter 9

A Conceptual Model for Exploring Innovation in Family Firms: Integration of Socio-emotional Wealth and Resource-based Theory Perspectives

Shweta Dewangan[a], Sanjeev Kumar[b], Pyali Chatterjee[a] and Ankit Dhiraj[b]

[a]*ICFAI University, India*
[b]*Lovely Professional University Punjab, India*

Abstract

The socio-emotional wealth (SEW) framework and the resource-based theory (RBT) offer two valuable perspectives on innovation dynamics within family firms. Through the SEW lens, family firms may prioritize preserving their traditions and core values, potentially resisting the adoption of new technologies and modern business methods. In contrast, RBT suggests that family firms can gain a competitive edge by harnessing and nurturing their unique resources and capabilities, such as collective experiences, market reputation, and established networks, to foster innovation and secure a strong market position. By integrating these two perspectives, family firms can achieve sustainable competitive advantages by balancing the tensions between tradition and innovation. This comprehensive approach allows them to innovate while preserving their SEW, ensuring long-term success in the ever-evolving business landscape.

Keywords: SEW; RBT; family business; innovation dynamics; competitive advantage

Entrepreneurial Behaviour of Family Firms:
Perspectives on Emerging Economies, 183–205

Published under exclusive licence by Emerald Publishing Limited
doi:10.1108/978-1-83753-934-520241009

1. Introduction

Family firms have always occupied a special place in the expansive realm of business research. They are not only economic entities but are deeply intertwined with a family unit's emotions, traditions, and dynamics. Given their unique position, they sometimes approach business strategies differently than non-family firms, particularly innovation. This confluence of practice and the need for novelty makes studying innovation in family firms riveting (Yazici et al., 2023).

This chapter introduces a theoretical framework to understand the intricacies and underlying mechanisms driving innovation in family firms (Schillaci et al., 2013). The main objectives of this chapter are the following: to explore the influence of SEW in defining the innovation strategies of family firms, to evaluate the ways in which family-specific assets and skills impact innovation in family firms, to examine how RBT and SEW preservation interact to influence innovation outcomes, and to determine useful ramifications and suggestions for encouraging innovation in family firms while safeguarding their distinct socio-emotional riches.

Small sole-proprietor's firms and large firms run from one owner to another (Fig. 9.1). Today's generation families in large groups perform more within the stipulated time, and family members contribute more efficiently. The dual nature of family and business systems operating in tandem is at the core of family firms. Each method has values, priorities, and goals that can sometimes conflict but synergize unexpectedly. For example, while the business system may prioritize profit and growth, the family system might emphasize stability and legacy (Haynes et al., 2021). This duality creates a unique innovation environment, with enabling and constraining forces at play.

SEW refers to the non-financial aspects of the business that provide emotional value and satisfaction to the family members. It encompasses elements like family identity, binding ties, and emotional attachment. SEW can influence innovation in two ways: (a) *conservatism:* high SEW may lead to risk aversion as families seek to preserve their legacy and status quo. It might hinder radical innovations but can lead to sustained incremental innovations, building on existing capabilities; (b) *commitment:* the emotional attachment can also lead to long-term commitment and perseverance in innovation, even in the face of initial failures or slow results (Rodrigues et al., 2023).

Generational transitions are pivotal moments in family firms. New generations bring fresh perspectives, skills, and a willingness to adopt newer technologies or

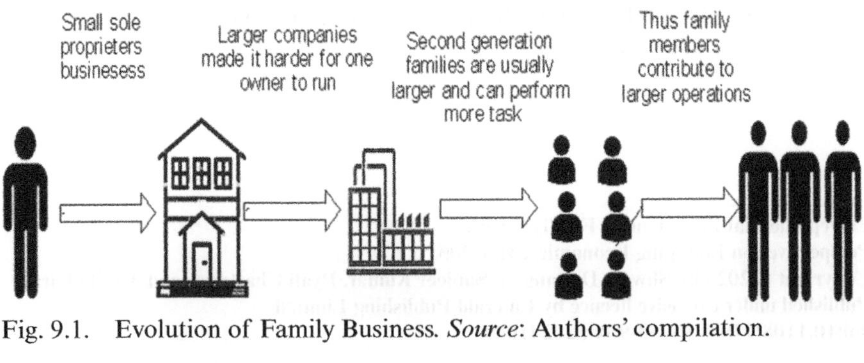

Fig. 9.1. Evolution of Family Business. *Source*: Authors' compilation.

business models. The interplay between the incumbent and the successor generation shapes the innovation trajectory (Hillebrand, 2019).

Family firms do not operate in a vacuum. The cultural, social, and economic environment can shape their innovation behaviour. For instance, in cultures that value tradition, family firms might be more conservative, while in cultures that encourage entrepreneurial risk-taking, family firms might be more innovation-driven (James et al., 2021).

Furthermore, the governance structure, including the role of the board, the involvement of external members, and the decision-making process, can significantly impact innovation. A diverse panel including non-family members might bring varied perspectives, leading to a richer innovation ecosystem (Guimarães et al., 2023; Parada et al., 2020).

2. SEW and RBT Foundations

Family business focus area and their contributions are presented in Fig. 9.2. According to the data provided there, 39% show long-term viability, and 65% bring more innovations and development with the latest trends in the family business. The total contribution of advancement and digital transformation is 80% and 82% business extension in future prospects (Times of India, 2022). The nexus between family firms and their innovative strategic behaviours can be better understood when we integrate two dominant theoretical perspectives, SEW and RBT. This combined lens provides a holistic view of the driving forces behind strategic decisions in family firms.

SEW emphasizes the non-financial utilities that family members derive from the firm, such as identity, influence, and the ability to maintain family bonds. These emotional aspects can significantly influence the firm's strategic direction and risk appetite. RBT postulates that firms achieve and sustain competitive advantage by deploying unique, valuable, inimitable, and non-substitutable resources and capabilities. This perspective often explains why some firms outperform others based on their internal resources.

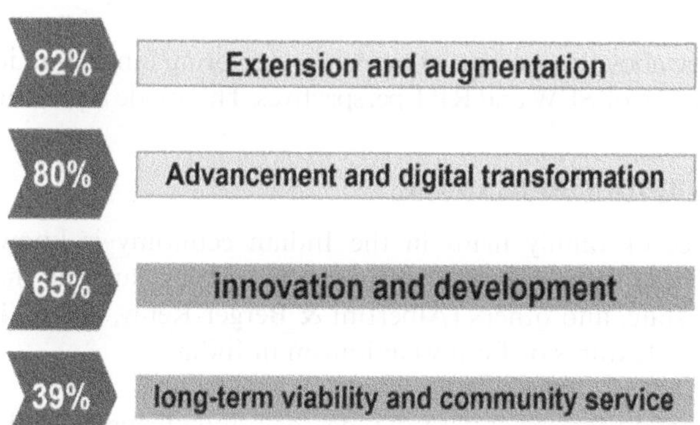

Fig. 9.2. Primary Focus Areas for Family Firms in India. *Source*: Based on Times of India (2022).

Intergenerational family sustainability refers to the ability of family firms to endure and thrive across multiple generations (Clauß et al., 2022). It encompasses financial success and preserving family values, traditions, and relationships. In understanding this phenomenon, SEW and RBT offer enlightening perspectives (Moreno-Gené & Gallizo, 2021).

SEW includes several perspectives on intergenerational sustainability, as following:

- *Emotional continuity*: SEW emphasizes maintaining family emotions, identities, and connections. From this perspective, intergenerational sustainability implies passing down the emotional and relational aspects of the business from one generation to the next (Makó et al., 2016).
- *Legacy and identity preservation*: Family members derive emotional satisfaction from preserving their legacy and identity. Intergenerational sustainability ensures that the business remains a testament to the family's history and values (Ferrari, 2020).
- *Challenges*: Overemphasis on SEW can lead to resistance to change, which might be necessary for business adaptation and survival. Ensuring that SEW supports rather than hinders adaptability is crucial for long-term sustainability (Smajić et al., 2022).

RBT perspectives about intergenerational sustainability are the following:

- *Resource stewardship*: RBT underscores the significance of valuable, rare, inimitable, and non-substitutable resources. Family firms often act as stewards of these resources, nurturing and passing them on to subsequent generations.
- *Knowledge transfer and capability building*: RBT suggests that intergenerational sustainability is achieved when older generations successfully transfer knowledge and capabilities to the younger ones. It ensures that the business maintains its competitive edge across generations (Habbershon & Williams, 1999).
- *Challenges*: The dynamic business landscape may require shifts in resources and capabilities. Balancing the preservation of legacy resources with the need for new stuff is crucial for intergenerational sustainability (Hansson, 2015).

Based on the above, a conceptual model for exploring innovation in family firms through integration of SEW and RBT perspectives. This mode is presented in Fig. 9.3.

3. Family Capitalism in India

The dominance of family firms in the Indian economy is known as 'family capitalism'. These firms operate in various industries, such as manufacturing, services, real estate, and others (Albertini & Berger-Remy, 2019). The following are some crucial features of family capitalism in India:

- The history of India is rich with the idea of family firms. India had a bustling community of regional traders, business owners, and merchants before British colonial control began.

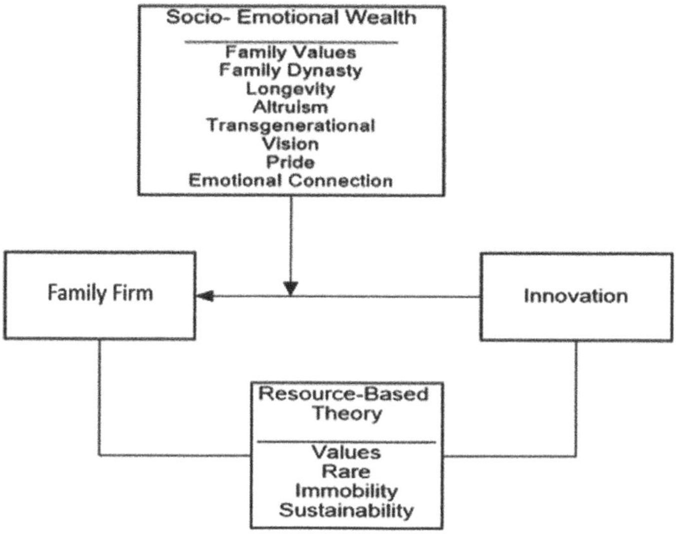

Fig. 9.3. Conceptual Model. *Source*: Authors' compilation.

- Following India's independence in 1947, the government embraced socialism and imposed stringent restrictions on private businesses. Family-owned firms persevered and adjusted to the shifting market despite these obstacles.
- Leading family-owned corporations like Tata, Birla, Reliance, and Mahindra have significantly impacted the development of India's industrial environment. These organizations have varied portfolios that cover a range of economic areas.
- The problem of succession is one of the main issues with family firms. While some families have successfully transitioned to the next generation without incident, others have experienced conflicts.
- Family firms in India have had to adjust to the changing business climate due to globalization and rising competition. Many have made management more expert, added outside knowledge, and gone global.

3.1. The Role of Familial Bonds in Strengthening Indian Family Firms

Indian culture, emphasizing family ties and relationships, reinforces the family business model. The familial bond is a source of trust, commitment, and continuity. India's rich cultural, religious, and social traditions have shaped its unique identity, strongly emphasizing familial ties and relationships. These bonds dictate personal dynamics and heavily influence the country's business fabric. Family firms in India demonstrate how family values shape its economy (Memili et al., 2015). Since Indian families share beliefs and visions, trust and reliability are crucial. This corporate similarity aligns with long-term goals and strategies. Multi-generational Indian family firms pass on expertise, experience, and history.

Family members care about the business's success since it represents their forefathers' hard work. Shared accountability makes family firms more resilient during economic downturns or crises. Due to less bureaucracy, family firms are more adaptive. Elders in the family often play a mentoring role, ensuring the younger generation is well-equipped with the necessary skills and knowledge (Lanz, 2015).

However, familial bonds also present challenges, such as conflicts arising from personal relationships and emotional decisions clouding rational judgement. However, family firms can effectively navigate these challenges with a clear distinction of roles, open communication, and professional management.

3.2. The Importance of Family Firms in India's GDP and Employment

Family firms make up a sizable portion of India's workforce and GDP. They support innovation and entrepreneurship and are essential to many different industries. In India, family firms account for 79% of the GDP. Additionally, they employ 60% of Indian labourers. India is home to 111 publicly traded family companies valued over USD 839 billion, making it the country with the third highest number of family firms worldwide (Astrachan & Shanker, 2003). Family firms in India employ 60% of the Indian workforce and have 111 publicly traded family companies valued at USD 839 billion.

The family business sector plays a significant role in the economic output of both developed and developing countries, contributing approximately 60–70% of their respective gross domestic product (GDP). India is not an exception. Business families may encounter distinctive management issues due to variations in the attitudes and goals of their family members. Maintaining the cohesion between the family and the business becomes an immense undertaking as successive generations get involved in the firm (Basco, 2015; Jahmurataj et al., 2023). Specific individuals prioritize maintaining family unity over the success of their commercial endeavours, whereas others prioritize the prosperity of their businesses at the expense of familial relationships. Research findings indicate that only 13% of family firms endure into the third generation, with a mere 4% surpassing this threshold (Zaefarian et al., 2016).

Furthermore, it has been noted that around one-third of business families experience dissolution due to conflicts arising from generational differences (Feltham et al., 2005). The cohesive nature of familial relationships, which promotes collaboration alongside adherence to domestic principles and deference to older family members, has proven essential in the prosperity of numerous family firms. Family firms in India are pivotal in the country's economy, serving as its foundation. Consequently, it is imperative to enhance the longevity of these family firms to ensure that the economy continues to reap the advantages derived from their significant contributions (Bertrand & Schoar, 2006).

Starting or operating a family business may require a long-term commitment, family unity, and customer and employee loyalty. Success depends on expanding your business and the long-lasting relationships you maintain with those around you. Several positive characteristics are associated with family firms, including increased financial success, a longer lifespan, and massive consumer trust. In addition to these advantages, managing a family business presents challenges, so I compiled this list of excellent solutions! Let's examine the obstacles and solutions to several prevalent family business issues (Vu, 2017).

3.3. Hindu Undivided Family in India: Balancing SEW and RBT Perspectives

India's Hindu Undivided Family (HUF) business structure is deeply rooted in traditional family values and socio-cultural norms. Simultaneously, from the RBT perspective, HUFs rely heavily on their inherent resources, primarily ancestral assets, and face challenges in leveraging external resources. This dual focus on preserving socio-emotional assets while optimizing material resources creates a unique dynamic where HUFs must constantly balance their intrinsic family values with the pressing need to adapt and thrive in a competitive business environment (Das Gupta & Gupta, 2017). HUF uniquely blends Indian culture and business. HUFs prioritize intangible assets like family pride, identity, and succession through the SEW lens, leading them to make decisions that may seem unfavourable to outsiders but are essential to them. Their reliance on socio-emotional value systems typically drives their reluctance to compromise family power, even if it means losing external investments or collaborations. However, RBT emphasizes using tangible and intangible assets for competitive advantage. It frequently involves strategic management of ancestral properties, family reputation, and indigenous business knowledge in HUFs. However, the largely inward-focused nature of HUFs can sometimes limit their ability to tap into external resources, hindering scalability and adaptability. This just a position between the emotional pull of SEW and the pragmatic strategies suggested by RBT results in a complex decision-making landscape for HUFs. As modern business practices and global competition permeate India's economy, HUFs find themselves at a crossroads, tasked with evolving while preserving their cherished SEW (Letonja & Duh, 2016).

A research project, named 'The Bind that Ties: Socio-emotional Wealth Preservation in Family Businesses', explains that family firms often prioritize factors like family ties, tradition, and reputation over just financial gains (Avabruth & Saravanan, 2018). While the decisions of family firms might seem illogical from a purely monetary perspective to an outsider, these businesses emphasize non-financial aspects such as maintaining familial succession and preserving core values. These intangible elements, while challenging to quantify, resonate deeply with family firms. In a study involving family-run olive mills in Spain, many chose not to join a local cooperative despite clear financial incentives and market stability. They prioritized family autonomy, independence, and the potential to carry on their legacy, even if it meant less profit. At first glance, this is a poor business decision. However, these firms often prioritize their core values, community image, and reputation. They're more inclined to partake in initiatives that boost social responsibility, earning them respect and pride rather than just revenue. They're also cautious about their financial dealings, steering clear of aggressive tax strategies and dubious earnings management to protect the family's reputation and legacy.

Though they operate with different values, family firms are often as profitable as their non-family counterparts, if not more so. It's worth noting that this sentiment rooted in socio-emotional values isn't rare. 95% of all businesses are family-owned in Asia and the Middle East. In the United States, family-founded or owned entities make up 70% of publicly traded companies, employing a significant 80% of the workforce. Moreover, big names like Microsoft, Hewlett-Packard, Cisco, and Motorola began as small home ventures (Hisrich & Ramadani, 2017).

In many developing nations, family firms dominate the economy. Such firms often have distinct objectives compared to publicly traded companies, primarily because a substantial portion of the family's wealth is typically tied up in the business. While some might think that family firms would be more prone to earnings manipulation, their business strategies usually have a long-term focus and are conservative. This conservatism often leads to reduced instances of earnings management. Family firms, while often perceived as entities striving for heightened shareholder value, have objectives that delve deeper. A core intention for many is to bolster the SEW within the family, even if it means consolidating resources in ways that might sideline minority shareholders. In some scenarios, this entrenched approach could pave the way for amplified earnings management. The empirical evidence on this topic showcases a divide: while specific research indicates a propensity among family firms for increased earnings management, other studies argue the contrary. Notably, research focused on Indian family firms did highlight signs of opportunistic earnings management. The findings emphasized that when a family's ownership is pronounced, there is a veil of opacity over the financial statements, facilitating both accrual and natural activity-based earnings management. In the Indian context, most family firms operate under the HUF banner. It is not merely an economic structure but also holds socio-cultural significance. Mainly prevalent among Hindus, HUF is both a legal and social entity. Rooted in the annals of Hindu jurisprudence, it mirrors an age-old business organization model. The importance of HUFs in India's financial landscape is undeniable, especially regarding wealth management and estate planning. They serve as vessels for pooling family assets and revenue while presenting tax advantages. Yet, the legal intricacies and tax stipulations related to HUFs can be labyrinthine. It becomes imperative to seek expert advice from legal and fiscal professionals when initiating or overseeing an HUF. Recognized as a distinct taxable 'person' as per Section 2(31) of the Income-tax Act of 1961, an HUF can possess its own permanent account number and is obligated to file income tax returns autonomously. Like individuals, HUFs declare their earnings, claim deductions, and are responsible for their tax dues. They also enjoy specific tax reliefs and exemptions contingent upon the prevailing tax code and the nature of their income. The act of partition in an HUF, entailing the distribution of assets and revenue among its members, can come with tax ramifications. Post this division, the tax obligations for the HUF and its constituents might diverge. Frequently employed as instruments for adept tax planning, HUFs enable the amalgamation of familial assets and revenue, possibly leading to an optimized tax scenario.

Compliance with income tax regulations, maintaining proper records, and filing accurate tax returns is essential for HUFs. Changes in tax laws can impact

HUF taxation, so it's advisable to stay informed about the latest provisions and consult with tax professionals for guidance on tax planning and compliance. That said, over time, the Ambani family has been involved in various business ventures under the Reliance Group, and they have their family dynamics and structures (Singh & Goodrich, 2006). However, the initial growth and success of Reliance Industries can be primarily attributed to Dhirubhai Ambani's vision and efforts as an individual entrepreneur. Joint Hindu family firms, rooted in tradition, carry certain inherent demerits that can pose challenges in today's evolving business landscape. One central area for improvement is the reliance on limited resources, predominantly ancestral property, which constrains their ability to secure external capital and expand, often leading to reluctance from financial institutions to extend credit. Additionally, the unlimited liability of the Karta, who plays a central role in decision-making, exposes their assets to cover business debts, introducing substantial risk. The dominance of the Karta, while holding decision-making authority, can also lead to conflicts within the family, hindering cooperation and effective governance. Furthermore, Karta's potential lack of managerial skills may result in suboptimal decisions and management practices. Notably, the declining relevance of joint Hindu family firms in contemporary times can be attributed to changing family structures and preferences, prompting many to explore more adaptable and modern business structures.

3.4. Family Firms and Covid-19 in India

Despite the pandemic, Indian family firms have shown they can weather the storm. Even while the poll found that 52% of Indian family firms experienced a drop in profits over the previous year, just 30% required additional capital at some point during the year, even while it is unknown whether the current environment and the ongoing second Covid-19 wave in India may dampen such confidence, the majority of family firms were bullish about recovery, with 88% predicting growth by 2022. Improving digital capabilities; expanding into new markets and client groups; providing unique products and services; and rethinking, modifying, or adapting the business model are significant initiatives for Indian family firms in the next two years (Sharma et al., 2023; Zainal, 2022).

Most Indian family firms believe they do not possess the digital experience and tools to maintain a competitive edge. The survey found that only 26% of Indian family firms claim digital solid capabilities, significantly lower than the global average of 38%. In addition, only 15% of Indian Facebook users believe they have reached the end of their digital trip, showing that most users still have a considerable distance to travel. Only 42% of Indian family firms have a formulated and communicated strategy for sustainability, which indicates that concerns connected to environmental preservation are lower on the priority scale. It is unexpected in light of the robust CSR focus of Indian family firms and their contributions to the communities in which they operate. 68% of family firms in India believe there is a chance to lead the way in sustainable business practices, compared to only 55% of family firms globally that hold this view (De Massis & Rondi, 2020).

Family firms go through a conventional life cycle, starting with the founding generation and progressing through the informal structure. The growth phase involves expansion, formalization of processes, and challenges related to scalability, raising capital, and professionalization. The sibling partnership or conflict phase involves sibling involvement, leading to complex organizational structures and potential conflicts. The cousin consortium or expansion phase involves multiple generations, formal governance structures, succession planning, professionalization, and institutionalization. The generational transition phase involves leadership transition, continuity and innovation, and legacy building. Successful family firms adapt to changing circumstances and proactively address challenges at each stage to ensure long-term sustainability. Effective communication, clear governance, and a commitment to shared values are key factors in navigating the family business life cycle. The younger generation may bring fresh perspectives and ideas to the business (Le Breton-Miller & Miller, 2022). In conclusion, family firms go through a life cycle of challenges and opportunities. Successful businesses adapt to changing circumstances and proactively address challenges to ensure long-term sustainability. Effective communication, transparent governance, and a commitment to shared values are critical factors in navigating the family business life cycle.

The survey also investigates the level of trust and cohesiveness within the families. Most of Indian family firms believed their family values helped the firm during the Covid-19 pandemic. Indian family firms tended to support their personnel, suppliers, and communities more than the typical family business worldwide did. Indian family firms were also more inclined to make some financial sacrifices. Despite the fact that the majority of Indian family firms have a favourable outlook on the quality of leadership within the firm as well as the levels of trust, communication, and transparency, just 67% of family firms believe there is family alignment in the direction of the firm (Leppäaho & Ritala, 2022). Regarding governance, Indian family firms are substantially behind their worldwide rivals. Only 55% of Indian family firms have some authority, and only 20% have a solid and documented succession plan (compared to 79% and 30%, respectively, for global family firms).

Even while going digital has been a top priority, especially in light of the recent Covid-19 pandemic, most of Indian family firms have a long way to go before becoming fully digital. These firms must develop robust digital capabilities to increase their adaptability, profitability, and future readiness (Kraus et al., 2021). Environmental, social, and corporate governance and sustainability are also gaining a lot of attention. However, there is much for Indian family firms to do in this area. With their strong family values and the trust and goodwill they enjoy in their communities, family firms are in a prime position to refocus on and lead the charge for sustainable practices (Anggadwita et al., 2023).

3.5. Forward-thinking Strategy for Indian Family Firms

Indian family firms require a long-term vision and plan to succeed. This strategy should emphasize succession planning, digital transformation, market expansion, innovation, flexibility, sustainability, governance, family alignment, and financial resilience. A solid succession plan reduces interruptions and assures a seamless leadership transfer. To compete in the changing corporate landscape, digital transformation requires current tools and techniques. Market growth means entering new markets and broadening clientele. To gain a competitive edge, innovation and R&D should be prioritized. The firm model should react to market changes. Sustainability and CSR can create a worldwide and socially acceptable sustainability plan. Governance and openness are essential for accountability and decision-making. Maintaining family harmony requires family alignment. Managing economic uncertainty requires financial resiliency.

Indian firms have a long-term plan to survive the pandemic: reinforcing fundamental principles, regularly analysing risks, and pursuing sustainability. Most organizations survived the epidemic because survey respondents emphasized wealth management and profitability for sustained development. Accountability, fairness, responsibility, and risk management helped them obtain internal and external stakeholder approvals; thus, corporate solid governance was reinforced. Digital transformation in manufacturing and marketing is essential in this age of fast technological change. These techniques helped Indian firms succeed during this challenging era according to the poll. To grow, Indian family firms must preserve unity, firm continuity, asset management, and legacy preservation. These pillars include open communication, dispute resolution, succession planning, a shared vision, professionalization, financial restraint, innovation, diversity, professional advisers, and governance. Forthcoming meetings, dispute resolution, and strategic planning unite families. Business continuity requires professionalism, strategy, financial prudence, innovation, diversity, and management.

Wealth management involves diversification, professional advice, and transparent governance structures. Legacy preservation involves philanthropy and CSR initiatives, documenting family history and mentoring younger family members. Engaging external advisors, such as family business consultants, can help navigate the unique challenges family firms face in India.

3.6. Early Expansion and Success in Family Firms

Family firms in India have a rich history, tracing several generations and contributing significantly to the economic landscape. These firms often start as small traders or community-based businesses and expand over time, such as the Tata Group, one of the world's most prominent conglomerates. The joint family system in India ensures that firms are passed down from generation to generation, ensuring continuity and sustained growth.

Family firms often start with a single industry focus but diversify over time, helping them hedge against economic downturns in one sector (Fig. 9.4). They also show remarkable adaptability and innovation, adopting modern management practices, technology, and global business strategies. Many Indian family firms operate on a solid ethical foundation, often rooted in Indian philosophical and moral values, which has helped them gain the trust and respect of stakeholders.

Community networks, often based on caste or regional affiliations, provide capital and moral support during the early phases of the business. After India's independence in 1947, the government's protectionist policies limited foreign

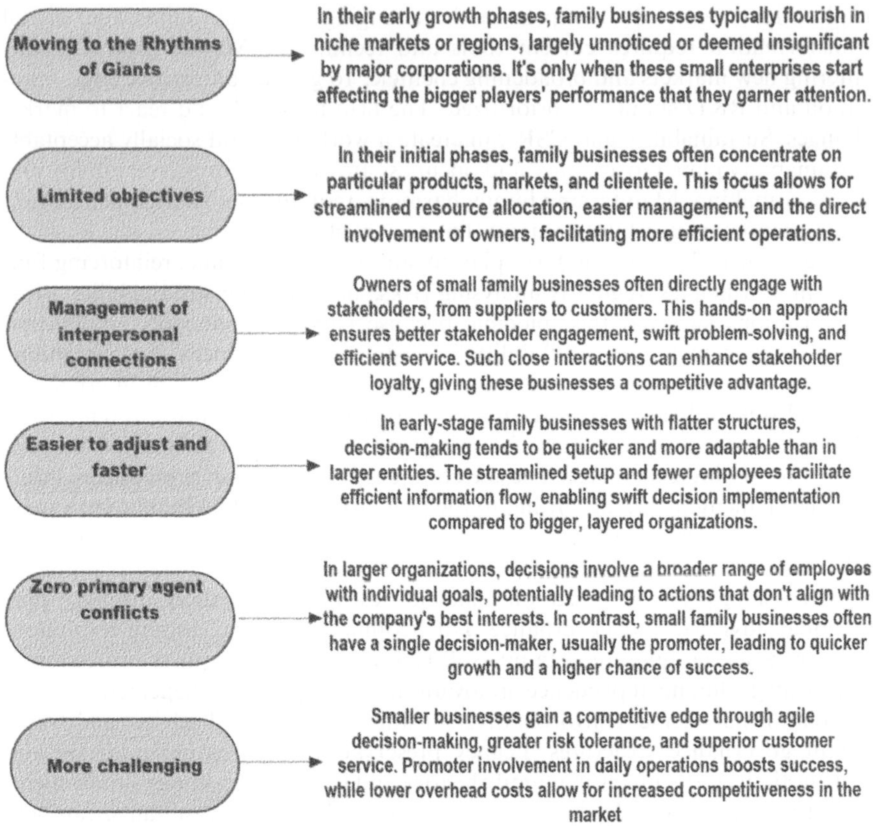

Fig. 9.4. Principal Factors and Catalysts of Initial Expansion. *Source*: Authors' compilation.

competition, allowing family firms to thrive and establish themselves in various sectors (Bahng et al., 2016).

In the post-liberalization era, many family firms expanded globally, taking advantage of opportunities offered by globalization. Professional management, hiring professionals from outside the family, brought in fresh perspectives and expertise.

Family firms in India have been at the forefront of philanthropy, earning goodwill and establishing them as responsible corporate citizens. In conclusion, the early expansion and success of family firms in India can be attributed to cultural, social, and economic factors. Family firms often expand quickly due to the promoter's attention, desire, and efforts. They can outperform established organizations with the promoter's efforts, a smaller setup, and a targeted strategy. They can make faster judgements, handle connections, and control expenses better, giving them a niche market advantage. To approach innovations in family firms through the combined lenses of SEW and RBT, the one would typically follow these steps:

(a) Comprehending the fundamental principles:

- *SEW*: This involves the family's emotional attachment to the business, the importance of family identity in the business, and the desire for family control and legacy.
- *RBT*: Focuses on the unique resources and capabilities of the firm that provide competitive advantage, like specialized knowledge, customer relationships, or efficient processes.

(b) Evaluate the present condition of the family firm:

- *Identify SEW factors*: *Evaluate how family values, traditions, and relationships impact the business. This could include family members' commitment, the significance of maintaining family control, and the impact of family dynamics on business decisions.*
- *Evaluate resources and capabilities*: *Identify the unique resources and capabilities within the family business that can be leveraged for innovation, such as specific knowledge, network connections, or financial resources.*

4. Innovation in Family Firms

Innovation is important for Family firms because it can help them sustain themselves through generations (Baltazar et al., 2023). Family firms are often considered to be innovative, but they can also be slow to make changes. One of the cornerstones of any prosperous firm is innovation. Family firms are perceived as being conservative when it comes to innovation since this idea stems from the risk taken that might alter a firm's history, reputation, and level of consumer trust in its goods and services. Family firms are motivated by various social and psychological factors, such as corporate strategy, the fear of losing the business, family traditions that constantly encourage innovation or creative ways to maintain the brand name, or the involvement of family members in business management (Canziani et al., 2020). Below are presented some recommendations how innovation can be spurred in family firms through SEW and RBT perspectives:

(a) SEW and RBT alignment for innovation:

- *Leverage family values and identity for innovation*: Use the family's unique values and identity as a source of inspiration for new ideas. For example, a commitment to sustainability could lead to innovative eco-friendly practices or products.
- *Utilize family resources for innovation*: Apply the family's unique resources, like networks or knowledge, to support innovative projects. For instance, leveraging long-standing customer relationships for feedback on new product ideas.
- *Balance SEW preservation and innovative risk-taking*: Innovations should be aligned with preserving SEW elements. For example, exploring new markets or technologies while ensuring family control and legacy are maintained.

(b) Formulate a strategic plan for innovation:

- *Integrate SEW and RBT in strategy*: Formulate a strategy that harmonizes the family's socio-emotional objectives with the practical utilization of business resources.
- *Encourage inclusive innovation culture*: Foster a culture where all family members feel encouraged to contribute ideas, respecting both SEW elements and business acumen.
- *Implement and monitor innovation initiatives*: Launch innovation initiatives that reflect this dual approach and regularly review their impact on both the family's SEW and the business's competitive positioning.

(c) Continuously evaluate and adapt:

- *Monitor impact on SEW and business performance*: Regularly assess how innovations impact both SEW (like family unity and identity) and business performance (like market share or profitability).
- *Adapt strategies as needed*: Be prepared to adjust your innovation strategy in response to changes in family dynamics, market conditions, or the firm's resource base.

5. Obstacles and Challenges

High promoter participation and a lean organization structure are two practices that have historically resulted in substantial profits but may currently need to be revised for expansion. Additional difficulties can arise from family disputes and organizational reluctance to change.

Among the most pressing challenges are the following:

(a) *Bandwidth management*. In most cases, a few promoters and trusted employees will be at the helm of a large group of 'executors' in a family firm. Many organizations need more robust middle management because decision-making authority is concentrated at the top. When a firm grows, it must deal with broader issues, including location, product line, employee count, and clientele. On the other hand, with a family-run corporate structure, authority remains concentrated at the top. Having to rely on limiting business performance is the inability to make decisions quickly and effectively because of the influence of a few people. Strong relationships between management and diverse stakeholders are another early feature of family firms; however, as the organization grows, it may become difficult for a small group of managers to continue to foster these relationships (Chaudhary et al., 2021).

(b) *Risk associated with key personnel*. Critical duties and knowledge are frequently concentrated with a few workers in smaller family firms. Firms often struggle to build back-ups for these persons. These workers' unexpected temporary or permanent departures could disrupt business operations (Mkansi, 2022).

(c) *Power centre development*. Individual family members are frequently entrusted with overseeing significant responsibilities and business divisions under legacy arrangements. Departments inside businesses often evolve into self-contained units. Communication between departments is generally dominated by management, with little engagement between lower-level people. Decisions can be made more quickly and easily on a local level. However, at a bigger size, the available managerial bandwidth may create bureaucracy and decrease productivity. Management infighting among departments has the potential to dampen communications between departments further. As different departments expand, power centres may cause duplication of organizational roles and functions like finance, human resources, sales, data management, and others that could be better served through shared teams, decreasing operational efficiency and increasing costs (Panjwani et al., 2008).

(d) *Change resistance*. With today's ever-changing market environment, businesses and internal business dynamics are increasingly compelled to adapt to change and evolve. After attaining a certain level of success, family firms often develop a sense of complacency, assuming that the actions that led to victory in the past will continue to yield positive results in the future. As a result, the employees need to be more comfortable and precise. These difficulties can be exacerbated when newer, second-generation business owners join the firm and introduce innovative ideas and procedures (Chahal & Sharma, 2020).

(e) *Complexity grows, and the importance of functional expertise rises*. Early-stage family firms frequently need more delineated divisions. First-principal management refers to delegating authority and responsibility for making decisions and running the business to a limited group of promoters and long-term workers. This method promotes speedy decision-making and adaptability in small firms (Chuenyindee et al., 2022). However, sales teams must adjust as the firm expands and processes become more complex. Finance management becomes more complex, marketing operations need to adapt, and supply chains need to produce a broader range of products over a more extended period to cater to a larger group of customers with increasingly diverse expectations – a larger area of the world. The operation of a family firm could be hampered by the use of traditional, unsystematic decision-making methods and by a lack of expertise in critical functional areas.

6. Investments, Key Partnerships, and Long-Term Goals

It might be easier for one person to accomplish the three long-term goals with assistance from others. The idea that coordinated efforts will be maintained throughout time should be no surprise. Collaboration with the new ecosystem rapidly changing and permanently reshaping market dynamics is another option to expand and build a firm, in addition to business acquisitions, which are an obvious way to accomplish these goals. It is how it works out. Conventional players leverage emergent ecosystems to create change. Increasingly involved with the start-up ecosystem to develop more substantial and trustworthy interactions with various stakeholders along the value chain. The overwhelming majority of responders supported the idea of exploring. As one might expect, partnerships with newly established businesses in supply chain management. A sizeable portion of respondents made financial investments in the business model of the next generation for new firms with ground-breaking products and services. For an Indian family business, long-term goals, investments, and essential partnerships all play a big part in how the business grows and stays in business (Ungerer, 2004). These things affect Indian family firms in the following ways:

(a) Investments:

- *Capital investment*: Family firms, like family savings, usually get the money they need to run and grow from within the firm. To become more efficient and successful, businesses often put money into things like infrastructure, technology, and human resources.
- *Diversification*: Some family firms may invest in new segments or industries to spread risk and exploit growth possibilities.
- *Real estate*: Many family firms in India invest in real estate by buying industrial properties or land and building on them.

(b) Key partnerships:

- *Supplier relationships*: Maintaining solid relationships with suppliers, especially in industries like manufacturing, is crucial for securing a steady supply of raw materials and components.
- *Distribution partnerships*: Family firms often collaborate with distributors and retailers to expand their reach and gain access to broader customer bases.
- *Joint ventures*: Entering into joint ventures with other businesses, including international partners, can be a strategy for growth and accessing new markets or technologies.
- *Franchise agreements*: Some family firms opt for franchise agreements to expand their brand presence and leverage the capabilities of franchisees.

(c) Long-term goals:

- *Succession planning*: Family firms typically have long-term goals related to succession planning. It involves grooming the next generation to take over leadership roles and ensuring a smooth transition of ownership and management.
- *Sustainability*: Many family firms in India emphasize sustainability and responsible business practices as long-term goals, aligning with the growing global focus on environmental and social responsibility.
- *Market expansion*: Long-term goals may include expanding the family business's presence into new geographic regions or international markets.
- *Legacy building*: Some family firms prioritize building a lasting legacy, which may involve philanthropic initiatives, cultural preservation, or community development efforts.

Family relationships and governance dynamics can significantly influence investment decisions, partnerships, and long-term goals in family firms. Maintaining transparency, effective communication, and a well-defined governance structure are critical to managing these aspects successfully. Additionally, Indian family firms often face unique challenges related to cultural values, tradition, and the need to balance family interests with business interests. Therefore, family firms in India need a well-thought-out strategy that considers the specific context in which they operate while pursuing investments, partnerships, and long-term goals.

7. A Co-evolutionary Framework for Sustaining Family Firms in India

Family firms in India, rooted in centuries-old traditions, play a crucial role in the nation's economy. A co-evolutionary framework is essential to sustain them, highlighting the interplay between these businesses and their environment. This approach involves understanding co-evolution, which represents the evolution of two or more entities that influence each other's development. Indian family firms often draw strength from core values, close-knit relationships, and a deep-seated sense of responsibility towards employees and communities (Magrelli et al., 2022).

Adaptive challenges for these businesses include generational transitions, technological disruptions, and global competition. They may adopt digital transformation, diversify product portfolios, or enter new markets to overcome these challenges. Modern governance should seamlessly integrate with traditional decision-making processes, such as setting up professional boards and adopting data-driven strategies. Balancing family interests with business imperatives and continuous learning and innovation are essential. Succession planning is critical for long-term sustainability, and effective stakeholder engagement is vital. Cultural revolution, embracing diversity and inclusivity, and adapting to global best practices can enhance the resilience of family firms. A long-term vision is also essential, with short-term gains not overshadowing the overarching concept of creating a lasting legacy that benefits multiple generations (Arregle et al., 2021).

By adopting a co-evolutionary approach, Indian family firms can navigate the complexities of modern markets while staying true to their roots and values, ensuring sustainability, relevance, and growth for the long term.

8. Next-Gen Survival in Indian Family Firms: What's Next?

Being the Next-Gen (the next generation of family members) and surviving and succeeding in an Indian family firm may be both a rewarding and challenging path (Song et al., 2022). Here are some essential things to think about as you get ready to join the family business and ensure its long-term success:

- *Development of education and skills*: Spend money on your education and professional growth. Get the education, credentials, and training you need for your position by pursuing applicable degrees, certifications, and training courses. To obtain real-world experience, look for internship and on-the-job training opportunities inside and outside the family business.

- *Recognizing the industry*: Spend some time fully comprehending the nuances of the family firm. Learn about the firm's activities, history, sector, and market competition. Learn from seasoned family members and co-workers who may offer insightful advice and mentoring.
- *Professional conduct*: Take a professional approach to your job. Show that you have a good work ethic, are trustworthy, and are dedicated to the firm's development. Keep your personal and business life apart to preserve a productive workplace.
- *Relationships and networking*: Create and maintain connections with colleagues, mentors, and business partners. Networking can lead to insightful connections and cooperative opportunities. Develop relationships with co-workers and employees to foster a supportive and collaborative workplace.
- *Leadership training*: Taking on leadership tasks gradually based on your interests and talents. Take on minor tasks at first, then bigger duties as you progress. To improve your leadership skills, think about receiving formal coaching or training.
- *Conflict resolution and communication*: Develop practical communication skills with all family members as well as external stakeholders. Building trust and resolving disputes need effective communication. Foster a culture of accessible communication and welcome constructive criticism.
- *Transition planning*: A clear succession plan should be developed in cooperation with the elder generation. Discuss the leadership transition's duties, responsibilities, and timetables. Make sure the succession plan is in the firm's best interests.
- *Adaptation and innovation*: Encourage creativity and adaptability. Keep abreast of market developments and technological advances to keep the firm competitive. Be receptive to fresh perspectives and promote employee creativity.
- *Honouring traditions and values*: Be respectful of the family's customs, principles, and business history. Integrate the need for innovation and change with tradition. Talk with family members about ways to preserve and develop the family legacy.
- *Seek outside counsel*: Consider consulting outside advisers, such as family business consultants, to ensure seamless transitions and handle challenging challenges.

Always should bear in mind that Next-Gen's path in a family business is a marathon, not a sprint. The most important qualities are perseverance, commitment, and a readiness to change and grow. To succeed in an Indian family business like Next-Gen, family members must work together and be dedicated to the firm's long-term prosperity.

9. Conclusions, Implications, and Future Research Avenues

Integrating SEW and RBT perspectives offers a robust theoretical framework to decode innovation in family firms. While SEW underscores the intangible facets, emphasizing family-cantered non-economic goals like identity, pride, and succession, RBT emphasizes the strategic management of tangible and intangible resources for gaining a competitive edge. Together, they provide a holistic lens, acknowledging family firms' emotional and pragmatic dimensions.

By intertwining these perspectives, family firms can effectively balance their deep-rooted values with the imperative to innovate, ensuring sustainability and growth in a dynamic business landscape. Therefore, this convergence of SEW and RBT serves as a beacon for family firms, illuminating their path towards successful, value-driven innovation in an ever-evolving marketplace. Family capitalism in India, dominated by family firms, is a resilient and economically impactful tradition. Despite facing challenges like government restrictions and globalization, these businesses have adapted and innovated. Their success is rooted in familial bonds, trust, commitment, and long-term vision. Addressing succession issues and leveraging their unique strengths is crucial for their longevity.

In summary, for the upcoming generation in Indian family firms, the journey is filled with both opportunities and hurdles. To safeguard the enduring success of the family firm, Next-Gen leaders must focus on continuous learning, upholding professionalism, and honing leadership skills, all while valuing age-old traditions and ethos. Open dialogue, teamwork, and meticulous succession plans are indispensable. Equally crucial is the zeal for innovation and adaptability. Turning to external consultants or mentors can be immensely beneficial, offering fresh perspectives. At its core, the transition and growth of Next-Gen in a family business demand unwavering commitment, perseverance, and a collective vision for the firm's future and sustained growth.

In sum, Next-Gen's trajectory in India's family firms is akin to navigating a vast sea with calm waters and stormy patches. While the very essence of these businesses is deeply rooted in history, tradition, and familial bonds, the modern landscape demands agility, foresight, and strategic thinking. The Next-Gen is not just inheriting a business but a legacy, a set of values, and a shared family dream. They must recognize the weight of this responsibility, drawing strength from the past yet looking ahead with a global and innovative mindset.

Furthermore, in a world characterized by rapid technological advancements and changing consumer behaviours, Next-Gen must proactively integrate technology, sustainability, and ethical practices into its business models. By doing so, they can ensure not only the longevity of their firms but also their relevance in a constantly evolving marketplace.

Fostering an inclusive and diverse work environment can bring fresh perspectives and innovative solutions to age-old challenges. By welcoming voices from different backgrounds and experiences, Next-Gen can propel their businesses into the future, ready to tackle challenges unknown to the previous generations. Embracing change while preserving the core will be the key. It's a delicate balance, but with the proper guidance, continuous learning, and a deep respect for the old and the new, the Next-Gen of India's family firms will undoubtedly write a success story that future generations will be proud to inherit and continue.

There are several implication from this chapter:

- The integration of theories is a fundamental framework that combines two significant perspectives, SEW perspective, which highlights the non-financial components of the business with an emphasis on the family-centric approach, and RBT, which stresses the strategic management of resources. This integration provides a comprehensive comprehension of the manner in which family firms engage in innovation, effectively managing the interplay between financial goals and familial principles.

- The framework has the potential to offer valuable insights into the decision-making processes inside family firms, specifically in terms of their resource management for innovation, while concurrently safeguarding SEW.
- The framework has the potential to assist family firms in effectively managing their distinct resources, such as family culture and relationships, with the aim of achieving long-term competitive advantage through innovation.
- The framework's findings have the potential to provide policymakers with valuable information regarding the distinct requirements of family firms in promoting innovation. This, in turn, might result in the development of more customized assistance programmes.

The present study aims to explore the influence of digital transformation on innovation in family firms, within the framework of the digital era and technical breakthroughs. The integration of sustainability and social responsibility features into the existing framework is imperative in the contemporary business landscape. Further investigation in these domains could substantially augment our comprehension of innovation within family firms, thereby furnishing invaluable counsel for professionals and scholars alike. The following are some of the further research avenues:

- *Empirical testing*: Subsequent investigations may undertake empirical testing of the suggested theoretical framework across various contexts and categories of family firms, with the aim of substantiating its application and enhancing its refinement.
- *Comparative studies*: Examine the differences in innovation strategies and performance between family and non-family firms have the potential to provide valuable insights when employing this paradigm.
- *Cross-cultural analysis*: The investigation of how cultural disparities impact the assimilation of SEW and RBT inside family firms operating in diverse countries or regions.
- *Longitudinal studies*: These are a valuable research approach that can be employed to examine the long-term dynamics of SEW and resource management within family firms across several generations.

References

Albertini, E., & Berger-Remy, F. (2019). Intellectual capital and financial performance: A meta-analysis and research agenda. *Management*, *22*(2), 216–249.

Anggadwita, G., Permatasari, A., Alamanda, D. T., & Profityo, W. B. (2023). Exploring women's initiatives for family business resilience during the COVID-19 pandemic. *Journal of Family Business Management*, *13*(3), 714–736.

Arregle, J.-L., Chirico, F., Kano, L., Kundu, S. K., Majocchi, A., & Schulze, W. S. (2021). Family firm internationalization: Past research and an agenda for the future. *Journal of International Business Studies*, *52*(6), 1159–1198. https://doi.org/10.1057/s41267-021-00425-2

Astrachan, J. H., & Shanker, M. C. (2003). Family businesses' contribution to the US economy: A closer look. *Family Business Review*, *16*(3), 211–219.

Avabruth, S. M., & Saravanan, P. (2018). *Earnings management preferences of family firms and its impact on the market value of the firm*. Springer. Available at SSRN 3102030.

Bahng, Y., Yang, J.-H., & Reilly, A. (2016). A qualitative approach to understanding Hawaiian apparel manufacturers' exports: Strategic marketing resources, dynamic capabilities and export barriers. *International Journal of Export Marketing*, *1*(1), 96–113.

Baltazar, J., Fernandes, C., Ramadani, V., & Hughes, M. (2023). Family business succession and innovation: A systematic literature review. *Review of Managerial Science*, *17*(8), 2897–2920.

Basco, R. (2015). Family business and regional development – A theoretical model of regional familiness. *Journal of Family Business Strategy*, *6*(4), 259–271.

Bertrand, M., & Schoar, A. (2006). The role of family in family firms. *Journal of Economic Perspectives*, *20*(2), 73–96.

Canziani, B. F., Welsh, D. H. B., Dana, L. P., & Ramadani, V. (2020). Claiming a family brand identity: The role of website storytelling. *Canadian Journal of Administrative Sciences*, *37*(1), 68–81.

Chaudhary, S., Dhir, A., Ferraris, A., & Bertoldi, B. (2021). Trust and reputation in family businesses: A systematic literature review of past achievements and future promises. *Journal of Business Research*, *137*, 143–161.

Chahal, H., & Sharma, A. K. (2020). Family business in India: Performance, challenges and improvement measures. *Journal of New Business Ventures*, *1*(1–2), 9–30.

Chuenyindee, T., Torres, R. B., Prasetyo, Y. T., Nadlifatin, R., & Persada, S. F. (2022). Determining factors affecting perceived quality among shoe manufacturing workers towards shoe quality: A structural equation modeling approach. *Journal of Open Innovation: Technology, Market, and Complexity*, *8*(2), 82–96.

Clauß, T., Kraus, S., & Jones, P. (2022). Sustainability in family business: Mechanisms, technologies and business models for achieving economic prosperity, environmental quality and social equity. *Technological Forecasting and Social Change*, *176*(3), 121450.

Das Gupta, C., & Gupta, M. (2017). The Hindu undivided family in independent India's corporate governance and tax regime. *South Asia Multidisciplinary Academic Journal*, *15*(1), 1–15.

De Massis, A., & Rondi, E. (2020). COVID-19 and the future of family business research. *Journal of Management Studies*, *57*(8), 1727–1731.

Feltham, T. S., Feltham, G., & Barnett, J. J. (2005). The dependence of family businesses on a single decision-maker. *Journal of Small Business Management*, *43*(1), 1–15.

Ferrari, F. (2020). Exploring the side effects of socio-emotional wealth. A multilevel analysis approach to the dysfunctional dynamics in family business succession. *International Journal of Entrepreneurship and Small Business*, *40*(1), 128–146.

Guimarães, J. S., Fernandes, C., Veiga, P. M., & Ramadani, V. (2023). The relationship between entrepreneurial ecosystems and digital transformation. *FIIB Business Review*. https://doi.org/10.1177/23197145231173850

Habbershon, T. G., & Williams, M. L. (1999). A resource-based framework for assessing the strategic advantages of family firms. *Family Business Review*, *12*(1), 1–25.

Hansson, P. (2015). Resource based theory and the family business. In M. Nordqvist, L. Melin, M. Waldkirch, & G. Kumeto (Eds.), *Theoretical perspectives on family businesses* (pp. 253–272). Edward Elgar.

Haynes, G., Marshall, M., Lee, Y., Zuiker, V., Jasper, C. R., Sydnor, S., Valdivia, C., Masuo, D., Niehm, L., & Wiatt, R. (2021). Family business research: Reviewing the past, contemplating the future. *Journal of Family and Economic Issues*, *42*(1), 70–83.

Hillebrand, S. (2019). Innovation in family firms – A generational perspective. *Journal of Family Business Management*, *9*(2), 126–148.

Hisrich, D. R., & Ramadani, V. (2017). *Effective entrepreneurial management*. Springer.

Jahmurataj, V., Ramadani, V., Bexheti, A., Rexhepi, G., Abazi-Alili, H., & Krasniqi, B. (2023). Unveiling the determining factors of family business longevity: Evidence from Kosovo. *Journal of Business Research*, *159*(4), 113745.

James, A., Hadjielias, E., Guerrero, M., Discua Cruz, A., & Basco, R. (2021). Entrepreneurial families in business across generations, contexts and cultures. *Journal of Family Business Management*, *11*(4), 355–367.

Kraus, S., Jones, P., Kailer, N., Weinmann, A., Chaparro-Banegas, N., & Roig-Tierno, N. (2021). Digital transformation: An overview of the current state of the art of research. *SAGE Open*, *11*(3), 1–15.

Lanz, S. (2015). *Goal orientation and its relationship to the business family, and family business performance, within the UK's family owned and managed mid-sized businesses*. Aston University.

Le Breton-Miller, I., & Miller, D. (2022). Family businesses under COVID-19: Inspiring models – Sometimes. *Journal of Family Business Strategy*, *13*(2), 100452.

Leppäaho, T., & Ritala, P. (2022). Surviving the coronavirus pandemic and beyond: Unlocking family firms' innovation potential across crises. *Journal of Family Business Strategy*, *13*(1), 100440.

Letonja, M., & Duh, M. (2016). Knowledge transfer in family businesses and its effects on the innovativeness of the next family generation. *Knowledge Management Research & Practice*, *14*(2), 213–224.

Makó, C., Csizmadia, P., & Heidrich, B. (2016). Succession in the family business: Need to transfer the 'Socio-Emotional Wealth' (SEW). *Vezetéstudomány-Budapest Management Review*, *47*(11), 16–28.

Magrelli, V., Rovelli, P., Benedetti, C., Überbacher, R., & De Massis, A. (2022). Generations in family business: A multifield review and future research agenda. *Family Business Review*, *35*(1), 15–44.

Memili, E., Fang, H., Chrisman, J. J., & De Massis, A. (2015). The impact of small- and medium-sized family firms on economic growth. *Small Business Economics*, *45*(3), 771–785.

Mkansi, M. (2022). E-business adoption costs and strategies for retail micro businesses. *Electronic Commerce Research*, *22*(4), 1153–1193.

Moreno-Gené, J., & Gallizo, J. L. (2021). Intergenerational differences in family business management and their influence on business profitability. *Sustainability*, *13*(12), 6979. https://doi.org/10.3390/su13126979

Panjwani, A., Aggarwal, V., & Dhameja, N. (2008). Family business: Yesterday, today, tomorrow. *Indian Journal of Industrial Relations*, *44*(2), 272–291.

Parada, M. J., Gimeno, A., Samara, G., & Saris, W. (2020). The adoption of governance mechanisms in family businesses: An institutional lens. *Journal of Family Business Management*. https://doi.org/10.1108/JFBM-07-2019-0054

Rodrigues, A. O. A., Marques, C. S., & Ramadani, V. (2023). Artisan entrepreneurship, resilience and sustainable development: The quintuple helix innovation model in the low-density and cross-border territories. *Journal of Enterprise Information Management*. https://doi.org/10.1108/JEIM-02-2023-0066

Schillaci, C. E., Romano, M., & Nicotra, M. (2013). Family business foundations: Theoretical and empirical investigation. *Journal of Innovation and Entrepreneurship*, *2*, 1–19.

Sharma, G., Kraus, S., Talan, A., Srivastava, M., & Theodoraki, C. (2023). Navigating the storm: The SME way of tackling the pandemic crisis. *Small Business Economics*, *63*(1), 221–241. https://doi.org/10.1007/s11187-023-00810-1

Singh, M., & Goodrich, J. A. (2006). *Succession in family-owned businesses: a case study of reliance industries-India*. http://dx.doi.org/10.2139/ssrn.954715

Smajić, H., Palalić, R., & Ahmad, N. (2022). Future perspective of socioemotional wealth (SEW) in family businesses. *Journal of Family Business Management*, *13*(4), 923–954. https://doi.org/10.1108/JFBM-05-2022-0070

Song, S., Zhou, L., Sindakis, S., Aggarwal, S., & Chen, C. (2022). The impact of intergenerational succession intention on family firm's innovation strategy: Evidence from China. *Journal of the Knowledge Economy*, 1–34. https://doi.org/10.1007/s13132-022-01078-8

Times of India. (2022). *Ushering India's family businesses into a new era of endless possibilities – Times of India*. https://timesofindia.indiatimes.com/education/news/ushering-indias-family-businesses-into-a-new-era-of-endless-possibilities/articleshow/89500724.cms

Ungerer, M. (2004). *Developing core capabilities in a financial services firm: An intellectual capital perspective*. University of Johannesburg.

Vu, H. N. (2017). *Relationships between entrepreneurial orientation and firm performance: The role of family involvement amongst small firms in Vietnam*. [A thesis presented in partial fulfilment of the requirements for the degree of Doctor of Philosophy in Management]. Massey University.

Yazici, O., Memili, E., Patel, P. C., & Ramadani, V. (2023). The determinants of non-family employees' turnover intentions in family firms. *International Journal of Entrepreneurship and Small Business*, *49*(4), 577–604.

Zaefarian, R., Eng, T.-Y., & Tasavori, M. (2016). An exploratory study of international opportunity identification among family firms. *International Business Review*, *25*(1), 333–345.

Zainal, M. (2022). Innovation orientation and performance of Kuwaiti family businesses: Evidence from the initial period of COVID-19 pandemic. *Journal of Family Business Management*, *12*(2), 251–265.

Printed and bound by CPI Group (UK) Ltd, Croydon, CR0 4YY

15/09/2026

14962489-0003